STAR WARPED

Machine-written from original screenplay
Gorgeous 'Lukin' Ass

<u>*Guaranteed*</u> body-harming hilarious!!!
If you do not physically injure yourself and/or
need hospitalisation through laughing at this book,
then Victor Gollancz will *not only* give you your
money back *but also* undertake to pay your
children's way through university.[1]

Six parodies for the price of one point four!

---

[1] This statement is true only for a given value of 'you'. At present 'you' is 'Fredric Gelman of Elm Tree Crescent, Egham'. This may change at any moment: check the website for further details. (Note: Forfurtherdetails.com is not owned by Victor Gollancz publishing, and the publishers are not responsible for anything that might be up there.)

A long time ago in a galaxy far, far away, A3R Roberts wasn't A3R Roberts at all, but the Robertski Brothers: the illustrious and justly-famed duo responsible for *The Mcatrix Derided*. And before that, when soddits were real soddits, dwarves were real dwarves, and Smug the magic dragon was *Really* Smug the magic dragon, A3R Roberts was A.R.R.R. Roberts, who wrote *The Soddit* and *The Sellamillion*. ('Neither of which form the first few minutes of prologue in A MAJOR NINE HOUR MOTION PICTURE EPIC!'). And in a galaxy not so far away or long ago, as Adam Roberts, he also found the time to write some proper books, like *Salt*, *On*, *Stone*, *Park Polar*, *Jupiter Magnified*, *Polystom* and *The Snow*, which are *much* better, though not as funny. Not intentionally, at any rate.

STAR WARPED

A3R ROBERTS

GOLLANCZ
LONDON

'This *is* the book you're looking for' Wobbli Bent K'nobbli, Jobbi Knight

'Magnificent is this. In it, sauce of wisdom will you find'
Yodella, Great Jobbi Master

'NOT BAD, BUT TO BE HONEST I THINK MY STUFF'S FUNNIER.
DON'T YOU?' Dark Father, Dark Lord of the Psmyth

First published in Great Britain in 2005 by Gollancz
An imprint of the Orion Publishing Group
Orion House, 5 Upper St Martin's Lane, London WC2H 9EA

1 3 5 7 9 10 8 6 4 2

A CIP catalogue record for this book
is available from the British Library

ISBN 0 575 07688 7

Star Warped

Once Upon A Time in a Far Away Galaxy there was a Beautiful Senator who fell in
love with a Lowly Slave Boy. After many Adventures in the galaxy he became a Great
Knight to whom love was forbidden, so the Beautiful Senator gave birth to their twins
in secret. But there was Great Evil in the galaxy, which turned the Great Knight into an
Evil Dark Warrior. Many years later a Beautiful Princess was captured by the Evil Dark
Warrior for his Evil Ends, but she was saved by a Lowly Boy on a Quest to become a Great
Knight, an Old Wise Man, and a Sexy Smuggler. They had many Adventures before the
Lowly Boy and Beautiful Princess realised they were twins and the Evil Dark Warrior was
their father. Between them, they saved the Evil Dark Warrior, defeated the Great Evil,
fell in love with the Sexy Smuggler and Lived Happily Ever After.

This isn't the parody of that story.

Typeset at The Spartan Press Ltd,
Lymington, Hants

Printed in Great Britain by
Clays Ltd, St Ives plc

www.orionbooks.co.uk

to Princess Lily

Contents

. . . A long time in the future, obviously (this being science fiction) . . .

. . . In a Galaxy – well, to be honest, in the Galaxy in which we all live now . . .

A NUDE HOPE

THE IMPERIAL EMPIRE OF THE IMPERIUM SEEMED TRIUMPHANT,
EVERYWHERE CRUSHING OPPOSITION BENEATH THE IRON HEEL OF
THEIR METAPHORICAL BUT NONETHELESS PAINFUL IRON JACK-
BOOT, SMASHING ALL WHO OPPOSED THEM WITH AN IRON FIST
SHEATHED INSIDE THE IRON GLOVE OF 'IMP-EMP-IMP' PROPAGANDA.
ONLY A SMALL GROUP OF REBELS RESISTED THE UNSTOPPABLE,
ONWARD-SLIDING MOVEMENT OF THIS IRON – THE 'REBELEND'
(SO CALLED, IN FACT, BECAUSE THEY WERE 'REBELLING' TO BRING
AN 'END' TO THE IMPERIAL EMPIRE, YOU SEE) FOUGHT FOR FREEDOM
AGAINST TYRANNY, FOR CHAOS AGAINST ORDER, AND FOR 'ROCK
AND ROLL AND DOING WHATEVER YOU FEEL LIKE AND STUFF'
AGAINST RESPECT FOR AUTHORITY, KNOWING ONE'S PLACE IN
THE HIERARCHY OF SOCIETY, DUTY AND SOCIAL RESPONSIBILITY.
WITH ALL MODES OF INFORMATION DISSEMINATION UNDER THE
TIGHT CONTROL OF THE IMP-EMP-IMP PROPAGANDA COHORTS, THE
REBELEND WERE REDUCED TO ASSEMBLING GIANT FLEETS OF
ALPHABETTI SPACECRAFT (FROM A- THROUGH TO Z-WINGS) IN SPACE,
SPELLING OUT THEIR SIDE OF THE CASE, AND FLYING THE MESSAGE
AWAY INTO THE GALACTIC DISTANCE BEFORE THE WONDERING EYES
OF ORDINARY CITIZENS. MESSAGES, INDEED, RATHER LIKE THIS ONE . . .

Chapter One

The Beginning

A tiny spacecraft flees zigger-zagger, passing over the pole of a yellow-brown desert planet and flying into the distance.

And, a moment later—

—an absolutely *massive* spaceship appears in pursuit, as if flying directly over your head: a vast crenellated white-metal ziggurat of a spaceship, larger than a cathedral, larger than most cities. On and on it comes; it just seems to *keep on coming*, steamrollering with insolent force over the top of your line of sight; its ten thousand space laser cannons blasting, its bay doors opened ready to gobble the little craft up. It is by far the more powerful and massive of the two craft. The little spaceship doesn't stand a chance.

So tell me: which of these two spaceships is more likely to enlist your sympathy? Just on your gut response?

Yes, I thought so.

Well, since you've already made up your mind, is there likely to be any mileage in me describing the small ship as 'a terrorist craft', flown by 'dangerous criminals, murderers, smugglers and social deviants'? Or in referring to the big ship as 'an official law-enforcement vessel', staffed by 'dedicated law enforcement officials doing a difficult job under trying conditions for too little money'?

No, I didn't think so.

Alrighty then. So, the small ship, called *Viva Galaxia Libre!*, carried aboard it a tired crew of heroic freedom fighters, who had flown half the width of the Galaxy to escape the remorseless tyrannical pursuit of the Imperial Empire of the Imperium. The large ship, on the other hand, was the *ISS Order Through Fear and Obedience XVII*, a Phagocyte class space destroyer, and the very embodiment of Imperial repression, oppression, depression, and four or five other words ending in -pression. Its holds held forty thousand fanatical shock troops, dressed in shiny white plastic space armour. It easily accelerated its colossal engines and pulled alongside the *Viva Galaxia Libre!*, grabbing the hull of the tiny battered ship with massive grapnels and hauling it inexorably into its cavernous cargo bay.

Aboard the *Viva Galaxia Libre!* a young woman was crouching next to a 'Dusty Bin'-shaped robot, looking nervously over her shoulder. She had good cause to be nervous; for there was a secret stored inside the robot; and no petty secret. It was the biggest Secret of all, the Secret her mother had entrusted her with, the Secret that was the key to Everything, that explained the entire cosmos, the continuing battle between the forces of good and evil – the Great Secret. This Secret was so secret, in fact, that even the Princess did not know it. She merely carried it, locked away inside a specially designed data containment cube. But now that the Imperial Empire of the Imperium had captured her ship she did not dare allow this cube to fall into the hands of the forces of evil. And so she lodged it inside the little droid, and sent it on its way.

Acting on the orders of the young woman this little robot, and his robot 'friend' (or 'longtime companion'), hopped straight out of an airlock, and plummeted directly to the planet below. Being robots, they were not discommoded by the vacuum of space, or the heat of re-entry, although the humanoid-shaped robot landed on his legs and compacted them by eleven per cent of their length, which annoyed him, and gave him an unfortunately stumpy look.

What's that? You want to know what the Secret was? This immense Secret that this Princess considered more important than her life?

All in good time, dear reader. You must be patient.

Why? *Because*, that's why. Because I'm telling you to be patient, that's why.

What's that? Well – if you *really* want to know the nature of this Secret right now this minute – if you're *that* impatient – then I can only suggest you flick to the back of the book, where the devastating Universe-changing reality of the secret is finally unleashed upon a startled Imperial Order. Go on – if you want to – just ruin the book for yourself. Why don't you?

Still here, eh?

I thought so.

Now. Where was I?

And meanwhile, aboard the *Viva Galaxia Libre!* the Imp-Emp-Imp forces prepared to board. They primed the airlock. The ship's own crew waited nervously, guns ready.

Then, with a flash that looked like (but, obviously, which *wasn't*) a cheap firework, the door (which, being a spaceship main airlock, was made of dense metal, clearly, and not hastily painted wood – although the force of the explosion *might* give an observer the impression of the latter) blew in. Sterntroopers came stumbling through the smoke, firing their laser rifles and occasionally smacking their heads on the low overhangs. Bolts of red laser light of a surprising uniformity and consistent thickness bloomed amongst the smoke and dust. This laser fire was not only uniformly thick, but also came in surprisingly short bolts (imagine how briefly you'd need to press the trigger in order to get a laser bolt rather than say, a line). Although each laser bolt looked, perhaps, no more dangerous than the sort of thing you'd find in a provincial disco, they had a dramatic effect on any Rebelend soldier they happened to strike, who tended to fling their arms wide and hurtle backwards to lie, motionless, on the floor.

The *Viva Galaxia Libre!* was lost, captured, gone, defeated, overwhelmed. It and all its passengers were in the grip of the ruthless Imp-Emp-Imp space fleet.

Against the backdrop of the vastness of space, the *ISS Order Through Fear and Obedience XVII* flew inexorably on.

And on the planet below them, two droids hit the sand with the force of a double meteorite, throwing up a huge mass of sand. It's a strange, and little-known, fact about sand: that any impact which throws up a huge mass of the stuff will tend to make the sand thus thrown look as though it has been superimposed upon an otherwise placid desert scene. Funny, that.

Chapter Two

In which Luke, on the planet down below, learns that his Uncle Sven is not truly his father after all, but only his uncle

Luke Seespotrun had clothes on again.

He was working on his hovercar in the garage in one of the outbuildings of Uncle Sven's farm, and he had put on slacks and a top. Experience had taught him that naked male bodies and whirring metal motors did not make a good combination. But, as if by a sixth sense, Uncle Sven was calling to him from the main house. 'Luke! Luke!'

Luke sighed. Holding out his sonic screwdriver, he adjusted one of the sonic screws.

Uncle Sven came barrelling into the workshop, his naked flesh jiggling with the effort of running. 'I knew it!' he cried. 'I knew it. You're *clothed*, disgustingly *clothed*.'

'I'm sorry, Uncle,' said Luke, eyes downcast.

'We are Swedes before we are Galactic citizens!' barked Uncle Sven. 'We *will* be true to our heritage. We *will* be naked.'

'Yes, Uncle.' Wearily Luke unzipped his pants.

'You can go wearing your fancy clothes,' said Uncle Sven, his belly quivering with indignation, *'after* you've left the farm to join the Imperial Empire of the Imperium's flying squad. Not before. Do you hear? Not before.'

'No, Uncle.'

'Well,' said Sven, his anger calming a little. 'I won't go on about it. Come through and have breakfast.'

'Yes, Uncle,' said Luke, obediently.

'Come and have breakfast,' repeated Sven. 'I have something important to tell you. Something of the utmost importance. A most important thing. A thing of ut importance.'

Intrigued, a now naked Luke followed his uncle out of the workshop.

Auntie Svenessa was in the kitchen, nude and pendulous, reading a news-flimsy with close attention and popping slices of yam toast into her mouth at regular intervals. She greeted her husband with a peck on the cheek, and Luke with the same gesture, although aimed at a different cheek.

Sven lowered himself onto his PVC-upholstered kitchen stool with a sound not unlike a smoochy kiss. He began tucking into breakfast. Luke sat down too,

11

although, as was often the case, the sight of his naked relatives eating had robbed him of what little appetite he possessed.

'Luke,' said Uncle Sven, his mouth full of cream curd, 'I have something important to tell you, Luke.'

Luke looked up expectantly, but Uncle Sven did not meet his gaze. For a while there was nothing but the sound of eating. Luke waited.

'I am not your father, Luke,' said Uncle Sven, shortly.

'Which would be why I call you uncle,' replied Luke. 'It makes sense. So who *is* my father?'

'I cannot say, save that he is dark.'

'How do you mean? Are you talking of his skin colour?'

'No – no – in terms of ethical bias. He has gone over to the Dark Side of the Farce.'

'The Farce?'

'A universal quantity of tremendous supernatural power. It has a Dark Side, and a Pale Side. He, your father, is definitely on the former of these two sides. Hence he, your father, is dark.'

'Strange,' mused Luke, 'that I have never heard of this "Farce".'

'Few have,' said Uncle Sven.

'Even though it is universal and tremendously powerful?'

'Yes,' said Uncle Sven, looking at the floor in a faintly embarrassed manner.

'Odd, that.'

'Some people might say so,' said Sven, disdainfully.

'So,' said Luke. 'My father has converted to the Dark Side of this Farce, has he? He could have chosen the Pale Side, but instead he has chosen the Dark, has my father. What is his name?'

'I cannot say,' said Uncle Sven.

'Why not?'

'I just can't.'

'I see,' said Luke, uncertainly.

There was an awkward silence in the kitchen-diner-area.

'Dark Father's in the news again,' said Auntie Svenessa, turning a page of the news-flimsy. 'Apparently he has killed another one of the Security Council.'

'Who's that?' said Uncle Sven. 'Did you say Dark Father?'

'Dark Father, yes.'

'Sorry,' said Luke. 'I didn't quite catch that. *Dark Father*, did you say?'

'Dark Father, yes.'

'Dark Father.'

'Hmm, Dark Father.'

'He's a dark one, that Dark Father,' said Uncle Sven. 'Killed another one of the Security Council, has he?'

'That he has,' said Svenessa. 'Throttled him with his bare hands.'

'Bare? No gloves?'

'Indeedy. No gloves. Or skin. Or bone. So bare, in fact,' Svenessa went on, reading slowly from the newspaper, 'that he didn't even use his hands.'

'Not at all?'

'Apparently he held his hand in front of the councillor's throat and made this little beaky pinching motion with forefinger and thumb, and the councillor was throttled. Here,' she added, 'see for yourself.' She passed the news-flimsy over to Luke.

DARK FATHER KILLS THIRD-IN-COMMAND, ORDINARY SOLDIER

Throttles them 'without even touching their necks, how weird is that' says eyewitness

[*Deep space, Thursday*] In a move guaranteed to enhance his power base amongst hardline Imp-Emp-Imp supporters, military leader and Imperial *eminence noire* Dark Father today handed out on-the-spot execution tickets to two members of his loyal and terrified staff. 'Grand Muff o' Tartan had called a meeting of the Security Council,' recalled Imperial Sterntrooper 3449#6a889~1447 Larry Drehe, who was on guard duty that day, 'and Deputy of Internal Repression the Lord Myna Bridishacta raised a point of protocol under point seven of the agenda. So Dark Father, like, totally crushed his windpipe. Without even getting out of his chair. He just sort of held out his black gloved hand and made this, like, pincer gesture, and the Lord Bridishacta started gargling and wheezing, and pretty soon he was solid *gone*. To say it was cool,' Drehe added, making a circle shape with his thumb and middle finger and wagging it in the air in front of him, 'would be, like, *understatement*. It was *way* cool.'

Myna Bridishacta was the third most powerful officer in the Imp-Emp-Imp military machine, in the line-of-command directly behind Dark Father himself and Grand Muff o' Tartan. 'The other guy on guard duty,' said Drehe, 'was my pal George' [Manzarek, Imperial Stern-trooper 3449#6a889~1466] 'and we were pretty impressed, behind our helmets, I don't mind telling you. But when the Lord Bridishacta fell to the floor, George made this sort of *eek* noise, almost under his breath, so Lord Father squashed his thorax as if he was testing a tube of pasta with his fingers to see if it was cooked. And all without actually making contact with him! Like, wow.'

Item seven on the agenda for that meeting questioned the appropriateness of continuing to refer to the 'Jobbi religion' as 'a Galactic-wide movement' when there is presently only one registered worshipper.

A spokesman for Dark Father's press office later issued the following statement: 'Myna Bridishacta was 100% loyal to the Empire, to the Emperor and to Dark Father himself, and was a fanatical believer in the Imperial ideology of Order. But it transpires that he was only 97% terrified of Dark Father. Frankly, the trillions of decent

Imp-Emp-Imp citizens are no longer prepared to put up with that level of insubordination.'

OLAF, the leading Citizens Group of the Empire has declared itself '100% behind the Imperial policy of randomly killing off senior members of military staff for trivial reasons.' 'What you must bear in mind,' said Blun 'Boba' Kett, Chairman of the 'Our Loyalty and Fear Are 100% In the Service of the Imperial Programme of Order Through Oppression' organisation, 'is that this is the only language these people understand.'

'That's pretty Dark behaviour,' said Sven. 'Even for Dark Father.'

'I don't understand,' said Luke. 'If he's going to the bother of holding out his hand, why not just throttle the guy? Or if he's going to use dark telepathy to throttle him, why bother with the hand? Why not just do it from his chair? I mean he could presumably do it with his arms crossed, or in his pockets, if he wanted to.'

'How do you mean?'

'All I'm saying,' said Luke, 'is that it seems to me a little *superfluous* to hold one's hand out in mid-air in front of a person's throat if one has the power to throttle a person with thought alone. What purpose does the hand-holding-out bit serve?'

'It's a puzzle,' agreed Sven. 'But there are many mysteries about Dark Father.'

'Perhaps it was, at root, a theatrical gesture?' suggested Auntie Svenessa. 'Done less for reasons of telepathic communication and more for the benefit of the others watching? It says here that he was wearing his stage magician cloak, and his special helmet.'

'Ah,' said the others, as if that explained everything.

Chapter Three

Concerning the Purchase of Some Robots

Just who is this Luke Seespotrun, you ask? It is a good question, and one I am inclined to answer, since he will play a significant part in the adventures to come.

He is a young lad, handsome though carbuncular, with a tendency for his acne to resolve into unsightly whiteheads rather than the blotchy but slightly less repulsive redheaded spots that are, I suppose, more common. But at seventeen he could be forgiven his repulsive skin condition, it being, after all, a common fate for the young male teenager.

'I've bought two new adendroids,' Uncle Sven announced one day. 'Luke. I want you to take them into the garage and get them cleared up.'

The robots certainly did not look particularly state-of-the-art. One was a dustbin-shaped robot of rather grubby external appearance, and the other a gold-skinned humanoid-shaped robot whose legs were ridiculously stumpy and disproportionate.

Luke led them through into the garage. 'Hi,' he said to the smaller of the two droids. 'What's your name?'

'Eeeeek!' replied the tin, wobbling energetically on its two huge motile globes. 'Eeeeeeeek!' it said again, turning through one hundred and eighty degrees. When its viewing lens was facing the blank wall it seemed to calm down a little.

'OK,' said Luke, only partially discouraged. Turning to the golden adendroid with the stumpy legs he asked, 'What do *you* do?'

'I have a number of functions,' said the golden man. His voice was elegant yet somehow grating. 'I *am* a thesaurus. And a dictionary. I can process words. But mostly I'm programmed to wind humans up; to lead them on only to disappoint them at the most crucial moment, and generally to get them choleric and heart-attack-proximate.'

'What's your designation?'

'See-thru Peep-hol-bra. It's on my chassis.' The robot inverted its arm, and Luke caught a glimpse of a logo: 'C3U-πP-HOL-8RA.'

'That says "Seethreeu Pie-p-hol eightra",' he pointed out.

'No it doesn't.'

'Yes it does . . . just look there. "Eight-ar-ay".'

'By no means. It so happens that they pronounce "8" as a "B" on the planet Antjuice.'

'Do they?'

19

'Which is where I was assembled.'

'Was it?'

'Yes.'

'That's how they pronounce "eight" on that world?'

'Yes.'

Luke was silent for a little space.

'*Is* it, though? Really?'

'Yes.'

'And π?'

'*Pee*,' said the golden robot, loudly. '*Pee*, I tell you.'

'Alright, alright, keep your hair on. What's your friend called?'

'His name is stamped on his back,' said C3U-πP, 'if you were prepared to go to the bother of actually looking. Unless you're blind? Are you actually blind, by any chance?'

'No,' said Luke. 'Of course not.' He walked over to the wall and examined the bin-shaped droid. On the machine's back it said: $RC\text{-}DU^2$.

'Are CDs U2?' he tried.

'A noble attempt,' said See-thru, with a patronising tone of voice. 'Actually it's "Arcy Doo-doo".'

'I think I prefer *Are CDs U2*,' said Luke. 'So he's an RC unit, is he?'

'Yes.'

'Good. Right. An RC unit. Excellent.'

Through the garage door the Tatuonweiner sky was visible, a flawless blue, the air was hot. Desert stretched in every direction. A Tatuonweiner mosquito, roughly the size of a chihuahua, buzzed lazily past on gauzy wings.

Eventually Luke said, 'Right,' again, and then, 'good, excellent, an RC unit. Alrighty-tighty, RC unit, very much *so*. Oh yes.'

'You don't know what an RC unit is, do you?' said See-thru.

'No, no, I don't,' Luke conceded immediately.

'Self-Portable Commode,' said See-thru. 'Another one of humankind's brilliant inventions. First you invented toilets. Then portable toilets. Then self-portable toilets with minds of their own, toilets that can chat to you whilst you relieve yourself. Arcy here can even show you footage of your favourite 3DTV show whilst you're – you know, occupied. Very useful.'

'Well that's all very well and good,' said Luke. 'But we don't need a new toilet on the farm. We've already got one. Two, if you count the pomegranate storage hole. What *we* need is a droid to help out around the farm, so I can leave to join the Imperial Space Navy. A droid to help with planting, harvesting, threshing, gleaning.'

'Oh, he wouldn't be much good at any of that,' said See-thru. 'No arms, you see. Just that bin-like body with the automated swing-top. That and those big motile wheel-globes at the base. Good for flat surfaces, less good on stairs. Considerably less good. Nothing much there to help with farm-style chores.'

'Oh,' said Luke, disappointed. 'And yourself?'

'Well, I'll be honest with you,' said See-thru. 'I'd very promising on the farm. I'd agree to do all sorts of chores, help out, all that sort of thing. But just at the crucial time – say during the precise five-minutes when dew-fruit must be harvested or it'll spoil, and you're really relying on me to get the whole harvest in . . . then I'd freeze up on you. And no amount of yelling at me, or banging the top of my head with your shoe, would unfreeze me.' See-thru shrugged. 'That's just the way I'm programmed.'

Luke felt desperation start gnawing at him. 'But this is terrible! If we don't buy two new droids then I'll be stuck on the farm for another year! You don't understand – it's been my dream to join the Space Navy for as long as I can remember! You've got to help me. Can't you help me?'

'Narp,' replied See-thru, obscurely.

'Narp,' repeated Luke. 'OK. Don't know what that means. Don't really care.'

Luke tried to clean the RC unit, but when he approached the motile commode it cried out 'eeek! eeek! eeek!' and scuttled to the corner. So he turned his attentions to preparing an oil-bath for the C3U unit.

'Tell me,' Luke asked, nodding in the direction of the shivering RC unit in the corner. 'Why does he talk like that?'

'Like what?'

'The only word he seems to use is *eek*. What is that? Is he speaking fax?'

See-thru seemed to find this inordinately funny. 'Fax?' he chortled. 'Him? That trundling poo-bin? – speak *fax*? Oh you tickle me, you really do.'

'Have I said something amusing?'

'Fax—' said See-thru, getting his laughter under control. 'Fax is like the robot Latin. There's no *way* he's got the education necessary to speak Fax. He's a mobile *dump-bin*, in the most scatological sense of that phrase. Fax? Don't make me laugh.'

'So why does he speak that way?'

'Well, the truth is,' said See-thru. 'he's humano-phobic.'

'Say again?'

'He's afflicted with a morbid fear of humans. He can't help himself.'

'I've never heard of that. Is it common amongst adendroids?'

'Why, yes,' said See-thru. 'A lot of robots have it, some more severely than others.'

'But why?'

'Well, there are conflicting theories. It may be castration anxiety. Or it may just be that he can't deal with the squishy, hairy, blobby *horribleness* of the human form. From a robot perspective, you see, humans are more or less repulsive and hideous. You all lack *definition*. There's not enough metal in your constitution. Not enough sharp edges. And when you consider what he was built for, does it surprise you that he's a little, shall we say, person-averse?'

'I see,' said Luke. 'Well that's very interesting. But now it's time for your oil bath.' He stepped back to give See-thru a clear view of the two-metre hole sunk into the garage floor, filled now with gloopy black lubricating oil.

See-thru inclined his head. 'I beg your pardon?'

'There you go,' said Luke. 'I've prepared a nice oil bath for you. After your long trek through the sand wastes, I bet a nice long oil bath would feel really nice.'

See-thru approached the oil bath, dipped a golden finger in, and held it up to his optical inputs. 'You want me – what? To clamber *into* this?'

'Yes.'

'A bath, you called it?'

'An oil bath, yes.'

'That's *bath* in the sense of "container used for immersing and washing the body, usually filled with a mixture of hot water and soap, whereby dirt and sweat is removed from the skin", is it?'

'Well,' said Luke, a little uncertainly. 'Yes.'

'And you've filled this bath with *crude oil*, have you?'

'Don't you fancy it?'

'Fancy it?' repeated See-thru, sarcastically placing his forefinger against the cleft of his metal chin in a mocking imitation of deep thought. 'Well, let-me-see, if it *so happened* I was afflicted with an overall level of *cleanliness*, and I wanted to get rid of that in a bath of stinky *mucky oil* and generally *befoul* myself – under those circumstances I *might* be tempted to clamber into your rank little hole.'

There was a pause.

'That's a no, then, is it?' asked Luke.

'A big hole full of *oil*? What were you *thinking*?'

'I was thinking that you're – you know – a robot.'

'Exactly,' said See-thru, with a witheringly scornful tone of voice. 'A robot. Not a diesel *tractor* from the *1950s*. Do you really think my joints are lubricated by *oil*? I'm a state-of-the-art cybernetic organism. I'm designed to operate in all environments from pure vacuum to the deep ocean. What do you think would happen to oil in the vacuum of deep space if my designer were stupid enough to design me needing oil in my joints? Give it half a thought. Give it a quarter of a thought, if you can afford that much. I mean, *really*.'

Luke stood looking down at the oil bath. 'Well what am I going to do with this two-metre-deep hole full of oil?'

'Narp,' said See-thru, strutting over to his RC-unit friend. 'Not a robot problem.'

Luke shuffled over beside the two robots and sat down, his back to the wall. See-thru Peep-hol was looking standoffish. Arcy Doo-Doo was shuddering with barely controlled panic at the proximity of this human.

'I feel a bit sheepish,' Luke admitted, shortly. 'I've so much to learn about robots.'

'That,' said See-thru, 'you have.'

'Still,' said Luke, regaining the optimism for which he was so famous. 'You guys will teach me – won't you?'

He slapped Arcy on his dome-like crown. In reply the droid said 'eek! eeeek!' He lurched away from Luke, collided with a stack of Froom!® cans sending them scattering skittle-like, tumbled down the three steps to the lower portion of the garage, and landed on his side. A blue light at his side flickered into life and a hologram materialised. It projected clearly, but at ninety degrees.

It was a hologram of a naked woman. It was a kind of nakedness quite new to Luke. He had spent his life surrounded by naked people; but, apart from himself and Uncle Skinny from Skörsgad (who was in his nineties) all the naked people he had ever seen weighed between eighteen and forty stone. Never before had he realised that nakedness could be an attractive or alluring thing. Until now. For this young lady, who looked to be no more than nineteen years of age, was naked in a way wholly new to Luke. Her sinuous, naked form affected him in a way that he couldn't quite put his finger on. Or, to be precise, he *could* put his finger on it, but didn't want to do so in front of the two droids. She was simply gorgeous: smooth skin like satin that had never been sat on; hair a wild tangle of chestnut curls (chestnut in colour, that is, not shaped or textured like chestnuts, which would just be silly); eyes like blue diamonds, and a figure so curvaceous that to run one's hands over it from top to bottom would be, in effect, to mime enthusiastic applause.

As the horizontal holographic naked woman writhed and danced, she opened her perfect, plump red lips and spoke: *Hey! Come on down to the Bada Big-Bang Bar, Main Street, Moz Isleybrothers. Dancing girls from seven different species! Fatalities amongst clientele down by thirteen per cent from last galactic year! Drinks half-price every other Thursday! Come on, big boy – you know you want to.*

And the vision of naked loveliness vanished.

'Hey!' Luke yelled. 'Play that again!'

'Eeeeek!' shrieked RC-DU^2, struggling like an up-ended beetle to get back on its legs. 'Eeeeek!'

No matter how Luke cajoled, or ordered, or threatened, the little RC unit, it refused to replay the beguiling image of perfect human nakedness. C3U-πP-HOL promised to help by persuading the RC droid (now upright and quavering in a corner with its visual inputs to the wall) to replay the image, but after lengthy and elaborate preparations it instead fell into a sleep-like comatose state.

Mildly infuriated, Luke wandered off to his own bed.

Meanwhile, far over his head, the Imp-Emp-Imp Star Destroyer orbited. Aboard this craft Dark Father brooded. Brooding, in fact, was one of his favourite pastimes. But this was brooding with a purpose. He had sent Princess Leper, under guard, to be interrogated far away by the feared Grand Muff o' Tartan, and he was confident that the Princess's secrets would soon be the Imperial Empire's. And once the Rebelend was crushed, total Galactic domination would swiftly follow.

Dark Father cleared his wheezy throat with a punchy cough, and began laboriously to practise his 'evil genius' laugh. You need to work at these things sometimes.

Chapter Four

Old Bony K'nobbli Shows Us Round His Compact and Bijou Desert Hermitage and Talks Frankly About Life as One of the Few Remaining Jobbi Knights Left Alive in the Galaxy

In the morning Luke came down to find the two droids gone. This annoyed him, but it was easy enough to see in which direction they had travelled by the two rows of tracks in the sand. More, in the garage the golden droid had left a post-it, stuck to a post in the garage that happened to function as an item of information technology hardware. It read:

After you went off to bed, RC-DU² stopped being so terrified, his mind cleared and he remembered that he was supposed to go to see Wobbli Bent K'nobbli, who lives, apparently, a few kilometres from you. We would have woken you up, but you seemed to be sleeping so peacefully, sincerely yours, C3U-πP-HOL-8RA.

Dispirited, Luke moped into the kitchen and found his aunt and uncle, naked as jellyfish, eating maple baps. 'Those two droids you bought yesterday, Uncle.'

'Yes?' said Sven, his attention on his breakfast.

'Well they've gone off,' Luke explained.

'Gone off?' said Sven, looking up at Luke. 'Like week-old milk left out of the Friggomat?'

'Off in the sense of departing this place. Said they had to go find Wobbli Bent K'nobbli, whoever he is. Do you think he might be a relative of Old Bony K'nobbli?'

'Completely different person,' said Sven confidently, returning to his breakfast slurping. 'Different names, you see? That's how you tell.'

'I see,' said Luke, sagely. 'Well I think I'll go after them anyway.'

'Why?' asked Aunt Svenessa, sharply. 'Do you think that old fool can tell you something about your father? Just because he knew him and fought beside him for years in the Colon Wars, that doesn't mean he's got anything edifying to say on *that* subject.'

'OK,' said Luke, uncertainly. 'I think I'll go anyway.'

'But you haven't had any breakfast!' Sven objected. 'There's a bucket of yoghurt behind the chair over there.'

'No thanks, Uncle.'

'Be careful of that old wizard,' Svenessa warned as Luke slipped away. 'If he tries to sell you any rabbit's-feet or crystals or tries to get you to go on a quest to dispose of a ring of power or anything like that, just say no.'

Meanwhile in the deep Tatuonweiner desert, a troop of Imp-Emp-Imp Sterntroopers stood looking at the tracks left in the sand by two droids. One was riding a really quite amazingly vivid and life-like-looking Giant Lizard. Another scanned the horizon with up-to-the-minute digital binoculars. 'This way,' he announced to his colleague. 'I think they went this way.'

Luke's journey across the sands was uneventful. He knocked at the hovel door and was granted admission.

'How wonderful to see you, my boy,' said the Jobbi knight. His words were freighted with a strange weight, as if they carried a greater significance than their simple meaning merited.

'Hi, Old Bony,' said Luke.

Old Bony K'nobbli shuffled painfully across the floor of his humble desert dwelling. 'There you go, young Seespotrun,' he said, handing him a cup of

some strange, hot juice, called, he said, 'tea'. This was
one of the old man's strange rituals; whenever a visitor
crossed his threshold (which was not something that
happened very often, of course) he brought out this
disgusting hot juice. 'There you go,' he said, with
tremendous self-satisfaction. 'Drink that.' There was
something rather impressive about the fruity, over-
done timbre of his voice; something oddly classy and
almost Shakespearian.

'Thanks,' said Luke.

'So tell me, young lad, what brings you out here?'

'I think you may have some droids of mine.'

'Ah. The droids,' said Bony. 'Come through.
They're in here. Bring your tea.'

The robots were parked in Old Bony's front room.
They did not seem especially happy to see Luke.

'Come,' said Old Bony, his joints creaking alarmingly. 'Sit down.'

The two of them sat down around the rude wooden
table on rude wooden chairs. Bony looked intently at
his young guest. Luke, a little embarrassed by the
unwavering nature of Bony's gaze, tried smiling
superciliously, shifted his weight on his chair, jolted
his teacup spilling a hefty splash of tea all over the
doily, lurched forward trying to prevent further spil-
lage and fell heavily off the chair, rolling under the

table. Trying to get to his feet he clonked his head on the underside of the table.

Sheepishly, he extricated himself, put his chair back on its legs, and sat down again.

'So lively!' said Old Bony, admiringly. 'So Farcical! So like your father.'

'You knew my father?' asked Luke, lurching forward eagerly, and spilling some more of his drink.

'I did.'

'How odd that we should be talking about this! Because I was, only yesterday morning, having a conversation about my father with my uncle. Over breakfast. So, what was he like? My father?'

'He was a handsome young Jobbi knight,' said Bony, meditatively. 'He and I fought side by side during the Colon Wars. The Farce was very pronounced in him. His name was Jane Seespotrun.'

'Jane,' said Luke. 'Right. Jane. Isn't that more of a *girl*'s name, though?'

'Mmm,' said Bony, nodding. 'He was very sensitive on that subject. It was best not to bring it up in his company, actually. *Very* sensitive.'

'Jane,' said Luke, trying to picture his father. 'Jane, my Dad. Strong in the Farce and a Jobbi master. Now, the Farce – as I understand it – is some kind of universal power or quantity. But who or what are the *Jobbi*?'

'I am one,' said Bony. 'A sort of – not military exactly, a, shall we say, *quasi*-military organisation. Highly armed and wearing a common uniform, but not affiliated to any particular government. An elite of trained warriors who command the Farce to – you know. Act as peacekeepers. Get into fights whilst all the time talking about how they don't want to get into fights. Chop people's arms off at the first sign of trouble. Spy on people. Break things. Stand in the background with arms folded, looking menacing. That sort of thing.'

'I see,' said Luke. 'So they're soldiers?'

'No. They have no official standing. They are only warriors in a loose sense of the word. They belong to no actual *army*.'

'More like Boy Scouts?'

Bony thought about this. 'Yes.'

'Excellent,' said Luke. 'So, only one question remains, a crucial question – what *happened* to my father?'

'Ah,' said Bony. 'Well, yes. Right. What happened?' Luke nodded.

'Well, let's see, let me see. Not to beat around the bush, Dark Father . . . um, well he *killed* your father.

35

Ah, yes, that's it. That's exactly what happened. He *killed* your father, killed him dead. Struck him down, killed him, slew him. In sum,' he concluded, 'killed your father.'

'I understand *killed*,' said Luke. 'But I'm not sure what you mean by that little gesture, the *tweaking* or *twitching* gesture you do with your two forefingers.'

'Gesture?' Old Bony looked confused.

'You did it when you said *killed*,' clarified Luke.

'I did?'

'Yes.'

'That's just a,' Bony said waving his hand vaguely, 'just a Jobbi thing.'

'Right,' said Luke, nodding. 'So to be absolutely clear. Dark Father *killed* my father. Do I understand you? Is that about the long and short of it?'

'Yes,' said Bony, nodding emphatically and squeezing, by the action, a startling series of crackling noises out of the bones in his neck.

'That's simply ghastly,' said Luke. 'I suppose I should vow revenge upon him, or something. Would that be the thing to do?'

'Good idea, good idea,' said Bony, distractedly, as if he wasn't really listening. He seemed more interested in the adendroid that they had rescued from the Offies.

'There is a message recorded inside that droid,' said

Luke, getting on the ground next to him. 'I got the first part of it this morning, but then it just fizzled out. But believe me, it would be well worth getting another chance to check it out. It was worth checking out.'

'Let me see if I can get it to replay,' muttered Bony, getting up and shuffling over to the robot. 'Here you go,' he said, jabbing RC-DU^2 in its metallic midriff.

A three-dimensional hologram immediately appeared on the dirt floor of Old Bony K'nobbli's hut. It was a two-foot tall, vivid representation of a well-built gentleman wrapped in a multicoloured toga of some kind.

Greetings! The hologram said, staring at the space directly between K'nobbli and Luke. *I am Nico Sigi Toussaint from the Planet Nigerium. I have forty million Imperial Credits trapped in a bank-account in the National Bank of Nigerium, and need a non-Nigerium friend to help me move it offworld. If you send me your bank details, a copy of your retinal scan and a simile of your signature, I will transfer the sum to you, and in return for your help will pay you twenty per cent of . . .*

Bony kicked the droid; the hologram scattered and fell into crumbs of light before vanishing altogether.

'That wasn't it,' said Luke. 'It was a naked woman. But thin. Not fat-naked, but really *nice* naked.'

Bony was peering at the insides of the droid.

'There's a bunch of junk in here, my young friend,' he said. 'Lightsword enlargement offers. Marketing software. Ah, here's a lady image, unless I'm very much mistaken.' He prodded, and the droid shuddered to life, projecting a second image.

This one was indeed of a lady, but not the naked female Luke had seen before. Instead she was demurely clad in a white dress, with a striking hairstyle, gathered in two continental-sausage-style curls on either side of her head. Luke's eyes were drawn to these, until he realised that they weren't coils of hair, but rather growths or tumour-like lumps of oddly symmetrical shape, one on either side of her face.

'Yuk,' he said. But the hologrammatical figure was speaking:

I can only hope, she was saying, *that my message reaches Wobbli Bent K'nobbli, and that you can do something to help me. Dark Father has captured the ship I was travelling on. On which I was travelling, I should say. That's how distressed I am right now. It's as if I no longer care about not ending my sentences with a preposition. Woe! Woe – but not to get distracted, included in this droid is, in coded form, the Great Secret, the Secret my mother passed to me in Secret, about which she swore me to secrecy, and which is so secret that even I have no idea what the Secret is, although nevertheless I believe it will bring about the end of the war between the Imp-Emp-Imp and the Rebelend. I hope that by passing this Secret on to you, Wobbli, I will be serving the forces of good. Please ensure that it gets to my adoptive father on the planet Ya!Boo!. Help me, Wobbli Bent; of my list of top hundred hopes you're in the upper fifty.*

'Wobbli Bent K'nobbli?'

'That's me,' said Bony. 'The early stages of my disease left me rather unsteady on my pins. Now that I'm almost bent double I find it easier to balance.'

'Do you know her?'

'Yes. Well, I knew her mother. Quite well. As it happens.'

'She has lovely eyes,' Luke mused dreamily. 'Although the unsightly fungoid growths on either side of her head are a little less prepossessing.'

'Yes. Of course, a gentleman might refrain from drawing attention to them.'

Luke blushed. 'What's her name?' he asked.

'Princess Leper. We must do as she says, and bring this droid to the rebel command. Assuming you don't mind getting involved in a rebellion against the Imperial Empire of the Imperium that might result not only in your own death, but the murder of your friends and family and the sowing of your family estate with Arcturan salt?'

'Well,' said Luke, 'I have been planning for ten

years or more to join the Imperial Empire of the Imperium Space Navy, going to open days, being an active member of the Junior Cadets, reading the literature endlessly, watching Imp-Emp-Imp propaganda soap operas on the 3DTV, especially *Fear and Obedience: the Young Generation*, and generally preparing myself for life as an Imp-Emp-Imp pilot. But, on the other hand, you seem like a nice enough bloke. I'm happy to throw out my entire life plan at the drop of a hat and go along with you.'

'I'll get the tarpaulin off my hovervan,' said Bent. 'I'd advise *you* to put some clothes on.'

Luke looked down at himself. As was often the case with long-term nudists, he had wholly forgotten that he was as naked as a chef. 'Right,' he said.

Chapter Five

The Empire, Dum Dum Dum, Duhm *∂'∂um,* Duhm *∂'∂um*

Princess Leper was being held captive in the deepest dungeon behind the most dedicated guards, deep inside the latest massive monstrous mechanical contrivance of the Imperial Empire of the Imperium. Officially called 'The Health Star', unofficially this construction was universally known – and feared – under a more chilling appellation: *The Death Spa*.

And what, you ask, is this Death Spa? Well, since you ask, I'll tell you.

The Imperial Empire of the Imperium had been secretly constructing this moon-sized movable machine over many months. With it they planned to bring muscle tone and detoxification to the entire galaxy, wiping out all sickness, lassitude and non-pertness. It was, in other words, the most horrifying prospect for ordinary non-fascist life. Under the hideous strictures of the Death Spa, the flabby, untoned flesh common to most of the trillions of non Imp-Emp-Imp citizens

would simply *disintegrate*. Very few individual con-
stitutions can withstand the sort of pummelling and
detoxification of intensive Death Spa attack.

Muscles grown flabby with years of disuse simply
tear when subjected to intensive exercise-massage-
electro-toning assault. Tendons that for decades have
been acting as little more than glorified string, holding
arms and legs to the torso, will *snap* when put under
the sorts of strain required by abrupt Death Spa
workout. The hearts beating in a trillion chests, humanoid and alien, have in almost all cases been required
– for decades – to do nothing more than squeeze a
handful of sludgy blood in the general direction of
'the bloodstream' a couple of times a second. Under
the effort provoked by the Death Spa's 'workout ray'
those hearts are all doomed. Only the very fittest,
hardest, thinnest and most beautiful – which is to say,
the fascist – will survive.

When the Emperor of the Imperial Empire of
the Imperium looked out amongst the yet-to-be-
assimilated worlds of the Galaxy, he saw planet after
planet populated by fat, exercise-averse slugs. Sometimes these slugs were actual slugs, native to the
worlds in question; but often they were humans
whose bodies approximated slug-like qualities on
account of the many years of eating nothing but

sugar- and lard-based food groups whilst slumped in front of the 3DTV. To such a population, the very idea of a Death Spa provoked terror beyond belief.

And so the Emperor had ordered one built.

But why (you ask) did the Emperor not simply utilise his enormous and finely trained space fleet, packed with millions of highly trained Sterntroopers, to conquer these as yet unconquered worlds? Was this vast military machine not (you continue, pressing home what you consider to be your advantage in this notional argument) sufficient to keep the already trillions-strong population of the Imp-Emp-Imp crushed and subservient?

These are good questions.

And the answers? The answers, not to hold you in suspense, are *no* and *no*.

Allow me to fill you in on the history and current disposition of the Imperial armed forces.

The Imp-Emp-Imp dominated the forty thousand colonised worlds of the Galactic Federation with a ruthless oppressive military force. Its fleet of spaceships was all-inspiring. Or perhaps I mean awe-inspiring. Yes, the latter. Their Battle Frigates were twenty miles long, titanic constructions of metal and plastic, hideously beweaponed. Yet, vast though they were, they were dwarfed by the Super Battle Dreadnoughts, which were a hundred miles from top to stern. And a hundred of these Super Battle Dreadnoughts gathered together could still nestle in the underbelly of the ExtraSuper-Size Colossal Megabucket Bigboy HyperCruiser, the biggest ship in the fleet. Which is to say, it *was* the biggest ship in the fleet, until the Imperial Emperor commanded the building of a Goliath Vastness Double-Cathedral Megasuperhyperdestroyer.

This fleet was launched upon the inky blackness of space to patrol and dominate, to hold the Imperial Empire of the Imperium together by sheer terror and brute force, by the forceful brutishness of its terrible, um. Its terrible *she-ers*, I suppose.

But this fleet, though awesome, was not terribly effective at actually defeating the burgeoning Rebel-end opposition. In a number of space engagements it was roundly defeated. There were, it seems, teething problems. In particular, the spaceships were so huge that it took them three weeks to slow to a stop. Their turning circle was seventeen parsecs. The rebel alliance slipped past them in much smaller and much more manoeuvrable craft.

And so the Imperial Emperor ordered the execution of the designers who had designed the various larger ships, and instead called for the creation of *Ti* (short for tiny)-*fighters*. Millions of these craft were manufactured: intricately designed spheres fitted with laser-bolt disruptor cannons, and also with two solar panels, one on each side, which were not of *much* use in the blackness of space, but helped the heating coil warm up on the onboard water tank, thereby reducing the craft's electricity bill by up to seven per cent, depending on available sunlight.

At the Battle of Progrok 7 the Emperor, and his terrifying second-in-command Dark Father, unveiled a fleet of one hundred thousand Ti-fighters and sent them out to defeat a much smaller Rebelend force.

But there proved to be a particular problem with the Ti-fighters, and it was this: flight controllers found themselves incapable of delivering the order 'fly tighter Ti-fighters' four or five times in rapid succession without, inadvertently, giving the order to 'flitter, fla-tatters'. The Imp-Emp-Imp pilots, hypno-trained to obey all orders immediately and without question, no matter how bizarre, tried flittering and made a range of guesses as to what fla-tattering involved. Many crashed into other craft. Some flew round and round in circles until the rebels blew them up. One or two flew away altogether.

The battle was a washout.[2]

---

[2] This is to say, one of those debacles which causes people to *shout wa!*

After an entire level of command officers were executed, it was decided to rename the spacecraft 'Imperial Empire of the Imperium Small-bore Designated Spacecraft Interceptors', which meant that the process of giving orders to the pilots, whilst slowed somewhat, no longer ran the risk of tongue-twisted misunderstanding. By the time the order 'fly tighter, Imperial Empire of the Imperium Small-bore Designated Spacecraft Interceptors!' was fully uttered, the moment had often passed, but at least there was no ambiguity about what was being said. Unfortunately, it now took so long for orders to be expressed battle was often finished by the time flight controllers could utter a complete order.

And so the Emperor and Dark Father had a right old confab. Yes indeedy, they settled down with a family-sized jug of Rutullian coffee and some amaretti biscuits and came up with a new plan.

The new plan was the Death Spa. And that is where Princess Leper was being imprisoned.

Grand Muff o' Tartan was standing in the control room of the Death Spa, wearing his tartan muff, his cadaverous face gazing impassively at the large-scale viewing screen before him. Two Sterntroopers brought Princess Leper to him.

'Tartan!' she spat, derisively. 'I might have known.'

'Might you?' sneered Tartan.

'You can torture me all you want,' said Leper, bravely, 'I'll never tell you the location of the Rebel-end main base.'

The Grand Muff looked surprised at this. 'There's a main base to the Rebelend, is there?' he asked. 'I didn't realise that. I thought you were scattered in many miniature little bases, round and about the galaxy.'

'Um,' said the Princess, looking about her as if for inspiration. 'Yes. *That's* it – scattered all over the place. Not what I said. What I said was a slip of the tongue. No main base, that's right, nothing like that. There is no main base.'

'Then why did you say there was one?'

'What I *meant* to say was – you can torture me all you like, but I'll, um, never reveal the locations of the many miniature little Rebelend bases scattered round and about the galaxy.'

'Presumably, as far as *location* goes,' said Tartan, 'that would be *scattered round and about the galaxy*. Am I getting warm?'

'Um,' said the Princess.

'But I'm more interested in this one *main* base you mentioned.'

'Me? I didn't say anything about the main base. I mean, I didn't say anything about any "main base".'

'I've been holorecording our conversation. Do you want me to play back your words?'

'Look – why don't I go out, you can have me brought in again by the guards, and we can start this all over again.'

'Where is the main base, Princess?'

'Oh no,' said the Princess, shaking her head wisely. 'You won't trick me. Just because you managed to trick me, there, at the beginning doesn't mean that I'm prepared to betray my friends. And even if you *tried* to attack Gregbare, what's to say that we don't have a massive defence shield and some really *really* big laser cannons?'

Tartan nodded slowly. 'Gregbare, is it?'

The Princess made a little gargling noise in her throat. 'Is that what you heard? Um, your hearing might be – for all you know, I said, um, Bedgare. Or Redhair. I certainly never said Gregbare. You must have misheard. In fact there is no central base. There's also no planet Gregbare. I just made it up. Um.'

'Thank you, my dear,' said the Grand Muff, gesturing to the Sterntroopers to take their prisoner back to the detention suite. 'You've been most helpful.'

'Wait!' cried Princess Leper. 'I demand a re-interrogation! I *demand* my right to be interrogated again . . .'

Her cries diminished to silence as she was dragged down one of the Death Spa's lengthy metal corridors.

Chapter Six

'These aren't – the droids – [wave of hand] you're looking for'

The ride into town in Old Bony's hovervan was not comfortable. The hovervan did a poor job of living up to its name, proving to be more of a dragalongthe-ground-van that banged and bounced on every pebble in the way.

But eventually they cleared a rise and rolled into Moz Isleybrothers, the main town of Tatuonweiner. At first view, this seemed nothing more than a few ram-shackle adobe houses, with a couple of humanoid aliens in smocks hanging about. But, strikingly, turning a corner the hovervan rolled through a vast open space in which a myriad of non-humanoid aliens sold bizarre wares, bickered with one another and generally rushed about, whilst in the distance a Sterntrooper mounted on another of those extremely realistic and vivid-looking giant lizards startled a seven-legged hovercyclist off his mount. Round another corner and the hovervan rolled through drab underpopulated streets once more.

50

Through seedy outskirts they rolled into the seedy inskirts, and did not stop until two Imp-Emp-Imp Sterntroopers waved them down at a roadblock.

'Halt!' called the first Sterntrooper stepping up to the side of the van. 'We have orders to search every car entering the port to locate two droids. These droids are Imperial property and will be confiscated. Anybody found trying to smuggle them in will be arrested.' He looked to the back of the hovervan where Luke's two droids were sitting, trying to look innocent. 'One is a golden annoyance-model,' the Sterntrooper continued, 'the other a motile commode.' He stared long and hard at C3U-πP-HOL-8RA and RC-DU^2. 'Have either of you seen any such droids.'

'Bony, what are we going to do?' staged-whispered Luke into Old Bony's right ear. 'They're looking for *our* droids – he said they're going to arrest us.'

'Don't worry my young friend,' said Bony. 'I have a plan to smuggle these illegal droids past the noses of these Sterntroopers.'

'You do?' whispered Luke. 'What's your plan?'

'You two realise,' said the Sterntrooper, leaning a little way into the car, 'that I *can* hear what you're saying? I mean, your whispers are pretty loud, even if my helmet weren't fitted with sound amplification technology. Which it is.'

Luke looked at the soldier aghast.

'The Farce can have a powerful effect on the mind unused to it,' Bony continued, oblivious. 'I'll use a special voice I can put on.'

'You see,' said the Sterntrooper, sounding a little peeved. 'I heard the whole of that. You just said "the Farce can have a powerful effect on the mind unused to it". I mean, you're not even *trying*. Shouldn't you have sorted out a plan *before* you got to our road-block?'

'My good fellow,' said Bony, addressing the Stern-trooper. 'These are not the droids you're looking for.'

'You mean,' said the trooper, ' "these aren't the droids *for which we are looking*." Don't you?'

Bony's brow furled and his smile sagged moment-arily, but then it returned to his face even more beamingly. 'I suppose I do,' he said.

The Sterntrooper stared at him. 'OK,' he said, eventually. 'If you say so.'

'Come on, Bony, let's go,' said Luke, urgently.

'Wait a moment,' said Old Bony. 'Watch this.' From the folds of his brown cloak he whisked an onion. 'Here you go, squaddie,' he said, handing it to the Sterntrooper. 'It's for you. It's a lovely *apple*.' He turned his head and winked at Luke.

'Bony,' urged Luke, in a panicky voice. 'Let's go, *now*.'

'Thanks,' said the soldier, sounding slightly surprised, but taking the onion.

'Aren't you going to take a lovely big *bite* from it?' prompted Bony. 'Eh? Eh?'

'Well, to do that I'd have to remove my helmet,' explained the Sterntrooper. 'And I'm not allowed to do that on duty. I'll save it 'til later. But thanks anyway.'

'Let's *gooo* Bony, *pleeease—*' begged Luke.

'Just a minute. I tell you what, Mr Sterntrooper. You know what I think? I think you're an *Arcturan Chicken*. Aren't you?'

'A chicken,' repeated the soldier, dubiously.

'That's right. A chicken. You really should be clucking, don't you think?'

'Cluck,' said the soldier cautiously, as if humouring the old man.

'I'd say it sounds more,' said Bony, encouragingly, 'like b'KAH-hk kluk kluk kluk!' He flapped his elbows up and down a little. 'You know – more chickeny.'

'You can go about your business,' said the Sterntrooper, waving them on. 'Go about your business. Please.'

❊

They parked outside a rundown and dodgy-looking bar. A neon light of tremendous length had been twisted and shaped to spell the words Bada Big-Bang Bar, and might have been illuminated, or not illuminated; it was difficult to tell in the piercingly bright sunlight of the Tatuonweiner morning.

'In here,' said Bony, 'we'll find a pilot in here to fly us to Ya!Boo! Now be careful . . . This is where the scum of the galaxy come to drink and eat nuts and play bar-billiards. And chat to their friends. And to put coinage in the fruit machines. The very *scum* of the galaxy. You'll need your wits about you.'

'I'm ready.'

'We'll leave the droids in the van.'

Together they stepped through the low door.

Inside it was dark, and nearly deserted. The bar smelt of those things a bar smells of at eleven in the morning: stale smoke, old beer, yesterday's fun. A baralien was sitting on a stool behind the bar. In one corner alcove a good-looking human man was sipping beer. Beside him was a huge yeti-like creature slumped over the table, apparently asleep. The bar was otherwise deserted.

'There's nobody in here but that man,' Luke said.

'Let's hope he's a pilot,' said K'nobbli. He creaked and shuffled his way over to them and took a seat.

'Hello there,' said the attractively-featured fellow. He really was a very good-looking chap; clear manly features, beautiful feathery hair layered perfectly and with not a single split end. 'Can I help you?'

'I hope so,' said K'nobbli. 'We're looking for a pilot.'

'I'm a pilot,' said the man. 'My name is Hand Someman, and I'm at your service. This is my co-pilot, Masticatetobacco. Don't disturb him; he's hibernating right now.'

'I'm Bony K'nobbli,' said K'nobbli. 'This is Luke Seespotrun.'

'What we need to know,' said K'nobbli impatiently, 'is, can we hire you and your ship to fly us off this world without the Imperial Empire of the Imperium capturing us?'

'Sure thing,' said Hand. 'How much you paying?'

'Ten thousand Imperial Credits,' said K'nobbli, with the air of a man who has no experience at all of money plucking a sum out of the air.

'That would come in very handy,' said the man. 'Because, as it happens, I'm in hock to a local gangster for precisely that sum. Do you know him? Pizza the Hutt, the disgusting alien creature shaped like a huge fluke, covered in revolting red pus and blotches, who rules this town with ruthless and violent cruelty?'

'I've never heard of him,' said Luke. 'But then again, I'm a nice middle-class lad. What's your ship like?'

'It's called the Millennium Bug,' said Hand Someman. 'Not a very good name, I know. I wanted to call it the Millennium Wasp, but that name was already registered. The same was true of Millennium Butterfly, Millennium Preying Mantis and Millennium Fly.'

'Pleasant though it is to chat like this,' said K'nobbli, 'I really think we should be going. Time being of the essence, and everything.'

'Right,' said Hand Someman. 'We'll have to carry my co-pilot.'

'*Carry* him?' said K'nobbli, freezing in the process of getting to his feet.

'Didn't you hear me? He's hibernating. He's a Woozie, from the planet Wooz. He hibernates for six months of the year. And a year on Wooz only lasts seven months. For the extra month he is awake, but not very with-it. Mind you, it's not surprising that he's tired during his month awake. He's got to cram everything into that one month – it's pretty exhausting.'

K'nobbli cast a rather aspersive glance at the snoozing hairy figure. 'What is he?' he asked. 'Some breed of giant dog?'

'Something like that,' said Someman. 'Come on, I'll

get under one armpit – you – Luke, did you say your name was? – you get under the other.'

There was an unpleasant surprise waiting for them outside.

'Hello,' said the Imp-Emp-Imp Sterntrooper. 'Remember me? It turns out I'm not a chicken. And that apple you gave me tasted *horrible*.'

'Ah,' said K'nobbli. Behind the Sterntrooper was a squad of soldiery. Behind that squad was another squad. All had laser rifles, and none looked unready to use them.

'You're *nicked*,' said the first Sterntrooper. 'Frankly. And we're confiscating your droids.'

'Quick,' panted Hand Someman, seriously weighed down and straining under half the weight of his sleeping companion. Luke, similarly burdened, had gone very red in the face. 'To the hovervan.'

'Fear not!' cried K'nobbli. 'I shall fight them off with my lightsword. You all get in my hovervan and escape – drive rapidly away, and get to Mr Someman's spaceship. Go!'

Before Luke's astonished eyes K'nobbli pulled a long, narrow glass tube from his gown. A moment's fumbling with a switch somewhere at the bottom of this object transformed it into a beaming, gleaming shaft of light, flickering slightly. As the Sterntroopers stepped back in amazement, K'nobbli wielded this gleaming object with practised sweeps, and took up a sword-fighter's stance.

'*En guard!*' said Bony. 'Watch yourself – *middle* guard! *Left* guard. *Right* gua – or, actually, not that last one. Have *at* you!'

He swung the gleaming blade right around his head and finished up with it held horizontally before his chest, his bony elbow poking out by his ear, and a menacing expression in his eyes.

The foremost Sterntrooper recovered himself and unholstered his laser pistol.

With a swiftness at odds with his apparently old and decrepit body, K'nobbli darted forward and brought the lightsword sharply down, to cleave the hapless soldier's shooting arm from his shoulder.

The lightsword collided with the upper arm of the armoured Sterntrooper. There was a loud cracking sound. The light went out, and the top of the glass tube broke away. Glass splinters scattered. The Sterntrooper's armour was unmarked.

'Um,' said Luke.

'Oh dear,' said K'nobbli, examining the shattered device. 'Actually, truth to tell, it's more of a cere-monial device.'

The Sterntrooper raised his laser pistol and fired. A bolt of red throbbing energy sped through the air, deadly, although it travelled, oddly, slowly enough for K'nobbli to move his head slightly such that the shot missed him by millimetres and instead struck Hand Someman in the chest. The pilot cried out 'agh!' and tumbled to the ground. Masticatetobacco collapsed on top of him, pulling Luke down too. When he came to rest, Luke's face was awkwardly close to a large wound in Hand Someman's chest: it was bleeding badly, and steaming a little. 'Oh no,' he said.

Hand Someman only groaned.

The next thing that Luke knew, he was being lifted by more-than-organic strength and tossed unceremoniously in the back of the open hovervan. K'nobbli was at the wheel, as C3U-πP-HOL hauled the supine forms of first Masticatetobacco and then Hand Someman into the car. 'It takes a robot to save the day,' he said. 'Away we go.'

'Go where?' demanded K'nobbli. Laser bolts from the many weapons of the Sterntroopers were flying through the air over their heads.

'Spaceport Hangar 337,' gasped Hand Someman, clutching his wound, his face a rictus of agony.

'Right ho,' said K'nobbli; and the van sped away, rocking as laser bolts collided with its sides and flew dangerously close to their heads.

Chapter Seven

Aboar∂ the ISS Order Through Fear and Obedience XVII *in orbit aroun∂ Tatuonweiner (Dum Dum Dum, Duhm ∂'∂um, Duhm ∂'∂um)*

High above, in polar orbit around the planet, Dark Father was in his extensive but minimally decorated quarters. He brooded. He had received reports from the Death Spa. He had communicated with the Imperial Emperor, who had foreseen that there was no further need to pursue the droids on the planet's surface below. There were new orders; to go to the planet Gregbare, the world amongst whose naked inhabitants the Rebelend command centre had been located.

But Dark Father brooded. All was not still in his mind. He summoned the Destroyer's Commander to his quarters, and with promptitude motivated by loyalty and terror, the Commander came.

'COMMANDER,' wheezed Dark Father, doomily.

'Yes, Lord Father,' said Commander Regla Onzed-cars, standing to attention and tucking his arms behind his back. The trick, he had decided after much thought, was to stare *not quite directly* at Dark Father's faceplate. To stare right into his big black cyborg eyes would be to give the impression of an insolent subordination, which would be tantamount to asking to have a reef knot tied in one's trachea. But to look pointedly *away* from Dark Father, as if he were too hideous to behold (as, obviously, he was) would likewise be courting disaster. Indeed it would be doing more than courting disaster. It would be plying disaster with drink and pressuring it to come home with you tonight. It would be actively stalking disaster, sending disaster persistent erotic emails and hanging around outside her front door trying to engage her in conversation as she dashed to the bus stop. Regla Onzedcars put all his energy into striking the exact balance between these two dangerous courses of action. He stood, motionless, at attention.

'YOU ARE TO BRING THE FLEET TO THE PLANET GREGBARE,' said Dark Father.

'Immediately, Lord Father.'

'THE DEATH SPA WILL FOLLOW.'

'Of course, Lord Father.'

There was an awkward silence, broken only by the

wheezy rasping that emanated from Dark Father's helmet. Commander Onzedcars waited, trying to maintain an absolute, respectful motionlessness. Fourteen of his predecessors had died because this same Dark Lord of the Psmyth, annoyed, had turned their gullets into cat's-cradles. He waited. It was not easy. There was a tickle right in the end of his nose that threatened to grow, as tickles will, into a full-blown sneeze if he wasn't careful. What with the recycled air in the starship-destroyer, and the fact that the thermostat always seemed to be turned up just a touch too high, Commander Onzedcars found himself sneezing quite frequently. That, and the constant coughing. He contemplated what Dark Father would do to one of his subordinates who had the temerity to sneeze upon his perfectly black cloak. He would be unlikely to be understanding. The fleet, after all, was three thousand light years from the nearest reputable dry-cleaners.

'COMMANDER . . .' said Dark Father, eventually.

Commander Onzedcars' heart gave a little stumble. He recognised that tone of voice. It was still doomy, profound, freighted with darkness and death, but added to that was the slight trace of . . . *ANXIETY*. When Lord Father was being murderously ruthless he was at least being *PREDICTABLY* murderously ruthless. But when he got into these sorts of moods, Commander Onzedcars felt an ontological terror yawn within him. And not yawn because it was tired and about to nod off; oh no. Yawn because it wanted to devour him – to swallow him whole and digest him in an agony of acid and crushing constricting muscles, to – actually, on second thoughts, perhaps 'yawn' wasn't the right word to use there in the first place. Gape. Open wide its grisly jaws and flash its razor teeth in the sunlight.

'Yes, my Lord?'

'COMMANDER . . . THE MEN . . .'

'The men, my Lord?'

'DO THEY . . . DO THEY EVER SAY THAT . . . THAT I HAVE NO SENSE OF HUMOUR?'

This was a tricky one. Onzedcars took a quick breath. 'The men are too terrified and loyal ever to talk about you, my lord – in any way.'

'GOOD,' said Dark Father. He turned his back on his Commander. 'GOOD. BECAUSE, YOU KNOW, I *DO* HAVE A SENSE OF HUMOUR. A VERY GOOD SENSE OF HUMOUR, AS IT HAPPENS.'

'Of course you do, my Lord,' said Onzedcars,

praying that Father would dismiss him now, or failing that, kill him quickly and put an end to his misery.

'WHY, ONLY THE OTHER DAY,' Dark Father wheezed in a doomy imitation of a lighthearted offhand interjection, 'ADMIRAL DADINT' OXO-FAMILY SAID TO ME, "DARK FATHER", HE SAID TO ME, "I FIND THESE REPORTS OF REBEL ACTIVITY IN THE HAMILTON QUADRANT VERY HARD TO SWALLOW", AND I REPLIED, "OH YOU *DO*, DO YOU? HARD TO *SWALLOW*, IS IT?" AND I CRUSHED HIS ENTIRE OESOPHAGAL AND TRACHEAL AREA USING ONLY THE POWER OF THE FARCE, AND AS HE LAY CHOKING AND DYING ON THE DECK I SAID "HOW'S ABOUT *THAT* FOR HARD TO SWALLOW?" EH?'

'Very amusing, my Lord,' said Commander Onzedcars. Sweat was creeping down the sides of his face, but he held himself motionless.

'I SAID IT IN A VERY COOL, SUAVE SORT OF WAY,' Dark Father added.

'I'm sure you did, my Lord.

'LIKE A YOUNG SEAN CONNERY. WITH A CONNERY SORT OF INFLECTION.'

'Yes, my Lord.'

'NOT A SUPERCILIOUS ROGER MOORE-ISH MANNER. I SAID IT IN A SUAVE-BUT-DEADLY WAY.'

'Yes, my Lord.'

'THAT'S FUNNY, WOULDN'T YOU SAY?'

'Very funny indeed, my Lord.'

Dark Father paced, with long strides, to the massive circular porthole that gave his suite of rooms so impressive a view of the khaki-coloured planet below. 'YOU SAY THAT,' he wheezed. 'BUT YOU AREN'T LAUGHING.'

'Ha,' said Onzedcars, slightly mad-eyed. 'Ha. Ha-ha-ha-ha.'

'COMMANDER, I FEEL *YOU* UNDER-STAND ME. YOU APPRECIATE THE DIFFICULTIES OF A MAN IN MY POSI-TION. OF *COURSE* I HAVE A SENSE OF HUMOUR. I HAVE A VERY WELL DE-VELOPED SENSE OF HUMOUR. I WAS WATCHING *NIGHT AT THE OPERA* AGAIN ON MY 3D HOLORECORDER ONLY LAST NIGHT.'

'A comic classic, Lord Father.'

'ISN'T IT, THOUGH? I MEAN, ISN'T IT? EVERYBODY SAYS SO. AND THE FUNNY ONE – HE'S VERY FUNNY, ISN'T HE?'

'The funny one, my Lord?'

'ZEPPO, IS IT? HE'S *VERY* FUNNY.'

The heart within Onzedcars's chest was like a hummingbird having an epileptic fit as he said, 'Zeppo, my Lord?'

'ZEPPO, YES. HE'S THE FUNNY ONE, ISN'T HE?'

'Er, well my Lord . . . that's as to say, many people consider, er, Groucho to be . . .'

'GROUCHO?' bellowed Father with a wheezy and doomy intensity.

'Or Harpo . . .'

'HARPO? BUT HE DOESN'T EVEN SPEAK. WHAT'S FUNNY ABOUT NOT SPEAKING?' Father seemed to be contemplating for several moments. 'PLAYING THE HARP?' he asked, eventually. 'WHAT'S FUNNY ABOUT THAT?'

'Funny about a harp, my Lord?'

'YES.'

'. . . nothing, my Lord.'

'I THOUGHT NOT.' Father seemed to con-template this essential and universal truth for a while. Then, as if noticing that Onzedcars was still there, he said: 'YOU ARE DISMISSED, COM-MANDER.'

'Very good, my Lord. Oh – Lord Father? There was one more thing.'

'YES?'

'I just thought I should report that our troops on the surface have located the two droids, together with a number of organic life forms we take to be members of the Rebelend. Shall we capture them and bring them aboard before departing for Gregbare?'

'YES, COMMANDER. THAT IS INDEED EXCELLENT NEWS.'

'Might I . . . er, might I *leave*, my Lord?'

'YES, YES,' said Dark Father, preoccupied with his own thoughts.

Gratefully Regla Onzedcars stepped smartly from Dark Father's quarters. Once in the corridor outside he started running.

Chapter Eight

Back on Tatuonweiner

But though Imp-Emp-Imp Commander Onzedcars was confident of capturing the droids, and the various humans who accompanied them, they themselves had not given up hope of escaping. Were they to escape, of course, they would be putting the Imp-Emp-Imp Destroyer Commander in a very awkward position: he would have to go back to Dark Father and admit that he had spoken too soon, which might have very unpleasant consequences for him. But it is a mark of the essential selfishness of the Rebelend forces that they neither knew nor cared about the fate of Regla Onzedcars. What can you say?

'If we can just get aboard the Millennium Bug,' gasped Hand Someman. 'If we can just get to my ship, we can fly out of here and get clear away.'

'Hold on,' said Luke, trying to take a look at Someman's wound. In the wildly rocking, veering and lurching van it wasn't easy. 'It looks nasty,' he concluded, leaning over the injured man's chest. 'If I remember my first aid training correctly we may need—' At this point the van turned sharply left and braked hard. The sleeping body of Masticatetobacco fell on Luke and knocked him over.

'We're here,' called K'nobbli, from the front. 'Come on everybody, let's get aboard. The Sterntroopers are only moments behind us.'

It took several minutes to transfer everybody aboard the battered-looking frisbee-shaped spaceship in the open-roofed hangar. Luke helped Hand to the cockpit. Everybody crowded in behind them. Through the cockpit windscreen they could see white-armoured Sterntroopers pouring into the hangar.

'Kid,' said Hand Someman, clutching the wound in his chest. 'I'm too shot up to pilot. *You're* going to have to fly the Millennium Bug owdda here.'

' "owwda"?'

'—out of.'

'I see. But wait,' Luke cried, 'I've never flown an interstellar spaceship! I've barely had time to practise on my uncle's flying golf cart. What does this lever do?'

Hand hauled his body forward in its chair, grimacing with pain, and squinnied at the level Luke was indicating. 'That – that's the Semileptonic Beta Invariant Drive Overload. It focuses the tau-leptons through the branching-ratio determinator, so that the neutrino condensate preserves a constant Vub balance and the thrust remains *in*clusive – apply that lever when the hyper-tau state, during the initial conditions for subspace separation, approaches a perturbative level – but *don't* in any circumstances use it to try to *reduce* the invariance of conventionally oriented sub-atomic tau-leptons, ya hear? – because then you'll run the *serious* risk of backing up semileptonic beta events, and if that happens then your tau-leptons will begin to cascade into *dilepton* formulations,' he gasped, through gritted teeth.

'I see,' said Luke, nodding knowledgeably. 'And this lever?'

'Cigarette lighter.'

'Right.'

Luke stared intently at the panel replete with flashing lights. There was a very large number of the flashing lights. There was also a large number of switches, buttons, levers and various other instrumentation. 'I think I can do it!' he called. 'I've been paying attention to all the stuff Old Bony has been telling me about the Farce. I think I can feel the Farce now – it will guide me. Strap in, everyone! We're leaving!'

Hand Someman, nearly fainting with the pain, pulled his seatbelt strap across his belly, and Old

Bony K'nobbli fitted himself into the adjacent one. Masticatetobacco was already slumped in a seat. The two droids extended grapples to clutch the metal deck beneath them.

Luke grasped the steering column with both hands. Through the windscreen he could see Imp-Emp-Imp troops setting up a tripod-mounted heavy-duty laser rifle. Once it was ready, the Millennium Bug would be easy meat. Their goose would be cooked. They would be in hot water indeed. They would be out of the frying pan and into the fire. Luke was beginning to assemble a fairly impressive mental list of cooking-based metaphors for their condition when the whole ship jarred and rocked. One of the Sterntroopers was firing at them with his hand-laser.

'Come *on*,' urged Hand, his face white. 'Let's *go*.'

'Right,' said Luke. He pressed the clutch, and pressed a button. Then he depressed the clutch, unpressed the button he had previously pressed and pressed another button. Then he squeezed the sub-atomic-condensate-gas pedal. He redepressed the clutch, repressed another button. The ship did not move.

A number of further laser bolts struck the craft. It rocked on its landing legs.

'Straight up there,' suggested Old Bony, pointing at

the large square of blue sky visible directly above them.

'I know,' said Luke, peevishly. 'The ship doesn't seem to want to move.'

'Handbrake,' gasped Hand, as he passed from consciousness into a groggy pain-filled semi-conscious state. 'Ooh,' he added, and a few seconds later said 'oh-ahh'.

'Right – handbrake, yes.' Luke squeezed the little red button at the top of the handbrakeish black bar beside his seat, and pushed the lever down. Immediately his chair flopped backwards through forty-five degrees.

'I think that lever merely adjusts the orientation of the driving seat,' Old Bony suggested, 'and is not the handbrake at all.'

'Push me up!' urged Luke glowering at the ceiling. 'I can't see where I'm going!'

By the time they had the seat back in flying position, the Sterntroopers had assembled the tripod-mounted heavy-duty laser rifle, and were eyeing up the Millennium Bug through its sights. 'Hand Someman!' cried Luke. 'Which is the brake lever? Which one?'

But Hand was unconscious.

'Could we wake up his co-pilot?' Luke gabbled. 'The big hairy guy?'

'Hibernation is more usually a state of *not* waking up,' opined Bony. 'Or so I've always been led to believe.'

'But he can surely fly this ship, since he's the co-pilot,' pressed Luke. 'Could you – I don't know, use the Farce? Do something?'

'The short answer to that question,' returned Bony, 'would be no.'

'Droids?' Luke shrieked. 'Do you know which lever is the handbrake? They're about to fire the big tripod-mounted gun thing *right at us* – hey, droids?'

'Droids?' replied See-thru in an outraged voice, adding a piercing whistling sound that caused beads of blood to form on Luke's eardrums. 'Droids? *Droids?* Are you *trying* to be offensive, you great stinking inbred loonball albino freak-beak?'

'Not at all,' said Luke, desperately.

'We have *names*, I'll have you know, we have *names* and *feelings* too . . . is it,' he added, becoming even more agitated, 'is it because we are *metal* that you figure you can simply discard our names? What *century* are you living in? What kind of *attitude* is that? – how would you like it if I tried to attract your attention by calling out "hey! Sacks of Watery Protein!" eh? You'd be hurt, wouldn't you?'

'I'm sorry,' gabbled Luke. 'I'm sorry See-thru, I

was just hoping that you knew which lever was the handbrake. You see, we really need to get out of here. In a minute these Sterntroopers are going to fire this really really big gun right at us, and Someman has lapsed into unconsciousness, and Masticatetobacco is asleep.'

'You fill me with disgust and disdain,' said See-thru, disdainfully. Then he deactivated himself in disgust.

'Eeek!' shrieked Arcy Doo-doo.

'This one,' Bony said, 'I think. The handbrake – under the dashboard here.'

Luke grabbed the lever and pushed it down. At once the mighty engines of the Millennium Bug roared, the complex interdimensional gearing caught, and the spaceship lurched into motion.

It zoomed backwards and smashed into the rear wall of the hangar, with a devastating effect on the structural coherence of the Millennium Bug's rear-end. The crash jarred the engine out of gear, and with a grating whine the whole spaceship stalled. Masonry cascaded down like heavy, stony hail. All the lights on the dashboard went out.

For a moment it was chaos. Then everything was quiet. Hand groaned in his unconsciousness.

'The Farce tells me,' murmured Old Bony, his voice

deep with meaning and mystery, 'that you had inadvertently placed the ship in reverse gear.'

'Reverse gear,' said Luke, nodding.

Chapter Nine

Concerning the True Nature of the Farce

The Sterntroopers took them all into custody, shackled their wrists with *Shak-Lo! The Low-Price Handcuff Alternative*, and herded them into the hold of a Police Cruiser. Hand Someman was fitted with a *Cure-O-Girdle*, and left supine on the metal floor. Masticatetobacco was similarly shackled. Luke was treated with a device called *Stik-U-Don't-Like*, a heavy stick applied with some force to the top of his head.

He passed into unconsciousness.

The next thing he knew, he was waking groggily in an Imp-Emp-Imp prison cell. He sat up. 'Where am I?' he asked.

'Inside the Death Spa,' said a female voice. Luke turned his head.

Sitting on a metallic utility bench at the side of the cell was the woman from the toilet-droid's hologram, in the flesh. She was even more beautiful, and even more obviously diseased, in real life than in cheap holographic form.

'Princess Leper!' he cried.

'That's right,' she said. 'And you are Luke See-spotrun.'

Luke's heart spun. Young love coursed through his arteries, and came galloping back up his veins as lust. 'How can you possibly know that?' he asked, eagerly. 'Is it fate that we meet? Did destiny whisper my name to your heart?'

'*He* told me,' the Princess said, jabbing a thumb over her right shoulder. Stretched out on the bench to her right was Old Bony, fast asleep. 'Apparently you got my droid. But instead of taking it to Ya!Boo! and my adoptive father, where it might have done some *good* – instead of doing that, you took it straight into a heavy concentration of Imp-Emp-Imp soldiery.'

'Sorry about that,' said Luke, getting to his feet, and rubbing the back of his skull where it was sore.

'The Imp-Emp-Imp have the droid now,' said Leper, mournfully. 'It'll be a matter of time before they extract the Secret I stored on board it. And when that happens, we might as well give up all hope for the rebellion. The Imperial Emperor, and Dark Father, will beat the Rebelend. That's all there is to it.'

'You really think Dark Father would beat the Rebelend?'

'Oh he'll beat it. He'll beat it mercilessly,' said Leper.

'It's catastrophic.' Luke sat down next to her.

'Don't be too hard on yourself, kid,' wheezed a voice from the floor.

'Hand!' cried Luke. 'Are you OK? You got shot in the chest!'

'I did,' Hand Someman gasped. He was sitting on the floor with his back to the wall. His big hairy co-pilot was flat on his back beside him, snoring softly. 'The shot burnt out pretty much a whole lung. The Imp-Emp-Imp gave me a cybernetic lung, and patched up my skin – the better to interrogate me, I guess. It's not a very good medical prosthesis, this artificial lung, so I'm pretty breathless. It's a good job I still got one natural lung, otherwise I'd be just plain *puffed*.'

'This is just terrible! Prisoners inside an Imp-Emp-Imp facility! What's to become of us?' wailed Luke.

'What's to *become* of us?' repeated Princess Leper. 'That's an asinine sort of question. They're going to torture us, that's what. They've been torturing me for several days.'

'Great Thog, no!' cried Luke. 'That's terrible!'

Leper nodded sorrowfully. 'They had me on the treadmill for hours yesterday. For much of that time, they angled it at twenty degrees, so I was effectively *running uphill*.' She shuddered at the memory. 'Before that it was this cross-country-ski-simulator machine, with *both* leg *and* arm poles to operate. You can set that at "South Downs" or "Kathmandu" settings, and of course they set it at the latter. And after that the sauna . . . they really turn the heat up beyond the levels any medical practitioner would sanction in there.'

'We're doomed,' said Luke, simply.

'We are,' agreed Leper. 'And not just us. This Death Spa has the capacity to exercise and massage an entire planet to death. It's flying to Gregbare as we speak.'

'Gregbare? The planet originally colonised by naturist science fiction authors? Why there?'

'Because that's where the Rebelend central base is located.'

'On *Gregbare*? Why?'

'Because we were sure it was the last place the Imp-Emp-Imp would look. I mean, bearing in mind the nature of the settlers on that world, who would *want* to look there? Who in their right minds?' She shook her head. 'But now that they know that the Rebelend base is located there, the Imp-Emp-Imp will swoop and obliterate it. Once they destroy that the Rebelend will be at an end. It will be the end of hope for the whole Galaxy. The Imperial Empire will crush the whole universe beneath its jackbooted heel. Beneath its heeled jackboot, I mean.' She turned to Luke. 'Or, on second thoughts, perhaps the first one. As you put it so succinctly – we're doomed.'

'We,' said Old Bony, sitting up slowly, and stretching like a cat waking up, 'are *not* doomed.'

'And what do you know about it, grandad,' wheezed Hand Someman. 'You brought an entire troop of Sterntroopers right *to* us in that bar. It's your fault I got shot up. And *what – what* was that business with the glass tube?'

'Wait,' said Leper, holding up her hand. 'Wobbli Bent K'nobbli is a great, if slightly whiffy, old man. Let us listen to what he has to say.'

'Yes, Bony will advise us,' urged Luke. 'What should we do? How can we get out of here?'

'It's very simple,' said Bony. 'We must trust to the Farce.'

Hand Someman blew a quantity of air through his lips, thereby indicating that he was not inclined to follow Old Bony's advice in this matter.

An hour passed. Luke paced up and down the cell. He examined every nook and cranny, and found no bolts to unscrew, no air-ducts to climb into. There was no way out of this cell.

'Bony,' he said. 'I've been meaning to ask. What exactly is this "Farce" of which you speak so often.'

'Ah,' said Bony, tapping the side of his nose. 'The Farce. It's a powerful ally, the Farce, provided you know how to *work with it.*'

'That doesn't really answer my question.'

'The Farce is woven into the fabric of the universe. It is an all-pervasive power.' The old man's eyes glinted with enthusiasm. 'Let me put it this way: do you know *how the universe was made*? How it *came to be*?'

'The Big Bang,' said Luke.

'*After* that,' said Old Bony K'nobbli. '*After* the originary matter of the universe had been disseminated? Do you know where the stars and planets came from – why the cosmos isn't just a soup of undifferentiated matter?'

'Gravity?' Luke hazarded.

'But gravity is only the *form* taken by the Farce!' screeched Old Bony, terribly excited. 'The universe grew by *collisions*. By things banging into other things. By lumps of matters colliding stupidly with other lumps of matter. This is the underlying principle of the cosmos – this stupidity. Pratfalls! Tumbles! Crashings-into-things! Does the cosmos rest on the principle of walking smoothly out through a door? No! It rests on the principle of misjudging the exit and smacking your kisser against the doorframe, and *then* stumbling back, putting your foot in the wastepaper bin and tripping over your desk to land in such a way as to give yourself mild concussion. Do you see?'

'I think I do,' said Luke, tentatively.

'Matter bumping into other matter! Comets crashing into gas giants! Planets knocking moon-sized chunks out of other planets! It's all one universe-sized slapstick comedy! The cosmos could not have formed without it. This is the *Farce*. This is the principle that binds all living matter.'

'I see,' offered Luke. But there was no stopping Old Bony now.

'What is the force that causes your bootlaces to become undone at exactly the moment you step into the urinals at a spaceport bar, so that then they trail along the floor? It is the Farce. Why, when you move your hand to bring a slice of toast to your mouth whilst reading the morning news-flimsy does your movement result in you jabbing toast up your nose? How else to explain,' he added, growing wistful as if recalling a much-loved memory, 'bidding farewell to your beautiful young girlfriend as she mounts the Hoverbus – walking alongside the slowly departing vehicle keeping pace with her window seat – blowing kisses to her, as she blows kisses to you – interpreting her suddenly widened eyes and open mouth as her dawning remorse for her decision to leave town in the first place – widening your own eyes as you gaze into hers, and nodding, as if to say, *yes, my love, how stupid that we must part* – and then walking sideways into a lamp post and dislocating your jaw? There *is* no other explanation.'

'And how does this help us in our current situation? Exactly?'

K'nobbli looked mysterious. 'We must trust the Farce.'

'But how is that *actually, practically* going to help us?' Hand asked. 'All that fine talk – we're still stuck in here.'

There was a lurch, and the whole cell shuddered. 'What was that?' asked Luke.

'It felt,' offered Hand, 'like the Death Spa coming out of hyperdrive?'

'We must have arrived at Gregbare,' said Leper, and she put her face in her hands. 'It's all over. They'll be charging up their engines of death. The secret base of Rebelend activity – doomed. The whole world of Gregbare – all those buck-naked SF authors, doomed. And we're stuck in here, unable to help them.'

The occupants of the cell were silent for several minutes. Finally Luke spoke up.

'Did you say,' he asked, ' "buck-naked"? Or "butt-naked".'

Leper turned on him. 'Does it matter?'

'Well it's just that "butt-naked" is a much less pleasant image than "buck-naked". Or so it seems to me. In the sense that a naked butt is a less savoury thought than a naked buck.' Luke looked from face to face. 'Don't you think? I mean, I'm not even sure what a "buck" is, in this context, but I'm fairly sure that seeing it naked would be less upsetting than seeing a SF author's naked, um, er.' He stopped speaking.

Everyone went back to being gloomily silent.

Through the metal wall of the cell the sound of jackboots clanging on metal walkways became audible. It soon became apparent that the footsteps were approaching. Two Sterntroopers were marching smartly along the corridor outside, towards the cell.

They stopped outside. All the prisoners looked expectantly up at the door.

It slid upwards to reveal the two Sterntroopers standing in the corridor outside. Both had laser pistols in their hands. 'Prisoners!' barked one of the faceless soldiers. 'You will be interrogated one by one – starting with *you*.' He gestured at Luke with his pistol. 'Come now!'

Luke looked over his shoulder, as if there were

somebody behind him at whom the soldier might be pointing. 'Me?' he said. 'Oh crikey bikey,' said Luke, alarmed, getting to his feet.

The two soldiers took a step in unison to come into the cell. In unison their helmeted foreheads collided with the low overhang of the cell door. In unison they clattered backwards to the floor, to lie motionless.

Princess Leper was the person with the foresight to hurry over to the horizontal forms. 'They're both unconscious,' she announced, with a degree of amazement in her voice. 'They just walked straight into the door lintel. That's pretty clumsy – pretty amazingly clumsy if you ask me.'

'You see,' said K'nobbli, as if he had expected precisely this development. 'You must trust the Farce.'

Chapter Ten

Some rushing about, and general running to and fro, inside the Death Spa

Luke and Leper stripped the soldiers of their armour, took their weapons and utility belts and tied them up in the cell. In the process they ripped the armour in several places. 'Look at this stuff,' said Luke, pulling a chestplate into two pieces. 'It's fantastically thin. It's like the sort of plastic you make Christmas decorations out of. Or like the stuff microwave meals comes packed in.'

'It is flimsy,' agreed Leper.

'Why don't they give their soldiers more substantial protection?' asked Luke.

Old Bony chuckled to himself. 'You think the Imp-Emp-Imp make their soldiers dress up this way for their *protection*? Oh dear me no. You've seen how ineffective the white armour is – laser pistols go right through it. You can hit them with a lead pipe and knock them unconscious. In fact, you can more or less hit them with a *baguette* and knock them unconscious. No, the reason they make them wear the armour is precisely to *render them clumsy*. To occlude their vision, to impair their physical performance. By staggering around, falling over, by cracking their heads on the overhang as they attempt to step through a door, in all these ways they access the tremendous power of the Farce.'

'Except that it hasn't helped them out at all,' said Hand, looking down at the supine forms of the Sterntroopers.

'Ah yes – because *we* are stronger in the Farce than *they*,' explained Bony, nodding sagely. 'But *they* weren't to know that.'

'The power of the Farce does *seem* to be working in our favour at the moment,' agreed Leper. 'Come on – we've got to get out of here. And we've got to find my droid.'

'I say we concentrate on the first part,' panted Hand, 'and leave the droid to shift for itself.'

'No,' said the Princess, firmly. 'I sent that droid away precisely to *stop* it falling into Imp-Emp-Imp hands. Now that you lot have so effectively delivered it straight back *to* the Imperial Empire, we have a duty to get to it before any more damage is done.

'What's so important about this droid anyway?'

'It contains the only copy of a certain vital Secret,' said Leper.

'What Secret?'

'I don't know.'

'Why not?'

'Because it's secret,' snapped Leper, becoming cross. 'Obviously.'

'But then how do you know it's important?'

'I not only *know* it's important,' said Leper. 'I know it's the *most vital piece* of information in the Galaxy. With it the Imp-Emp-Imp will certainly crush all resistance. But if we can get it to my adoptive father on Ya!Boo! then it might just turn the tide in favour of the Rebelend. Now *let's go.*' She went to the cell door and peered out.

'So,' said Luke, sidling up to stand beside her. Despite being leprous there was something strangely alluring about this woman. 'You were adopted, were you?'

'Yes,' she said, brusquely, scanning the corridor in both directions. 'I never knew my actual father.'

'Get out!' said Luke, slapping her lightly on her shoulder. 'Me neither! Actually I recently discovered that my father was a great Jobbi knight, killed by Dark Father. I've vowed to take revenge on Dark Father, actually.'

'Is that right?' said the Princess, with the air of

somebody not quite paying attention. 'Come on, let's go.'

They made their way along the corridor cautiously. It was a lengthy metal-walled structure, pentagonal in cross-section: a curious design such that walking near either of the walls meant bending one's head down to avoid scraping it along the ceiling, although there was ample headroom in the middle of the floor.

The group had two laser pistols, one salvaged from each guard: Princess Leper had one and Luke the other. 'Wouldn't it be better,' he suggested, holding the weapon in his hands as if it were coated with some finger-rotting substance, 'if Someman had the gun? He's a rough-and-tough space-pirate figure. You want it?'

'I got my work cut out,' gasped the one-artificial-lunged pilot, 'dragging Masticatetobacco behind me.'

'Oh, *can't* you just wake him up?' Luke snapped, straying a little into the realm of tetchy.

'You obviously,' grunted Hand, hauling his co-pilot along the corridor floor, 'don't have much experience with hibernating Woozies.'

'Just point the thing at a Sterntrooper,' said Princess Leper, 'and shoot.'

'Oh, I don't know,' said Luke. 'That might well

involve killing. I'm not sure I can do that. I haven't really thought through the ethical implications of an act like that.' He tucked the gun into his trousers.

'Oh great globular clusters . . .' Leper muttered, half under her breath.

They had reached the end of the corridor. It opened into a control area: a series of large computer banks, flashing lights, whirring reel-to-reel magnetic tape, a box of punch-cards in the corner. Four Sterntroopers in full uniform were sitting in front of flickering green-lit screens. They looked up at once, and all of them immediately drew their laser pistols from the plastic holsters at their sides.

'I shall use the Farce,' announced K'nobbli, 'to disable them. Have no fear.'

With astonishing speed and a feral grace the old man darted forward, his hands poised before him karate-style, blades outwards. Before the nearest Sterntrooper had a chance to react, K'nobbli was on him.

'Hurrah!' cheered Luke.

It was all over in moments. The Jobbi knight barked his shin against the side of one of the control monitors, yelped, staggered to the left, put his foot in a small metal waste-bin, overtoppled, windmilled his arms, and rammed his head into the rifle-rack on the left wall, getting his cranium stuck hard between two of the charge-rifles fixed there. All that could be seen were the old man's hindquarters wriggling, his scrawny legs occasionally kicking up as he heaved and struggled to extricate himself. The waste-bin was still stuck on his left foot. His voice was heavily muffled and barely audible, but it seemed to be saying 'oh, for crying out *loud*' and 'my ears, my ears are trapped behind the trigger guards on either side, help! Oh my beautiful *ears*!'

'Oh,' said Luke, in much more subdued voice, 'dear.'

The four Sterntroopers, who had clearly never seen anything quite like this before, stared at the struggling form of the Jobbi knight. Trained with a ruthless efficiency to be efficiently ruthless, they faltered when presented with a situation for which their training had not prepared them. This was such a situation.

This gave Princess Leper all the time she needed. She was able to take careful aim, and squeeze off two bolts of laser energy, dropping two of the guards before they even realised they were under attack from a different direction. Even then, as the remaining two guards pulled out their weapons and attempted to return fire, they could barely prevent themselves glancing over at the wriggling, stuck form of the old man. They were easy targets for the Princess.

Smoke and the smell of burning plastic swirled around the small space.

Leper rounded on Luke. 'Were you planning on *using* your laser pistol any time soon?' she snapped. 'Or is it purely ornamental?'

'Well,' said Luke. 'Like I said, I'm not sure . . .'

They went over to Old Bony and heaved at him to dislodge him. But in doing so they yanked the two rifles out of their holdings, and this set off an Unauthorised Rifle Removal Alarm. It went like this: ouu-WAAAA! ouu-WAAAA! ouu-WAAAA!

'Great,' said Leper, sarcastically, shouting to be heard over the sound of the alarm. 'Come on – let's get out of here.'

There were two doors in the wall on the far side of the control room. The sign on one read 'Exit: Way Out'. The other read 'To the Innermost Portions of the Death Spa. No Way Out. Cul-de-Sac. Authorised Personnel only.' Leper pulled open the first door. It revealed a long corridor down which something like twenty Sterntroopers were jogging, heading directly towards them, rifles at the ready.

'Not that way,' she cried. 'They're sending a squad

straight here. Through the other door – quick, run. *Move it.*'

To be honest, Luke couldn't quite hear her words over the constant ear-breaking ouu-WAAAA! ouu-WAAAA! ouu-WAAAA! noise. But the urgency of her manner, and her desperate facial expression, added to the fact that she bodily pushed him through the second door, told him all he needed to know.

'Run!' he screamed. 'Every life form for itself! Run – we got to get *away*!'

He barrelled through the second door. He barely had time to register a cavernous hallway filled with what appeared to be rank after rank of deactivated battle droids, before he surged forward, and began running as fast as he could.

He was a young man, with long, strong legs, and he ran very quickly. His legs flashed beneath him, pummelling the ground, propelling him onwards. Pretty soon he fell into a sprinter's rhythm, sucking deep breaths and pushing them out again in time to his strides. Run – run – run –

Beside him Old Bony was making remarkably rapid progress, keeping up with Luke and even starting, very slowly, to overtake him. Luke was surprised to see the old man capable of such a lick of speed. Presumably he was scared enough of the approaching

Sterntroopers really to work his legs – or perhaps he was calling on the power of the Farce to move himself onwards so rapidly.

Then Hand Someman pulled past him. His speed was even more surprising, given that he was dragging the supine form of Masticatetobacco after himself. Even more surprisingly, he appeared to stop from time to time, to mop his brow and get his breath back, before picking up his co-pilot's legs and starting to haul again. Luke could not work out how he was able to do this whilst simultaneously running with all his strength, running so fast as to be able to keep up with Luke himself.

'Hey,' snapped Princess Leper. 'You. Stop mucking about, and get down off that running machine.'

Realisation dawned. Luke slowed his strides, and the conveyer-belt floor beneath his feet slowed too. Blushing a little with embarrassment, he hopped off the treadmill. 'Sorry,' he said. 'I got a little panicked, and accordingly a little distracted . . .'

The door behind them burst open. Ruby-coloured laser bolts seared through the air. Princess Leper span on her heel and fired off half a dozen expert shots with her pistol. The Sterntroopers in the door frame tumbled forward.

'Come on,' she yelled.

The party hurried through the hallway, past the rank upon rank and row upon row of empty running machines. At the far end was a broad doorway, through which they passed into a Free Weight Room. The walls were mirrored from floor to ceiling; padded benches were arranged in L and Π shapes; in the corner a 3DTV screen was showing *Hits of the 2440s! The Nonstop Aerobic and Vacuumobic Workout Channel* on a continuous loop.

The free weights themselves were arranged on racks along the far wall. 'I don't understand it,' said Luke. 'Free weights are supposed to be lots of different weights, from small weights to really big ones. They're supposed to be big, heavy *metal* discs, for you to fit onto your weightlifting bar.' He picked up one of the Death Spa free weights. 'These are all *plastic*, they're all the same size.' He tossed it up and down in the palm of his hand. '*And* they're all exactly the same *weight* – about the same weight as a piece of pitta bread. How is this supposed to help a person build muscular definition and upper body strength?'

'Don't you know anything?' snapped Princess Leper. 'The gyms on your homeworld must be primitive places indeed.' She pointed at the door on the far side of the room, and shoved Bony, Hand and Masticatetobacco towards it. 'You lot, through there.

Luke and I are going to use these to hold off the Sterntroopers for a while.' As the others shuffled through, she came to stand by Luke's side.

'They're adjustable weights,' she explained, pointing to the tiny red and green buttons in the centre of each disc. 'Pressing these modifies the artificial gravity device embedded in each of them; you can set it to any gravitational level you like, to vary the resistance. Have you really never seen one of these before?'

'I'm more a work-in than a work-out sort of guy,' said Luke, unsure what, if anything, the sentence meant, but liking the sound of it. Despite the hideous growths on the sides of her head, there was something very alluring about this princess; an ivory pureness and whiteness about her skin, a depth about her blue eyes, that whispered to his soul about moonlight and midnight, about the susurration of surf on a warm beach on an idyllic world, and the two of them could be together always, the new Adam and new Eve of a perfect new World of Love. Plus she smelt nice and had a great rack. He decided he *liked* it when she stood next to him.

'Here,' she said. 'Set the timer for, say, three seconds.' She did so on one of the discs. 'Then set the weight for Gas Giant. Then —'

Right on cue, the first of the pursuing Sterntroopers rushed through the entrance to the room as she spoke.

'—throw!' she cried, spinning the flimsy plastic disc, frisbee-like, at the soldier. It floated almost dreamily through the air, weighing a few grams. Then it struck the chest of the Sterntrooper weighing two-thirds of a metric tonne, breaking his ribs and crushing him instantly to the floor.

One after the other, soldiers popped through the door; one after the other, Luke and Leper tossed the lightweight discs just in time for them to turn into artificially-gravitational superdense bodies as they struck their targets. Several Sterntroopers fell straight down. One or two flew back through the air with their legs separated by angles of more than one hundred degrees. One did a perfect back flip and crashed through a table upon which year-old copies of various magazines were located for the reading pleasure of exercisers.

Finally the whole troop was lying, groaning, on the floor. Princess Leper dashed to the door and peered out. 'There's another battalion coming,' she said, hurrying back to Luke. 'Quick,' she gasped. 'Quick, after the others – through the back door.'

Together they ran through the exit on the far side of the room, neither of them noticing the sign over the door that read: 'Through here to the Sauna *Only*: No Exit. No Way Out.'

They didn't know it, but they were now trapped.

Oh *no*!

Chapter Eleven

Let us take it (the narrative) to the bridge

Dark Father strode onto the bridge, purposefully, evilly, menacingly. Seriously. I mean, he strode on seriously, which is to say in a serious manner. I wasn't exhorting you to take my words seriously, as if perhaps you had thought I was joking. Anyway. The ordinary bridge crew flinched and buried themselves deeper in their ordinary bridge duties, whatever they might be. Wherever he went, Dark Father carried with him an aura of hideous darkness.

Grand Muff o' Tartan was already there, staring at the huge display screen at the sight of the planet Gregbare laid out below. He was wearing his special ceremonial muff (Macgregor tartan) in honour of the terrible destruction they were about to wreak upon the helpless world below him – the first destructive action of the newly readied and fully operational Death Spa.

Through the viewscreen Tartan was watching with pleasure as one hundred and thirty thousand Ti-fighters deployed in brilliant formation. A hundred and twenty thousand Rebelend alphabetti spacecraft were dogfighting with them, dogging their tails and fighting with them in a general sense. The sight on the viewscreen was of myriad little sparks and explosions, as alphabetti or IEISDSI craft blew up; mixed with the flickers of laser strafing as the desperate battle continued.

The Rebelend had sent up all their alphabetti space-fighters in a desperate last-ditch defence of their main base. A- and Q-wings, Z- and W- and P-wings, and indeed the full range of letters together with !-wings, £-wings, $-wings, %-wings, and &-wings, hurtled through the void, swooping about the Death Spa in a vain attempt to attack or disable it.

'Greetings, my old friend,' said the Grand Muff as Dark Father stood beside him. 'Everything is in readiness.'

'THE REBELEND ARE RESISTING?'

'Yes, but punily. They are no match for the might of this Imperial Empire of the Imperium fighting force.'

'WHAT ARE THEIR TACTICS?'

'They keep flying into the long equatorial trench.'

'THE TRENCH?'

'Yes. It seems they believe that the end of the trench is a weak spot in the Death Spa's design.'

'I SEE. IS IT?'

'Not at all. It's just the water pipe through which we

fill the trench when we want to do some rowing practice.'

'THE REBELEND ARE FOOLISH AND MISGUIDED.'

'What puzzles me,' said the Grand Muff, 'is the way they fly into the trench a good eight hundred kilometres *away* from the portal, and then spend all their time buzzing along the length of it. What good does that do? I mean, granted, they're wrong to think it a weak spot; but given that they *do* believe that, why not just swoop down and blast it from above? Why enter the trench so far away from the target, and then fly along for – ooh, simply ages?'

'BAFFLING,' agreed Dark Father.

'Ah – there's another trench flier gone.' o' Tartan pointed. The flash of light and puff of rapidly expanding gases was clearly visible against the curve of the Death Spa's horizon. 'They don't seem to realise. It's for rowing practice, that trench, not for flying down. It's wide enough for an eight-person scull, not a ruddy great spaceship. Ah well. What is your news, my friend?'

'THE ouu-WAAA! ALARM HAS BEEN SOUNDED ON THE LOWER LEVELS. IT APPEARS THAT THE PRINCESS HAS ESCAPED FROM HER CELL.'

'Oh dear,' said the Grand Muff. 'And the other prisoners?'

'THEY HAVE ALSO ESCAPED.'

'Oh dear. Isn't Commander Rada Traynd in charge of the keeping of prisoners?'

'I HAVE ALREADY TOLD THE COMMANDER OF MY DISSATISFACTION WITH HIS COMPETENCY TO HOLD SUCH A SENIOR POSITION.'

'Have you also, by any chance, changed his throat from a three-dimensional to a two-dimensional structure, using only the power of the Farce?'

'INDEED. HE WILL NOT BE BREATHING THROUGH *THAT* ANY MORE.'

'Well, there's nowhere for the escaped prisoners to go. Do you want to watch the destruction of the Rebelend up here with me, or go down and chase after the prisoners?'

'IT HAS COME TO MY ATTENTION THAT THE PRISONER LOGGED UNDER THE NAME OF OLD BONY K'NOBBLI IS IN FACT A COMPLETELY DIFFERENT INDIVIDUAL, A PERSON NAMED WOBBLI BENT K'NOBBLI; AN OLD JOBBI MASTER AND ONCE MY TRAINER IN THE WAYS OF JOBBI.'

'Extraordinary. How did you ever deduce that?'

'I FELT HIS PRESENCE. ALSO I RECOG-NISED HIS MUGSHOT.'

'Oh – there goes another one!' Another fruitless assault along the trench had ended in explosion and death for its hapless Rebelend pilot. The Grand Muff clapped his hands together delightedly.

'I MUST CONFRONT K'NOBBLI. HE IS STRONG IN THE FARCE.'

'Well good luck with that, old friend,' said o' Tartan. 'How about we meet up for a fondue later? To celebrate our victory?'

'EXCELLENT.'

'My quarters, at twenty-hundred hours?'

'I'LL BRING SOME CRÈME DE MENTHE.'

'And I will unroll the Twister mat. I might give it a wipe down, actually, after last time. Goodbye for now, my friend!'

Dark Father strode impressively from the bridge.

Chapter Twelve

Exciting Denouement

The group made their way along a brightly-lit corridor, and then through a sliding door into a wood-panelled room.

'It's a dead end,' cried Someman. 'Quick – back the way we came.'

They hurried *en masse* back out into the corridor; but it was too late. The far end of the corridor was packed with Sterntroopers. They had all taken up firing positions, some on their knees, some on their fronts, the ones at the back standing up.

And through this mass of trained soldiers stepped Dark Father.

'It's Dark Father!' ejaculated Luke. 'He killed my father, did Dark Father! I don't even know who my father was, except that he was himself Dark, and ended up killed by Dark Father, in some mysterious manner!'

'Evil Dark Father,' cried Princess Leper. 'I will put an end to your evil-doing right now.' She stepped to the front of the group, lowered her laser pistol, and fired directly at the towering black-clad figure.

Her shot flew wide. She fired again and again, and each time the laser bolt missed its target. Dark Father made no attempt to avoid the shots; he merely stood, arms folded, wheezing slightly.

'I don't understand it,' Leper said. 'He's only twenty feet away, but I can't seem to hit him.'

'He is too strong in the Farce,' said Old Bony, stepping forward. 'Clumsiness, maladroitness and dyspraxia surround him like an evil forcefield. You will never muster enough co-ordination to fire accurately. This is a fight none of you can win. You must leave it to me.'

'Bony!' cried Luke. 'What are you going to do?'

'Give us a quick leg up,' he muttered to the young man. In a trice Luke had lifted his frail frame up to the ceiling, from where, with deft though gnarled fingers, the venerable Jobbi knight unscrewed one of the fluorescent lightbulbs from its fittings, power nubbin and all.

'Ow,' he said, when he was back on the floor. 'This is hot.'

'Bony!' cried Luke, again, in an agony of anticipation. 'Be careful!'

K'nobbli inched forward, holding the gleaming metre-long lightbulb in front of himself.

'Dark Father,' he said.

'WOBBLI BENT,' said Dark Father. 'IT HAS BEEN A LONG TIME.'

'Ages,' agreed Bony.

Dark Father unfolded his arms, reached inside his own robes and drew out a fluorescent tube of his own. When he activated this it glowed a pinky-red. He stepped forward as well.

'That's a nice red colour, Dark,' taunted K'nobbli. 'Planning on developing some *photographic plates*, are you?'

'DO YOU DARE BAIT *ME*?'

'Man, you are *ugly*,' baited K'nobbli, thereby confirming that indeed he did so dare.

'WHEN LAST WE MET,' said Dark Father, 'YOU WERE THE MASTER. NOW *I* AM THE MASTER. I AM A MASTER OF BAITING, AS WELL AS A MASTER OF LIGHTSWORD-PLAY – BY WHICH,' he added, shifting his weight from dark foot to dark foot and coming closer towards K'nobbli, 'I MEAN LIGHTSWORD-*PLAY*. AS OPPOSED TO *LIGHT*-SWORDPLAY. ON THE CONTRARY. MY SWORDPLAY WILL BE HEAVY, A HEAVY FATE FOR YOU.'

'Is that the best you can do, baiting-wise?' said K'nobbli. 'That's rubbish. That's hardly baiting at all.'

'MY SWORD WILL DO THE TALKING.'

'You can't defeat me, Dark. If you strike me down I shall become even more powerful.'

Dark Father seemed to think about this for a moment. 'AH – HOW DOES THAT WORK, EXACTLY?'

'It's one of the mysteries of the Farce.'

'BUT IF I STRIKE YOU DOWN YOU'LL BE DEAD.'

'Agreed.'

'IN WHAT SENSE ARE THE DEAD MORE POWERFUL THAN THE LIVING?'

'I'd rather not go into specifics,' said K'nobbli, circling his foe with his lightsword.

'MORE POWERFUL IN THE "LYING MOTIONLESS ON THE FLOOR, SLOWLY DECOMPOSING" SENSE OF "POWER-FUL"?'

'I might return in spectral form to haunt you.'

'OOO, I'M SCARED,' said Dark Father in the tone of voice of somebody not scared. 'WILL YOU BE ABLE, PHYSICALLY, TO INTERACT WITH ME IN ANY WAY? WHEN YOU

RETURN AS A SPECTRAL VERSION OF
YOURSELF?'

'. . . No,' conceded Bony, shortly.

'SO WHY EXACTLY WOULD I BE WOR-
RIED BY THIS DEVELOPMENT?'

'Well . . .' said K'nobbli, as if he was considering
the question for the first time. 'Look. Can we discuss
this later?'

The old Jobbi knight lurched forward and brought
his gleaming blade of white light down towards Dark
Father's head. But Father was ready with the parry,
swinging his own red-gleaming lightsword round to
intercept the blow.

The two blades clashed with a mighty clashing
sound. Instantly both lights went out, and broken
glass scattered to the floor.

'Oh, botheration,' said K'nobbli, looking dis-
consolately at the ruined lightsword in his hand.

'Oh I don't *believe* it,' gasped Hand Someman in
an infuriated voice, from his vantage point at the
far end of the corridor. 'They're *useless*, those lightswords.'

But at that precise moment, Dark Father jabbed
forward, burying the sharp end of his broken fluorescent light tube in K'nobbli's chest. The razor-sharp
shards of glass cut through the old man's torso like

something very sharp being rammed forcefully into
something comparatively soft.

Everybody gasped. Time seemed to freeze for a
moment.

'So *that's* how it's supposed to work,' gasped K'nobbli, looking down at the fatal wound in his own chest.
Then he collapsed to the floor.

'Quick,' screamed Leper. She hauled Luke back
through into the dead-end sauna, and punched the
door release. The heavy door slammed down, just as
the first Sterntrooper laser bolts crashed into it. Leper
aimed her own pistol at the door release, fired, and
fused the locking mechanism.

'That ought to hold them,' she said, through gritted
teeth.

'Old Bony is dead!' said Luke, aghast. 'I can't
believe it!'

'Believe it,' said Someman. 'Those lightswords are
plain stupid *qua* weapons.'

There was the sound of pummelling on the far side
of the door, interspersed with occasional though ineffective laser fire, and the odd muffled shout of 'Oi!
Watch out, nearly had my eye out with that.'

'They can't get in,' panted Hand Someman. 'But we
can't get out.'

'Checkmate,' agreed Luke, nodding his head.

Princess Leper looked at him. 'Don't you mean stalemate?'

'That's what I said,' said Luke, nodding vigorously.

'Damn!' said Leper, pacing about the sauna room. 'Trapped. We're no closer to finding those droids. And the Death Spa is about to unleash its terrible fitness ray upon the flabby, slack, unprepared naked SF authors on the planet below. They won't stand a chance. To say nothing of the Rebelend.'

She flung herself furiously onto one of the wooden benches. 'At least the banging on the door has stopped.'

Luke took a seat beside her. 'What shall we do now?'

'I'm working on that,' said the Princess.

Luke sat for a while. Then he started whistling. He stopped when Leper gave him a fierce look.

After a while he said: 'I can't believe Old Bony has gone!'

'It is a shock,' said the Princess.

'Princess,' said Luke, turning to her. 'Old Bony told me about you.'

'What?' she snapped. 'What about me?'

'About your – you know. Your leprosy.' Luke shook his head sorrowfully. 'That's a dreadful shame. It's a nasty disease.'

'It's not nice,' said the Princess, tight-lipped.

'Is it the – you know – the cause of those things?' He nodded in the direction of her head. 'Those growths on the side of your head?'

This seemed to anger Princess Leper even more. 'Don't you know anything *at all*? Are you the most ignorant individual in the *quadrant*? Leprosy is a disease of human beings caused by the bacillus *mycobacterium leprae*, which is characterised by lesions of the skin and superficial nerves. Destruction of the peripheral nervous system can result in a loss of sensation, which, when combined with progressive general degeneration of bodily tissue, often results in the extremities becoming eroded, although not in my case. Other symptoms can include a loss of skin coloration, inflammation of tissue beneath the skin. My leprosy, you'll be glad to hear, is kept well at bay by nanotechnology implants; it is arrested at an early stage. Leprosy as a disease does *not*,' she added, fiercely, indicating the growths on both sides of her head 'cause anything like *these*.'

'Ah,' said Luke. 'I stand corrected. Sorry. So – what are those, er, things then?'

'Mind your own business,' she snapped.

'OK,' said Luke.

'Hey, Princess,' called Hand. 'Our situation just got a lot worse.'

Leper and Luke got to their feet. There was no mistaking it: scalding steam was pouring in through a vent at the back of the sauna. In seconds it had filled the whole room, opaquing vision, filling lungs with a choking hot whiteness.

'They plan to steam us,' cried Leper. 'They can't get in here, so they plan to steam us to death.'

'Great Thog!' swore Hand Someman. 'The swine . . .' He waved his arms, but there was no dispersing the steam. It was hot as boiled soup in the little wooden room, and still the boiling white clouds were pumping in. 'I'm sweating,' he gasped. 'I'm seeing spots in my eyes. I can *feel* the core temperature of my body rising . . . it's horrible.'

'Yes,' said the Princess. There was despair in her voice. 'A few minutes of this and we will literally cook in our own juices. What a terrible way to die!'

'Curse them!' cried Hand Someman.

The Princess slumped back on her bench. 'I might as well die sitting down,' she said.

It was then that Luke had his brilliant idea. It was the first, although not the last, of his life. What is more, he had it at exactly the right moment.

'Wait!' he called. 'Don't give up hope – we can escape from here!'

'How?' asked Leper.

'Yeah, kid,' said Hand. 'What you got in mind?'

'We can crawl through the vent – the vent through which the steam is currently pouring.'

'Are you crazy?' said Hand. 'It's hot enough in *here* – can you imagine how hot it's going to be in that vent? To crawl towards where the steam is being generated? That's insane. That would only hasten our deaths.'

'Not,' said Luke, dramatically, 'necessarily. We have one weapon at our disposal that the Imp-Emp-Imp will not be expecting.'

'What?'

'We can *get naked*!' he cried, jubilantly.

There was silence in the little room for the space of a full minute.

'Right,' said Princess Leper, drawing the syllable out to three or four times its usual length.

'I'm serious, guys!' said Luke, pushing his way to the back of the sauna, where the steam was thickest, and starting to unbutton his pants. 'My whole life has prepared me for this moment. Without clothes we won't get quite as hot. We should survive long enough to wriggle down the steam duct and away from the whole sauna complex. Come on – I was raised by Swedes. I *understand* nakedness.'

'Well,' said Princess Leper, dubiously. 'I suppose

it's worth a shot. I'm prepared to try, provided you all promise not to – you know. Look.'

'What about Masticatetobacco? He can't undress, he's covered in hair.'

'We can shave him,' said a now naked Luke, fumbling in the billowing steam at the wall. 'There is a bank of personal grooming equipment on this wall, including clippers. But come on – *hurry*. We don't have very long.'

It took only one minute to shave the whole Woozie, although it took several more minutes to cram his slumbering form into the steam duct and kick it down. Hand Someman, naked, went next, pushing his co-pilot in front of him. Luke tried a 'ladies first' on Princess Leper, but she wasn't having any of it: so he went next, and she clambered in after him.

Naked, slick with sweat, panting and feeling as if his eyeballs were about to explode with heat, he wriggled down the duct. Luckily the duct was mostly angled downwards, so passage was not too hard. To begin with it got hotter, but after they passed a grille in the floor through which the steam was issuing, it began to get easier. The steam cleared quickly and the air temperature became more bearable. Soon enough Luke could see well enough to look ahead of him;

whereupon he caught a glimpse of Hand Someman from a rather unflattering angle. 'Ur!' he cried. He looked away as quickly as he could but the sight remained, somehow, burned on his retina.

And then, abruptly, they were all free of the duct.

They tumbled, one after another, into a vast inner metal cavern. Row after row of cars stretched in all directions.

Princess Leper found a sign printed on very thin plastic that said '*Level 14,566, Rank 345. Remember Your Location!*' By dint of much heaving and yanking, she managed to haul this off the wall and, by tearing rips in two opposing sides, she was able to wrap it around her naked body and fix it as a sort of lampshade-cum-toga. It was not very functional, since she had to keep a hold of it with her left hand to stop it falling off, but at least it was a form of clothing. Luke and Hand had to remain utterly naked. Masticatetobacco was still asleep; the strange thing was that, shaved as he was, he now resembled a rather handsome, if very tall, man.

'We seem to be in a car park,' Luke observed. 'A car park of gargantuan size.'

'It makes sense,' said Leper. 'A place this size – it's as big as a whole planet after all – that's a *lot* of commuters. Not to mention the visitors, the people who don't actually work here. They've all got to have somewhere to park their cars.'

'But – *cars*?' said Luke.

'You're forgetting how big this Death Spa is. It's planet-sized. How else you going to get around from place to place upon it or within it? You going to rely on public transport? Of *course* people bring their cars. Come on – we can't stay here. If they figure out where that duct in the sauna room goes, they'll be right on us.'

The group set off together, Hand still dragging Mastic' behind him.

Forty minutes later they were exhausted, and becoming more and more infuriated. 'This goes on forever,' Leper complained. 'I've never *seen* so many cars. Cars, cars, cars.'

'Like you said – what's the population of a place like this likely to be? Something like a trillion people live on Earth, but that's just the *surface*: this place has its surface *and* all the lower levels, right through to the core. The population may be millions of trillions. And of course they all want their cars.'

'Well,' said Luke. 'Thinking logically, there's going to be a balance, isn't there, between the number of people and the number of cars. If a large proportion of the inner space of the Death Spa is given over to parking, then people can't live there. So there must be a balance. There are probably only a few billion actually living here.'

'Yes,' conceded the naked Hand Someman. 'You're right.'

'Over there,' said Leper, pointing with the hand she wasn't using to hold up her rudimentary item of clothing. 'There's a light in the distance. Come on.'

Twenty more minutes brought them to a truly spectacular sight.

They were at the extreme inner edge of the car-parking level across which they had been walking. There was a low balustrade, and on the other side a dizzying vista of level after level, stretching away below – and above – into the far vertical distance. The sheer immensity of the sight was gobsmacking; so many layers curling round in myriad arcs, tightly packed one on top of the other. The perspective made the levels further away look like sheaves of paper. The central space around which these millions of car-parking levels were arranged was as big as a planetary sky; it was even possible to see faint clouds floating in the space. And far, far below them, below

the lowest of the car-parking levels – in, Luke esti-
mated, the exact centre of the Death Spa – was what
looked like a curled and brilliant ball of lightning. It
gleamed and flashed, lighting up the stacked storeys
of the carpark with dazzling electric blues and whites.

'The Death Spa's power source,' Hand said, peering over the brink. 'It's a folded black hole. They use
the event horizon to generate shearing pressures that
break photons into usable energy. It's spectacular, and
very efficient – nothing else would do for a device this
size. But it *is* inherently unstable. It can only process
photons – they're massless, you see. Anything with
mass would break through the operative layer and
collapse the whole system.'

Princess Leper was looking incredulously at Hand
Someman. 'Thank you for that little *lecture*, professor,'
she said in a mocking tone of voice. 'Now if you don't
mind, I'm getting tired of trudging around with this
wearisome piece of plastic wrapped about me. Can we
please find some clothes?'

They turned right at the edge, and walked alongside
the balustrade for perhaps a kilometre, eventually
arriving at a large blocky structure. An input ramp
was set through the ceiling, running from the layer
above onto the floor of this particular storey.

'This,' said Leper, 'must be where the cars arrive. Inside that hut there must be parking officials.' She hefted her laser pistol. 'Parking officials wearing *clothes*. You understand? And we are going to *get* those clothes. Come on!'

Hand left Masticatetobacco snoozing on the pavement outside, and the three of them burst through the door with their guns ready.

Inside, sitting motionless behind a desk, was C3U-πP-HOL-8RA.

'Hello,' he said. And then, 'Shouldn't you people be wearing some clothes?'

'See-thru!' cried Luke in delight. 'What are you doing here?'

The golden robot looked at Luke. Even though his face was incapable of expression, it was clear that he was looking with the robot equivalent of disdain. 'I'm *parking cars*,' he said. 'What else would I be doing in a car park?'

The words sounded strangely familiar to Luke, but he couldn't place them right away. 'I'm just really glad to see you,' he gushed. 'We've been looking everywhere for you.'

'Have you?' said the droid, sardonically. 'Have you *really*?'

❋

Leper found a cupboard at the back of this parking control lodge in which spare overalls were stored, and in moments the whole party was dressed.

'Is RC-DU^2 with you?' the Princess demanded.

'He is,' said C3U-πP-HOL-8RA. 'No chance of getting rid of him. He's out there now, parking a Fiat Pluto HLX Automatic. There's been a lot of coming and going recently.'

'Thank Thog!' the Princess exclaimed. 'I was so worried that he would fall into the hands of Dark Father.'

'Oh, Dark Father had him in his office for a while,' said See-thru, in an offhand manner. 'Half an hour or so. Then he sent him back out again. He and I were assigned here on car-parking duties. Been here ever since.'

'This is excellent news,' said Luke. 'See-thru, can you help us? We need to get off this world, and quickly.'

'Hmm,' said the golden robot. 'Well, I suppose I could commandeer a car. It's against regulations of course, but – well, the obeche tree native to Africa doesn't insist upon me following orders in a matter such as this.' His gold hand slipped inside a drawer and emerged with a fat, plastic key. 'A Vectra Vector-Elector 7,' he said, proudly. 'With double-cam overshafting. A plastic contractor from Sirius drove in with it today. He's at some squash match right now. I've *always* wanted to have a spin in one of those.'

'It's no good just driving around,' complained Luke. 'We need to get *right off* this Death Spa.'

'You think these are, what, bicycles?' said See-thru, with a return of his previous disdainful tone of voice. 'They're space cars. Wheels for the flat surfaces; thrusters and hyperdrive for the *open* open road.' He got to his feet. 'Shall we?'

'Wait,' said Princess Leper. 'You're suggesting we save our own skins, whilst allowing the entire population of Gregbare to die? What about the Rebelend?'

'You're right,' said Luke, punching his right fist into his open left palm. 'All those naked SF authors. And the freedom fighters.' He cast his eyes about the parking control hut. A series of broad windows gave the controller sitting in the hut a panoramic view of the immediate vicinity of the parking level, and also of the dizzying drop over the side of the edge into the inner depths of the Death Spa.

'See-thru Peep-hol,' he said. 'This office is plumbed into the main Death Spa computer, isn't it?'

'Of course,' replied the droid. 'It's how we log all the incoming cars, so the Imp-Emp-Imp can keep tabs on who's on board.'

'Exellent,' said Luke. 'See-thru, I'd like you to go outside, collect RC-DU^2, and pull up in that executive space car you mentioned. Honk the horn when you're ready. I take it you can drive the car out of here *quickly*?'

'Certainly I can,' said the robot.

'Good,' said Luke.

The golden machine toddled out of the hut, and Princess Leper hurried over to Luke. 'You're up to something,' she said. 'What is it?'

'Oh – nothing,' he said. 'It's just that my eye chanced upon *this*.' He pointed. On a control panel was a fat red button marked: AUTO DESTRUCT.

'Great Thog!' gasped Hand Someman.

'The paranoia of the Imp-Emp-Imp will be its downfall,' exclaimed Luke. 'They're evidently so worried about this mighty weapon of theirs falling into Rebelend hands that they've fitted it with a comprehensive system of auto-destruct devices throughout. The fools!'

'You're brilliant!' said Princess Leper, looking happy for the first time Luke could remember. 'I could kiss you!'

'Really?' beamed Luke.

The Princess leaned over and gave Luke a peck on the cheek. 'There you go.'

'Let's just hope the destruct countdown gives us enough time to drive out of this place,' said Hand.

'I'm sure it will,' said the Princess. 'I have a good feeling about it.'

Through the door of the hut came the sound of an expensive car-horn playing Purcell's *Trumpet Voluntary*. 'Go on, Hand,' urged Luke. 'Put Masticate-tobacco in the car. We'll be out as soon as we've initiated auto-destruct.'

Hand hurried out. Luke looked into Leper's beautiful blue eyes.

'You realise,' she told him, 'that you're about to become a hero of the revolution?'

'Really? I like the sound of that. Hero of the revolution, eh? Do they get any perks, heroes of the revolution?'

'Don't press your luck,' said the Princess, though not unkindly. 'Just press the button.'

'Here goes.' Luke leaned on the fat red button.

Through the window of the control office, they could both see what happened next. A huge metal claw, at the end of a fat and snaky metal tentacle, appeared from an enormous metal cube located a few metres beyond the office. The claw opened, darted down, grabbed one of the parked cars, and heaved it into the air. It swung back to its metal cube, and dropped the whole thing into a gleaming metal maw. Instantly the walls of this space pressed inwards, turning the car into a tiny cube of compressed metal in moments. The claw then lifted this miniature parcel, and tucked it away on a ramp at the side of the crusher. Then it disappeared back inside, and the lid closed over it.

'Auto destruct,' said Luke, 'in *that* sense. I see.'

'I retract my kiss,' said Princess Leper, coldly. 'You're an idiot.'

'How was I to know the Imp-Emp-Imp would be so committed to recycling?' cried Luke. 'Although, now I come to think of it, it's not very likely that the Imp-Emp-Imp would fit a button capable of destroying the entire Death Spa inside a lowly parking official's hut.'

'Come on,' said the Princess. 'There's no point in us hanging about in here.' She moved to the door.

Luke stared at the red button. There was a tingly feeling inside his gut. 'Wait a minute,' he said.

As if from some plane of existence beyond his own, he heard a ghostly voice intone: *use the Farce, Luke.*

'What?' he said, startled.

'What?' asked Princess Leper.

'What?' he said, looking at her.

'What did you say?' she asked.

'What?'

'*What?*'

'Did you say something? Did you say "use the Farce, Luke"?'

'No,' she said.

'Did you say anything that I might have mistaken for "use the Farce, Luke"?'

'No – now, stop stalling. Come *on*. I know See-thru Peep-hol. He's liable to drive off without us if we're late.'

'I've an idea,' said Luke. 'It's all coming together in my head.' Slowly, as if in a trance, he reached out towards the AUTO DESTRUCT button a second time.

'That again?' said Leper. 'We know *that's* no good.'

Luke grinned at the Princess, and pressed the button anyway. Through the window they could see the hood of the crusher slide back, and the giant metal claw emerge, snaking towards another of the parked cars.

Luke snatched up his laser pistol, aimed at the control panel, and fired. The panel exploded in a flash of smoking plastic.

Outside, the claw shuddered as if shocked, twitched, and then it started going mad. It grabbed the nearest car, and flung it wildly, like a spastic baseball pitcher. The auto flew over the balustrade

and started tumbling towards the centre of the Death
Spa.

'Run!' yelled Luke.

They got outside in time to see the Claw toss a
second car over the edge, and reach for a third, and
then they clambered inside the Vectra Vector-Elector
7. 'Thought you weren't coming,' grumbled See-thru
in the driver's seat. 'I was about to leave.'

'Go go go go!' cried Luke.

'Just "go" is enough,' said See-thru. 'And *please*
would be nice.' Then, looking through the front
windshield, the robot added in a more terrified tone
of voice 'oo-*er*!' The Claw, having disposed of the
cars immediately proximate to the crusher, was now
snaking towards the Vectra Vector-Elector. See-thru
floored the pedal, and the finely engineered executive
machine hurtled up the rank.

They sped through what seemed like endless
tunnels. Red lights in the walls flashed to their left
and right. There was a monstrous rumbling. Audible
inside the car, even over the various other noises, was
a recorded voice booming '*Warning! Warning! Evacuate! Evacuate!*'

'What did you *do* back there?' asked Hand.

'I used the Farce,' said Luke. 'I think I collapsed the
Death Spa power source.'

'You *did*? Fantastic, kiddo!'

'What'll that do?'

'It'll implode the whole damn thing!' whooped Hand. 'The black hole at its core will suck everything into a singularity. You've done it, boy!'

'We're not free yet,' said Leper. 'Look —'

The car had emerged from the tunnel into a huge departure–arrival chamber. Deep space was visible through an ingress/exit forcefield; but their way was blocked with hundreds of milling Sterntroopers. The nearest of these were waving the car down, rifles at the ready.

'GO,' yelled Luke.

The car went.

When they realised that this car was not going to stop the soldiers opened fire. Laser bolts thudded into the bodywork, leaving smoking craters but not penetrating the bodywork completely. The rear jet kicked into life, and the Vectra launched into the air, heading straight for the opening.

One lucky shot shattered the rear windshield with a terrifying noise; tiny particles of plastiglass fluttered around, and a warning siren sounded inside the car. Unruffled by the kerfuffle – indeed, constitutionally unrufflable – See-thru Peep-hol shut off the siren and pressed the button that activated the back-up wind-shield.

Then they were in deep space, and speeding away.

Through the rear window, Luke and Leper watched the vast shape of the Death Spa shudder across its enormous length. Fires burst from random portholes. Several of the larger towers buckled and collapsed. A ripple of shattering metal passed, like an earthquake, over the surface of the artificial world. Then, with a staggering, blinding detonation, the whole Death Spa exploded like a plastic globe stuffed with firecrackers. Or, on second thoughts, like a vast world consumed by a vast incendiary ball of light and fire, with a huge torus of white flame spinning out from its equator. A wall of white-hot flame wider than his eyes could comprehend hurtled directly at the escaping car.

'We left it too late!' cried Luke. 'We're going to be immolated.'

The wall of fire rushed towards them, impossibly fast. It almost touched the rear of the car – but then, as if pulled back by a phenomenal forcefield, it slowed, slowed, and, miraculously, centimetres from the back of the car – it stopped. Then, like film being shown backwards, it started retreating, sucked back along its path towards a supermassive central point, collapsing down, imploding gas and fragments all pulled into a central spot.

One moment the view from the back window was of a roiling sphere of superheated gas . . .

. . . the next moment, nothing. The entire Death Spa had been sucked into the artificial black hole at its centre.

The Vectra Vector-Elector 7 rolled on through empty space, in the general direction of Gregbare. From the back seat came a voice.

'Oh no,' said Hand Someman. 'Not again.' The one stray laser bolt that had penetrated the car during its last frantic escape had struck him in his good lung. A gaping, bleeding, and steaming wound was visible.

'Hand!' cried Luke.

'Well, *that's* a shame,' said the Princess. 'Because if it weren't for that accident, I'd be celebrating right now.'

THE EMPIRE STRIDES AROUND IN BLACK

THE DEATH SPA HAD BEEN DESTROYED, BUT THIS SETBACK HAD ONLY REDOUBLED IMPERIAL EMPIRE OF THE IMPERIUM'S WILL UTTERLY TO CRUSH THE REBELEND. IN FACT TO BE PRECISE, IT HAD *RETRIPLED* THEIR WILL UTTERLY TO CRUSH THE REBELEND, PROVIDED ONLY THAT BY 'RETRIPLING' WE UNDERSTAND 'MULTIPLY BY SIX-TIMES' AND NOT 'MULTIPLY BY NINE-TIMES', WHICH WOULD BE 'TRIPLE-SQUARING', AND WHICH WOULD RATHER OVERSTATE THE AMOUNT BY WHICH THE IMP-EMP-IMP'S WILL TO DESTRUCTION HAD BEEN MAGNIFIED. DARK FATHER, WHO HAD ESCAPED THE DESTRUCTION OF THE DEATH SPA BY A SERIES OF EVENTUALITIES (INTO WHICH WE DON'T REALLY HAVE TIME, IN THESE INTRODUCTORY ROLLING CREDITS, TO GO) WAS PERSONALLY MASTERMINDING THE HUNTING DOWN AND EXTERMINATION OF ALL REBELEND RESISTANCE TO THE POWER OF THE IMP-EMP-IMP. MEANWHILE ON THE ICE-WORLD BRATHMONKI THE REBELEND HAD GATHERED THEIR BATTERED FORCES . . .

Chapter One
The New Rebelend Base

The ice planet Brathmonki glittered in the eternal blackness of space, like a giant white pearl against a profoundly dark backdrop. Or, to be exact, of course, you need to imagine the dark backdrop as speckled with lots of little white dots. Imagine, for the sake of argument (bear with me here), imagine that you're doing some decorating, painting your ceiling with white paint, and to preserve your carpets you've spread a black velvet sheet over the whole floor. I don't know why you'd use black velvet – perhaps you're eccentric. Perhaps you don't have any cheap cotton sheets to hand. So there's this black velvet sheet all across the carpet below you, and you go about your painting with a gay abandon, and inevitably some spatters and drops (although no dribbles or larger spills, since that would ruin the simile) of white paint fall onto the black velvet sheet. Now, let's say you stop painting for a minute, possibly because you've got a crick in your neck, you know what it's like painting a ceiling, most exhausting decorating job there is, that, just murder on the neck and shoulders; and you reach in your pocket for a handkerchief to mop your sweating brow. But as you pull the handkerchief out you inadvertently tug free the large white pearl you always carry about with you. How large? I don't know exactly. Let's say ping-pong-ball sized. As the handkerchief comes free you realise that you've dropped the valuable pearl (or if you prefer it, the ping-pong ball) and you look down with horror on your face – just in time to see, albeit momentarily, this giant pearl, or ping-pong ball, in the process of falling away from you, visible against the paint-spattered black velvet – a sight so traumatic that it seems to freeze in time, the image burning into your memory, so you'll never forget it.

That's what the planet Brathmonki looked like from space.

Down on the planet, Luke Seespotrun was out in the snow, riding on a 'piggibakka' (a giant-woolly-kangaroo-style life form indigenous to Brathmonki). He was well swaddled against the minus 80° cold; a fake-fur parka with the hood raised and the zip done right up to his Adam's apple, and a pair of driving gloves. He rode his mount to the top of a snowy hill, and then he rode him down again. From time to time he would fit binoculars into the fur-fringed oval space at the front of his parka hood.

He was looking for signs of Imp-Emp-Imp activity, trying to decide whether the Imperial Emperor had discovered the Rebelend's latest hiding place. But he couldn't see anything. Nothing. Nada. Zilch. Nothing to see here, move along. Blankness. Whiteness. Zero. Plenty of not-one-thing. Snow, snow, snow, snow.

Luke pressed the button on his walkie-talkie. His ridie-talkie, I mean.

'Base?' he said. 'This is Seespotrun reporting. Over.'

The sound of static and cackling. '. . . *zzp–pzz–zyzg–* Hello Luke?*–pzaz–zzzzz–*'

'Princess Leper? Is that you? Over.'

'Good to hear your *crxzc* voice Luke,' said Leper. 'Over.'

'Well,' Luke said. 'I've been out here for hours and I haven't seen anything. Over.'

'*pz-pz-pz–*our automatic tracking puts you less than a klik from Mount Snowless Black Granite. You ought to be able to see the Giant Black Granite Mountain Range directly in front of you. Over.'

'Can't see anything at all. Only snow. Over.'

'Well it's a clear day, Luke–*pz!–*you should be able to see the wide blue sky above you.'

'Nope. Just snow. Over.'

'Can you–*pzz*–see your piggibakka beneath you? Over.'

'No.'

'Can you see your hand flapping in front of you?'

Flap. Flap. 'Nope. Over.'

'Luke – you may have a case of *cwzzzz–zazazz*. Repeat: You may *cwzzzz–zazazz* snow blindness. Be careful out there.'

'I'll be fine. Rooaaarrr!'

'Luke?' Princess Leper's voice sounded distant and tinny over the ridie-talkie device, but her concern was still very evident. 'Luke? Why did you say "rooaaarrr" at the end of that last sentence?'

'*I* didn't say "rooaaarrr". Over.'

'I definitely heard a "rooaaarrr".'

'Well it wasn't *me*,' said Luke.

'Rooaaarrr!'

'There it is again, Luke,' cried Leper. 'Get out of there.'

'It's OK,' said Luke. 'I can't see anything that might be dangerous to – *aaarrghh!*'

'Luke? Luke? Was that *you* saying "aaarrghh"? Or was that another roar-like noise from the unseen roaring creature?'

'No,' replied Luke. 'The "aaarrghh" was me. Over.'

'Luke? What's happening?'

'A huge shambling yeti-style creature seems to be *argh!! Argh! Ow! Ow! Ow!*' The fizz of static was all that could be heard for a full thirty seconds; but finally Luke added 'over' in a gaspy, hurt-sounding voice.

'Luke? Are you alright? Luke?'

But there was no reply. For long minutes, Princess Leper tried raising her friend on the radio link. But in vain.

'*crcrcrzzzz–zak–kak–*. . . rly hear you Luke . . . *pneeeeee!–zz–*you're breaking up . . .'

Luke had indeed been attacked by a gigantic yeti-style creature, a beast that had batted him from his piggi-bakka's saddle with one sweep of its huge hairy paw; and then swiped him again on the head just for the hell of it.

Luckily for Luke the yeti-style creature was not interested in eating him. It lacked the necessary enzymes in its yeti-style gut to digest a creature of Luke's (to him) alien provenance, a fact which made Luke's semi-conscious, groaning body about as ap-petising to it as a plate of sand would be to us. But he devoured Luke's piggibakka steed, and shambled away, leaving the sorely wounded young man mountless in the middle of the wilderness, and literally freezing to death.

Clouds boiled coldly into being in the sky, and soon it was snowing. A vicious wind gathered, shrieking and yanking rudely at Luke's clothes. Soon the wind started hurtling the snow around in a blizzard-like manner.

'Nooo . . .' Luke groaned. Or perhaps it was 'ooooh'. It's difficult to tell, actually, given the high level of ambient noise from the wind and the blizzard and everything. It was clearly a negatively framed utterance. Bearing in mind that he had been recently mauled by gigantic wild beast, left for dead in the middle of a raging snowstorm and everything, it's unlikely, to say the least, that he would make a positive or affirmational noise, a 'yes!' or 'yee-ha!' or 'Dolores!', or anything along those lines.

The blizzard swirled around his supine form. Then, oddly, the howling of the gale seemed to distort, the sound bubbled and lowed like cattle, and then, as if the very wind were haunted, Luke thought he heard the wind speak.

'Luke . . .' it said. And then, 'Luke Seespotrun . . .'

The voice was that of Old Bony K'nobbli.

But it couldn't be! Bony had died on the Death Spa, his corpse sucked into a black hole singularity

with all the other matter on that doomed construction.
It *couldn't* be!

'Bony?' Luke looked up. 'Is that you, Bony?'

'Luke,' said Bony. Looking up through the snow,
Luke could see a spectral shining form that bore a
fleeting resemblance to the old dead Jobbi knight.

'Luke, listen to me,' said K'nobbli. 'You must go to
Swamp World and seek out Yodella . . .' warbled the
hallucination.

'Yodella?' gasped Luke, as frostbite started biting
his face.

'He is a great Jobbi master. He can complete
your training in the ways of the Farce. I'm sorry I
didn't mention it before, actually; you know, when
I was actually alive. Slipped my mind. Shocking. I
can't apologise enough. Anyway, here I am, better late
than never. Late as in the sense of dead.'

'Bony!' gasped Luke. 'Bony!'

'Go to Swamp World!' said Bony, putting a fruity
low-level vibrato on the words, as if striving for mystic
resonance: 'It is your destiny! Go, Luke! Seek out
Yodella! Think positively! Have an aromatherapy
bath from time to time! – you deserve it! You can't
put a price on relaxation! Drawing the Death card in
tarot is not necessarily a bad thing, it may only mean
the death of old and bad habits or negative modes of

thinking! Wear Purple! These Crystals are available for only 29.95 Imperial Credits plus interstellar post and packing! Go into the Light! Think Pink! Go to work on an egg!'

'Bony – I'm losing you! You're fading out!'

'Luke!' Bony K'nobbli said, very faintly. 'Use the Farce . . .' But he was gone.

The snow flurried around Luke's supine form like an impossibly large quantity of soapflakes under the action of a powerful wind machine. And very cold soapflakes – I think we can take that as read. Soapflakes, shall we say, that had previously been stored in a super size plastic container in a walk-in refrigerator. It was very cold indeed, that's what I'm trying to get at.

Luke passed out.

The blizzard stopped. Sunshine shone on the virgin snowfall.

Hand Someman, riding his own piggibakka, knew that something was wrong. He could almost *sense* that Luke was in trouble, almost *telepathically intuit* his situation. He rode over the snow as if guided by some supernatural affinity with the wounded man. It helped, of course, that Luke was carrying a satellite tracking bug, and that his last known position was well established, and that his last communication had been 'arrgh!'

'Base,' said Hand into his radio receiver. 'I'm approaching Luke's position now.'

He galloped up the final slope to where Luke's body was lying. 'Hold on, kid,' he called, hopping off his mount and cradling the younger man in his arms, although in a 'life-saving' rather than 'romantically intimate' manner.

'Bony . . .' moaned Luke. 'Old Bony K'nobbli . . .'

'It's me, kid,' said Hand. 'Hand Someman. The guy with the two artificial lungs. Your buddy, yeah?'

'. . . Old Bony . . .'

'No, no,' repeated Hand. 'It's *me*. Hand Someman.'

'. . . K'nobbli . . .'

'You're rambling kid, I'm *Hand*. Not Bony K'nobbli. Hand. Me – it's me.'

Luke twitched as if in pain, but his incoherent burbling continued: '. . . saw *vision* of . . . Old Bony . . . in the blizzard . . . his spectral form seemed . . . appear to me . . . not *addressing* Bony K'nobbli right now . . . rather *recalling* previous vision . . . told me to go to Swamp World . . . meet Yodella . . .'

'You're not making any sense, kid.' Hand shook his head. 'I'm losing him to the cold,' he muttered. 'I'm going to have to take drastic action to warm him up.'

He reached into his rucksack and withdrew an absolutely gigantic Bowie knife, silver all over except for a single red zigzag near the top of the blade.

'Actually,' murmured Luke, opening his eyes a little '. . . feeling a bit better . . . if you could just . . . get me back to base . . . nice cup of hot sweet tea . . . blanket perhaps made of winceyette . . . around my shoulders . . .'

'Hold still, kid,' said Hand, his face grim. With one swift motion, followed up with twelve or fourteen desperate jabbing and stabbing motions, he cut open the belly of the piggibakka, allowing its foul-smelling viscera to tumble and pour all over the snow. The pale green guts steamed as they slopped out, but the fierce iciness of Brathmonki's climate soon chilled them.

'So cold . . .' said Luke.

'Here you go,' said Hand, scooping pile after pile of foul slippery intestine over Luke's body. 'This'll warm you up.'

'So cold . . .' Luke said again, his brow furrowing. 'And also, now, smelly. So cold and smelly. Not to mention slimy.'

'This is no good,' fretted Hand. 'These slimy viscera haven't retained their heat at *all* in this freezing environment. They're not going to insulate you at all. You need more effective up-warming than *this*.' He rifled around inside the opened stomach of the piggi-bakka's corpse for a while, pulling out the rest of the creature's intestines, and then grabbed Luke by the waist, and heaved with all his might, pushing him head first into the cadaver-cavity.

'Urh,' said Luke, his voice now muffled by the fact that his mouth was inside the dead body of a large shag-covered animal. 'Sooo cold . . . and also the bad smell *much* worse now . . . plus face being pressed uncomfortably against the inside of some dead thing's ribcage . . . very uncomfortable . . . and covered in foul gunk. And still cold.'

Hand stopped trying to heave Luke in with his hands. It wasn't working: it was as if the gut cavity of a creature the size of a large kangaroo wasn't large enough to fit a fully-grown human male. Clearly he needed more effective leverage. He stood up, and looked down at his friend, whose head and shoulders were inside the dead creature, but whose body was otherwise very much outside. The sounds Luke was making, although only half-audible, did not suggest a person in a state of comfort or health. This situation called for drastic measures. He hurried to Luke's feet, and sat himself down. Hand then fitted his own feet to the bottoms of Luke's feet, and pushed with both legs with all his might. A few more inches of the top of Luke's torso disappeared into the ragged hole cut in the piggibakka's gut, but no matter how hard Hand pushed he could not get more of him inside. 'Mmmbb, Bbbmmm,' said Luke. 'MmmmbBBbb! Mm! Mb!'

'What's that, kiddo?' Hand asked, getting back to his feet.

There was a rushing sound in the clear cold air, and a Rebelend hover-transporter swooped down to land a few yards from the scene. The side door slid open and Princess Leper leapt out, running over to Hand's side.

'Hand! Thank God you're alright! And Luke – is Luke OK?'

Hand looked into her beautiful face. Then he looked down at the scene on the snow before him: a dead piggibakka, intestines lying curled and scattered all about, and Luke's horizontal body lying with its top twenty per cent or so stuffed inside the carcass.

'Great Thog!' cried Leper in dismay. 'What happened here?'

Hand quickly weighed up the possible explanations. 'He was like this when I found him,' he said, setting his facial expression to 'sincere'.

'You're *kidding*?' said the Princess, aghast. 'Luke? – what did he *do* to his *mount*? I didn't think him *capable* of . . .' She stared in silent surmise at the figure of Luke for long seconds, before shaking her head and announcing: 'anyway, the Imp-Emp-Imp fleet has arrived. They've discovered our base. We have to evacuate. Come on, pull him out of there – we have to get back.'

'Excellent,' said Hand, brightly.

'By the way,' she added, as Hand clambered aboard the transporter. 'Where's *your* piggibakka?'

'Ah,' said Hand. 'Um. Yes.'

Chapter Two

The Emp-Imp-Emp. Or, no, that's Imp-Emp-Imp. Or is it the first one? One of the two, certainly

High above the icy planet, a fleet of Imperial destroyers circled relentlessly. Of course, that is in the nature of any orbit, its relentlessness. Unless it's relentless it's not really an orbit. A *relenting* orbit would be what we call 'a re-entry' or possibly 'a crash'. But I am using the word 'relentless' to convey not only a literal description of the spaceship's movement, but a metaphorical sense of their unstopping campaign of terror and oppression. You see.

On the command bridge of the Phagocyte class space destroyer *Oppression Through Fear and Terror is the New Freedom*, Dark Father stood, legs apart, face unreadable behind his terrifying black skull-shaped mask, staring into the inky blackness and black inkiness of deep space. He had come close to destruction aboard the Death Spa, and had only escaped at the very last minute in some rather implausible circumstances into which we do not, at the moment, have time to go. Suffice to say that he had indeed survived, and that he was not best pleased with the fact that a military facility costing 45,000,000,000, 000,000,000,000,000,000,000,000,000,000,000,000, 000,000,000,000,000,000,000,000,000,000 million Imperial Credits to build (not to mention the on-going salary of its seventeen million crew, and the various non-renewable statutory recovery overheads, payment vouchers and loss-leader profitability returns) – that such a facility could so easily have been snuffed out of existence in a trice!

After a tense meeting with the Imperial Emperor, during which a new Death Spa had been commissioned, Dark Father was sent out on a Galaxy-wide mission to track down the Rebelend and punish them by Death Absolute.

Now, after many months, the search had produced its result. Below them the Rebelend was concentrated.

Commander Regla Onzedcars approached the Dark Lord of the Psmyth with the trepidation he was finding it harder and harder to disguise. 'My Lord,' he said, standing to attention behind the brooding form of the evil Father.

'COMMANDER,' boomed Dark Father.

'We have located the Rebelend's new base on the ice planet of Brathmonki, below us.'

'GOOD WORK, COMMANDER,' boomed Father. 'ORDER THE FLEET TO ATTACK MODE. DEPLOY THE ONE-LEGGEDY AT-TACK CRAFT.'

'Yes good, my Lord. And . . . my Lord?'

'YES, COMMANDER?'

'That renaming order still applies, does it? The one telling all staff to refer to the attack craft as "one leggedy"?'

'IT IS THE IMPERIAL EMPEROR'S WILL, COMMANDER.'

'Yes, my Lord. Of course, my Lord. It's just that . . . some of the men feel that . . . "Monopod Attack Craft" was not only a more accurate name, but one more calculated to inspire the troops with proper battle fury. The problem with "One-Leggedy" is . . .'

'IT IS THE IMPERIAL EMPEROR'S *WILL* COMMANDER.'

'Of course, my Lord.'

There was an awkward, brooding, dark silence. Commander Onzedcars did not dare leave until dis-missed.

'COMMANDER,' boomed Dark Father. He turned to face his subordinate. 'I WANT YOU TO READ THIS.' He held out a jet-black folder, within which Onzedcars found several dozen plastic flimsies' worth of text.

'New orders, my Lord? Destruction to be wreaked on some other unsuspecting planet?'

'NO, NOT THAT. SOMETHING ELSE. ACTUALLY – THE FACT IS I'VE ADDED SOME DIALOGUE TO *A DAY AT THE RACES*,' said Dark Father. 'A FEW IMPROVE-MENTS HERE AND THERE, FOR INST-ANCE, AT THE BIT WHERE GROUCHO . . . YOU TOLD ME THAT GROUCHO WAS THE FUNNY ONE?'

Onzedcars swallowed nervously. 'Many people think so, my Lord. I mean . . . well . . .'

'YES, YES, WELL WHERE GROUCHO SAYS "I COULD DANCE WITH YOU 'TIL THE COWS COME HOME, IN FACT I'D RATHER DANCE WITH THE COWS 'TIL YOU GO HOME" – I'VE REWRITTEN IT SO THAT HE ADDS "YOUR COWS ARE AS *NOTHING* COMPARED TO THE DARK SIDE OF THE FARCE, I SHALL *CRUSH* THEM,

AFTER WHICH *I* SHALL REPLACE YOU AS
DARK LORD OF THE DANCING, IT IS MY
DESTINY".'

There was a period of silence.

'Very good, Lord Father,' said Onzedcars, nervously. 'Very . . . um. Good. A distinct improvement.'

'ANYWAY, ANYWAY, HAVE A LOOK AT
IT WHEN YOU'VE SOME SPARE TIME. I
DO THINK I'VE IMPROVED IT.'

'I'm sure you have, my Lord.'

'WELL, AS I SAY, HAVE A READ OF IT.
LET ME KNOW WHAT YOU THINK. BE
HONEST.'

'Of course I will,' said Commander Onzedcars.

'I MEAN,' said the Dark Lord of the Psmyth, with
a hint of uncertainty about the words, almost as if he
were hurt, 'I MEAN, IF YOU REALLY DIDN'T
THINK IT WAS FUNNY . . .'

'No, my Lord! It was hilarious my Lord – ha! Haha
haha!'

'. . . I'D ACTUALLY VALUE SOME GENU-
INE FEEDBACK. I REALLY WOULD.'

'Of course my Lord.'

'ANYWAY, ANYWAY. WHAT WERE WE
DOING?'

'Launching an attack on the Rebelend base below, my Lord?'

'AH YES. UNLEASH THE ATTACK FORCES.'

Chapter Three

Attack! Attack! Attack!

All was confusion in the Rebelend base. Rebelend soldiers ran hither and thither, many of them then returning to hither to collect stuff they'd forgotten in their haste to get thither. Panic was in the air. 'Evacuate!! Evacuate!!' screamed an automatic siren, resonating in every corridor and hallway. 'Evacuate!! Evacuate!! Hurry – they're almost upon us!'

To be frank, it was more counterproductive than productive.

'Hand!' cried Luke, as he limped awkwardly towards his own fighter. 'I have to go to the Swamp Planet and meet Yodella.'

'You're crazy, kid,' said Hand, heading towards his own Rebelend-allocated spaceship. 'I wish you luck.'

'I'll meet up with you at the Floating City.'

'Sure thing – and hey kid?'

'Yes Hand?'

'It's a long flight to Swamp Planet. Take an RC Motile Commode unit with you. You'll need it.'

'What about you, Hand?'

'I'm taking Leper to see an old friend of mine;
Landrove Afreelanda. She's got a bee in her bonnet
about the Great Secret secreted on board her droid. I
figured Landrove can download anything from anything – he's a computer genius. So we'll go see if he
can finally sort out what this Great Secret is, and
whether it can help us defeat the Empire.'

'Good luck then!'

'And good luck to you . . .'

The two friends shook hands. Hand raced to his
spaceship, and Luke got into his. Both craft zoomed
into the sky, and in moments were hyperspacing away
from Brathmonki as fast as their engines could propel
them.

There was no time to lose: the Imp-Emp-Imp had
landed its landers less than a kilometre from the
Rebelend base; and now it had loaded thousands of
Sterntrooper shock troops into the metal hulls of their
Monopod, sorry 'One-Leggedy', Attack Craft.

Dozens of these craft were now pogo-ing along the
ice-fields towards the Rebelend base. Huge metallic
hulls perched atop single spindly hydraulically-
operated robot legs, these terrifying engines of war
were capable of pole-vaulting over any defensive wall
constructed on a level, hard surface such as a salt flat

or horizontal grasslands. But they worked poorly in the soggy snow and uneven terrain of Brathmonki. As long as the snow lay on relatively flat fields, they could execute their bone-jarring and hair-raising leaps and jumps, bounding leadenly from spot to spot. But where the terrain shifted topography, slanting either up or down, they tended to topple forwards or backwards, to explode, or crack open, or just lie motionless. And once a one-legged creature without arms has fallen over, it is almost impossible for that creature to get itself back on its single leg.

I mean, think about it.

'Idiots!' screamed the Ground Commander, Idsthadguy Fromcorrie, from his vantage point at the beach-head. 'Fools! Idiotic Fools! Foolish Idiots! Why are you fooling around like this, idiots?'

'The terrain, Commander,' screeched one of his One-Leggedy Attack Craft Captains. 'It's just too tricky! Our gyroscope software cannot predict the lie of the land underneath the snow . . . woooooaaaah!' The line went dead. Away to Ground Commander Fromcorrie's left there came the wu-*oomf* noise of a machine exploding as it hit snow.

'Idifools!' cried Fromcorrie, bitterly. 'Fooliots! *Quickly*! Before Dark Father hears of this debacle – deploy the Doubledy-Leggedy Attack Craft.'

'Sir?' queried the second in command.

'The DuoPods!' Fromcorrie screamed. 'At once!'

From the Rebelend base, General Fishedd Onaslab was watching developments through a pair of digital binoculars. 'The Monopods have failed. It looks as though they're . . . yes . . . the drop hangars are opening their doors, and the DuoPods are emerging. Send the order down: plantains at the ready.'

The order was carried through the ice-trenches by a runner, who sprinted frantically down to the lower levels. 'Ready the plantains! Ready the plantains!'

Two dozen plantain cannons were already armed with the gigantic banana-like fruit, picked from the plantain-forests of Gigantia and shipped here in huge-hulled carriers, ready for just such an eventuality. Each individual yellow-green skinned plantain was twice the length of a grown man; the skins leathery yet easy to split, the pale fibrous fruit within soft and starting to go black and squishy at the edges. Each of these gigantic objects was loaded onto a massive catapult-style launcher, and aimed at the battlefield.

Within minutes the launchers could see their targets. Imagine aircraft carrier-sized boxes, hulls filled with expectant soldiery, each the product of a lifetime's training, all arranged in rows on rank after rank of benches, each with their armour on and their weapons ready. Now imagine the forward end of this giant hangar; up a metal staircase, and into the forward cockpit compartment. Here a trained walker was stepping with experienced ease on a treadmill; his trousers were wired with complex sensors that transferred his motion to the twin metal legs of the DuoPod. Now (to maintain the cinematic analogy) zoom out of the cockpit, into the chill air of Brathmonki, and pan down. You can see the enormous, sinuous legs of the craft: link after link of enormous circular metal connected into two strands, hundreds of metres long – resembling, in fact, the sorts of hose you get linking a showerhead to the shower itself – except that this hose is powered from within with complex heavy engineering.

The DuoPods marched inexorably over the landscape towards the Rebelend base. Having two legs, they were not incommoded by any changes in the elevation of the land beneath them.

General Fishedd eyed them up. When they were within range, he ordered the firing of the giant plantains. Dozens of the fifteen-foot-long fruit hurtled through the air in a graceful arc, to collide with the frosty permafrost: the inner fruit matter splatted on impact, spreading out in a puréed mess, but the skin spread into gigantic star shapes and slithered over the ice, to lie ready for the clunking metal feet of the gigantic DuoPods.

From his vantage point at the rear of the Imp-Emp-Imp lines, Ground Commander Fromcorrie sighed heavily, as, one after the other, his DuoPod attack craft slipped and tumbled to their doom. Some flew backwards, flapping their huge metal-tentacle legs high in the air. Some tried for several seconds to keep their balance by thrashing their feet about like a tap-dancer, but only managed to postpone the inevitable.

'Tripods! Set loose the tripods! At once!'

As the second-in-command hurried to execute this order, Fromcorrie put his hands to his face. This assault was going to take a long time to get right.

Chapter Four

Swamp World. It's Swampy

Luke zip-crashed out of hyperspace above a small green-green world. 'Somehow,' he said, speaking to the RC unit stashed beneath the cushionless seat on which Luke was sitting, 'I've got to track down a single Jobbi master on this place.'

'Eeek!' returned the droid.

The ship soared and dipped into the heavy atmosphere of the world, swooping low beneath the clouds to reveal a horizon-to-horizon jungle. 'How am I going to find Yodella in this vast jungle? It would be like looking for a needle in a huge stack of much bigger needles many of which tower over one's head and have sprouted leaves and other foliage.' He pondered his dilemma for some time. 'I must trust the Farce,' he said, finally. In line with this new resolution he flew his craft lower – low enough, in fact, to collide with a number of the taller trees. In seconds the complex wing-structure of his &-wing spaceplane was reduced to stumpage. The fuselage was striated by lower branches; Luke, in the passenger seat, was jolted and shaken so much that his teeth performed a drum solo, similar to one first performed by Keith Moon in the Who's *Live at Leeds* performance. Then Luke's trajectory brought him into jarring collision with a particularly big tree, and the dented remains of his spaceplane landed in a yard of mud, not far from a stagnant and foul-smelling pond, above which flew some foul-smelling fowl, amongst which was a particularly foul-smelling owl.

For several minutes Luke merely sat, until his eyeballs stopped shimmering and the humming in his ears receded. Then he pulled his helmet off, unbuckled his seatbelt, and pressed the cockpit release button. 'Time to go find this Yodella geezer,' he told RC. 'If I can . . .'

'Eeeek!' replied the little droid, emerging from underneath Luke's seat.

Luke surveyed the scene for a while, and then set off into the undergrowth. RC-DU^2 followed at a suitably cautious distance. 'I can only hope,' said Luke, as he tramped on, 'that by trusting to the Farce, and abandoning myself to – waaagh.'

He had fallen down a deep hole. 'Help!' he cried. 'I seem to be in a deep hole.'

'Down there, hello,' came a voice. Over the lip of

the hole Luke could see a wrinkled tortoise-like green
face looking down at him.

'Can you help me?'

'You will help I,' replied the figure.

'No, can *you* help *me*?'

'You answered have already I.'

'Oh, for crying out Thog,' said Luke. He pulled
himself up, and using his fingers – still sore and,
frankly, rather incomplete from their frostbite experience on Brathmonki – he scrabbled up the muddy,
slimy side of the hole into which he had fallen. At the
top he collapsed on the ground. 'Thanks for nothing,'
he gasped.

'Going are you where looking,' said the little green
man. 'Not,' he added, as if an afterthought.

'You what?' said Luke. 'Your command of Galactic
Standard doesn't seem to be wholly idiomatic.'

'tainly, Cer,' said the tiny fellow. He settled himself
on a log, the better to be able to converse with Luke.
It was a very large log; large enough, indeed, for a full-
grown man to fit inside it, had he wanted to. And had
the log been hollow. Which, of course, it wasn't. But
I'm only saying, to give you some sense of the dimen-
sions of the log.

Luke sized him up. This didn't take long, since he
was a very diminutive individual indeed: green of skin

and short of limb, and also green of limb, obviously, since his limbs were covered in his green skin. His face was wrinkled and curiously collapsed in on itself, and no hair grew on his green head. Most odd was his clothing: a green velvet waistcoat over a cream-coloured shirt, and tight leather short trousers that reached, barely, to his knees.

'I am looking,' said Luke, sitting up, 'for a mighty Jobbi warrior. Name of Yodella.'

'Yodella, am I,' said the little fellow. 'Yodel-idle-odle-idle-oh-*i-heee*, lonely goat-herd, sat a, high on a hill,' he added.

Luke stared at him for fully two minutes. At the end of this he said 'right' in a cautious tone of voice.

'Teach you I will,' said Yodella. '*Unlearn* you must, before you can learn. Feel the Farce, you will. Yodel-ay-*i-heee*! Yodel-ay-*i-hayy*! Yodel-idle-odle-idle-odle-idle-odle-ay-*i-heee*!' On these last few syllables the little creature's voice reached a pitch so high only dogs were able to hear it.

'. . . I'm sorry?' said Luke.

Yodella looked inscrutable. His mouth crunched up in a bizarrely non-human way, almost as if his entire cranial substructure of bone and sinew were actually shaped not as a smooth globe with a subordinate hinged jaw, but as a five-pronged medially-flattened

structure bent over itself, almost *hand*-shaped that
was rubbing its 'thumb' against its 'fingers'. Luke had
never seen anything like it before.

'Sacred song of the Jobbi, it is,' Yodella explained.
'Learn it, you will. Tight your trousers must be.
Yes. Help you *climb* it will, climb *every* mountain, yes.
Another song there is, for swinging through this
jungle on the vines, with myself on your back like a
little rucksack. Sing it I will—'

'That's alright,' interrupted Luke. 'There's no need.
So, um. Pleased to meet you. Could you, please, if it's
not too much trouble, train me in the rites and lethal
arts of the ancient Jobbi religion?'

'I will. Train you in the use of the lightsword I
will. And also in Farcical martial arts, Ecky-Thump,
moving pebbles with one's mind, smacking people in
the head with a plank carried over one's shoulder,
many other lethal skills. Not to mention dynamite-*ti-
heeee!* – yes with dynamite-*ti-heeee!*'

'Is it really necessary,' asked Luke, 'to end so many
of your sentences with the sacred Jobbi song?'

'Indeed, yes,' said Yodella. He appeared to have
got down from the log, although Luke hadn't actually
seen him move; and now he was making his way
through the dense undergrowth of Swamp World's
jungle floor. Luke couldn't see the little creature's legs

or feet, but took it on trust that he possessed these physical appurtenances. He certainly moved as if he were walking, rocking to and fro on (Luke assumed) his lower limbs. 'Come with me you will,' Yodella said. 'To my tiny little house, although inside you will be squashed, rather. There I shall impart to you the great secrets of the Farce.'

'Excellent,' said Luke.

'Yipee-ai-iiii-*i-hee*! Yipee-ai-ayyy-*i-hee*! Yipee oh *iii* a-yo, *iii* a-yo *i-hee*!' agreed Yodella.

Chapter Five

Floating City. Ah – now that's a nice location. Really pretty. You should check it out, if you ever get the chance. Real charming vacation destination. Lovely views. And if you can go off season, which is to say, if you don't mind taking the kids out of school for a couple of days, it's extremely reasonable. Really

Hand Someman piloted the spaceship *Rebel Yell He Said More More More IV* out of hyperspace with practised ease. He found it easy to pilot a ship out of hyperspace. He'd practised it. Beside him slept Masticatetobacco; some of his pelt had grown back, but no more than a thick stubble which made him bristly and unpleasant to handle. Accordingly, Hand had had a special lounger seat fitted to the bridge of the *Rebel Yell He Said More More More IV*, had hauled Masticatetobacco into it and more or less left him there to sleep.

Princess Leper had changed into an elegant dress fashioned from a single trouser-leg cut from a pair of really wide loon-pants. 'So tell me about this friend of yours we're going to visit?'

'Landrove Afreelanda? I've known him for years. He's managed to find himself a pretty cushy job as Overseer on the Floating City. If anybody can download this mysterious Secret from your droid it'll be him.'

'Are you sure he can download the Great Secret from the droid? I'm pretty frustrated with my inability to access this secret, you know. I'm sure that, if we could only get at the Secret, we'd be able to defeat the Imp-Emp-Imp in a trice.'

'If anybody can hack the droid,' said Hand, confidently, 'Landrove can. He will help us, I just know it.'

'I hope you're right,' said Princess Leper, as the spaceship crested the top of the planet's atmosphere and swooped through the air. 'There's a lot riding on getting at this Secret.'

Soon the Floating City itself, in all its gorgeous, floating opulence came into view. Shaped like a gigantic trifle made of metal and plastic, it hung in the mid-air with breathtaking hanging-ness. 'I radio'd ahead,' said Hand. 'Landrove is expecting us.'

He brought the *Rebel Yell He Said More More More IV* in to land at the city's main landing bay, turned off the engine, engaged the handbrake. Everybody unclicked their seatbelts, except Masti' (whom they left where he was). All of them capable of moving under their own power piled out of the airlock. The air outside smelt fresh and ozoney.

'Welcome to Floating City,' announced a smiling young man – good-looking even though he was wearing a cape, although not *quite* as good-looking as Hand Someman.

'Landrove, my old buddy!' cried Hand. 'How ya doing?'

'Hand! Hand Someman! Great gosh, it's good to see you!'

'This is Princess Leper,' said Hand.

'Enchanted to meet you. And where's Masticatetobacco?'

'Sleeping,' said Hand, nodding back towards the spaceship.

'Of course. But how great to see you all, here, on the Floating City,' said Landrove, beaming. He shook everybody warmly by the hand, including See-thru Peep-hol. 'It really floats,' he added. 'The city I mean. It really does hang in mid-air, a mile or so above the ground of this world. Really. It does.'

'So I see,' said Princess Leper, looking about her. 'The view is . . .'

'—It's *very* advanced technology,' interrupted Landrove. 'The city-float-up-make-happen, er, technology. Very advanced.'

'Right,' said Leper.

'We really do float up here. Skyhook-like. Suspended. We're not,' and Landrove started laughing unconvincingly, short bark-like little laughs, as though what he was saying were hilarious, 'we're not *perched* on top of an enormous *pole*, or anything like that! Ha! Ha! No, no, the *very idea* ha! – not that. No.' But his eyes were not laughing.

'OK,' said the Princess, uncertainly.

'Good,' said Landrove, rubbing his hands together. 'So we've cleared that up, have we? A *floating* city – *fl-oa-t*-ing. OK?'

'We understand,' said Hand.

Landrove looked from face to face, a little anxiously, before breaking into a wide grin. 'Excellent! Come along then! Refreshments.' He led the party along a series of white-painted corridors, all of them with hand-holds along the walls. These latter features were particularly useful, since the whole of Floating City seemed to sway alarmingly, angling slowly in one direction until the floor was at some fifteen degrees from the horizontal, then pausing, then slowly tilting back until it tipped about fifteen degrees in the opposite direction, before starting the whole cycle again.

'You'll get used to the slight tilt in no time,' said Landrove, beaming at them, and palming himself hand over hand until he reached a door.

'If you say so,' Hand said, through gritted teeth.

'I feel seasick,' said See-thru. 'And I don't even have an inner ear, let alone an internal digestive system.'

They hauled themselves into a room, and collapsed gratefully onto bright red faux-leather settees. A traction-robot crawled alternately up and down the same stretch of floor and brought them drinks, each served in toddler-style non-drip cups.

'Why does it sway so?' asked Leper.

'Sway?' said Landrove, as if he really hadn't noticed. 'Ah, you refer to the mild perturbations. Are you talking about the mild perturbations?'

'I guess so.'

Landrove waved a hand in the air. 'That's a minor glitch in the complicated traction-beam forcefield, um, laser, computer, er, keepie-uppie technology that, ah, powers the city.' He opened his smile to wide-beam. 'Believe me, you really won't notice it after a little while. *I* no longer do.' Abruptly the floor angled and lurched like a banking airplane, with such rapidity and force that Landrove was flung off the settee. He zipped through the air with a look of terror on his face, caromed off the wall, and smacked face-first onto the floor.

He picked himself up with some difficulty, and groped his way back to the settee.

'So,' said Leper, trying to make conversation while Landrove patted at his bleeding nostrils with a piece of tissue paper, 'what does the city specialise in? Is it a mining outpost?'

'No, actually,' replied Landrove, as if he were attempting a Melvyn Bragg impression. 'We offer specialised night classes and college educational courses.'

'How fascinating. In the humanities? Sciences?'

'In only one area, as it happens. City-floating technology.'

Princess Leper nodded as the dangling hair on either side of her face swayed back and forth like two clock pendulums. 'I'd be interested in taking a course like that.'

'It's more than one course,' said Landrove. 'The technology involved is so very complicated . . . most students need to pay seven-year's fees, at four hundred thousand Imperial Credits a year, before they are even allowed to study City Levitation 101. The average degree takes nearly twenty years, and only the *very richest* life forms can afford it. The very richest life forms,' he added, '*or* their parents. And if some super-rich parents wanted to get rid of a noisome, selfish kid for up to twenty years in a college suspended a mile above the ground from which escape is impossible, who are we to turn them down?'

'So how many people graduated with your advanced city levitating skills diploma last year?' asked Leper.

'Um,' said Landrove. 'But look through the window! Isn't that a lovely sunset?'

After an hour or so of small talk, Landrove excused himself and made his way along one of the ocean-liner-in-a-bad-storm corridors to another room. The door hissed open, and a familiar black-clad figure was revealed standing, rather uneasily, inside.

'LANDROVE,' said Dark Father. 'ARE THEY HERE?'

'They're here,' he announced. 'But one of them is an old friend of mine. I've changed my mind about betraying them and turning them over to you.'

Dark Father appeared to be contemplating the view of sky and clouds through the room's window. Either that, or he was contemplating throwing up.

'IT WOULD INDEED BE A SHAME,' he said, shortly, 'IF I WERE COMPELLED TO ORDER MY TI-FIGHTERS TO DESTROY YOUR CITY'S POLE . . .'

'Pole?' said Landrove, outraged. 'What do you mean, *pole*? What manner of unsubstantiated and wholly untrue accusation is this? There is no *pole*.'

'COME, COME, LANDROVE. THE LARGE POLE UPON WHICH YOUR SO-CALLED FLOATING CITY IS PERCHED. THE POLE YOU HAVE PAINTED SKY-BLUE. *THAT* POLE.'

'Ah,' said Landrove. '*That* pole. Well, it would be in many ways better, as far as we're concerned, if you didn't, you know, destroy that pole. Not that it supports the city,' he added, hurriedly, 'I'm not saying that, of course not, this city is suspended in mid-air by a miracle of futuristic technology, oh yes. But, that fact notwithstanding, it would probably be better if you – you know – *refrained*. From destroying the pole. Or even from mentioning the pole.'

'AND SOMEMAN?'

'I shall have him delivered to your Sterntroopers within the hour.' Landrove's voice was low, and bitter. Like a snail, you might say. But he knew when he had been beaten.

'DO WE UNDERSTAND EACH OTHER?'
'We do.'
'HAVE YOUR GUARDS PLACE THEM
ALL IN CUSTODY, BUT BRING HAND
SOMEMAN TO ME.'

'Hi there, guys,' said Landrove, returning to his
guests. 'More pimp-juice? Cranberry-and-apple?' He
sat himself down in one of the settees. 'What can I do
for you guys anyway? What brings you to my little
city-cum-university?'

'Landrove,' said Hand, leaning forward. 'I'll tell
you. You were the most skilful computer hacker I
ever knew.'

Landrove smiled modestly. 'It's true. They used
to call me "Hacker Bilk".' His smile faded, and he
became thoughtful. 'I never understood why . . .'

'Well, there's some secret data loaded into this
droid,' said Hand, gesturing towards See-thru. 'And
we wanted . . .'

'Not *that* droid,' interrupted Princess Leper,
crossly. 'The RC unit. I wouldn't trust *that* droid
with the secret plans of my granny's outside toilet.'

'Oh,' said See-thru in hurt tones. 'Thanks a lot.'

'The RC unit,' said Hand, uncertainly. 'Really?'

'Yes.'

'*Really* really? Or not really really.'

'Really really.'

'Ah,' said Hand. He looked at the undulating floor. 'Oh,' he said.

'You *did bring* the RC unit, didn't you?' said Leper. 'You didn't leave it back on Brathmonki to fall, once again, into the hands of the evil Imp-Emp-Imp?'

'No,' said Hand firmly. 'I didn't do that.'

'So where is it? Is it on the ship?'

'I gave it to Luke,' said Hand. 'I figured he'd need the motile commode, since he had this long flight to Swamp World to do.'

Leper's steely-eyed stare spoke volumes. None of the volumes contained any polite or flattering writing. 'I'm sorry,' she said, turning to Landrove, and speaking in a dangerously polite voice. 'I'm afraid we've wasted your time.'

'Ah well,' said Landrove. 'Never mind. Some other time, maybe. Now there's just one thing I wanted to talk to *you* about, and then maybe we can all grab some lunch.'

'Something you wanted to talk to us about? What's that?'

'I'm sorry to say that the Imp-Emp-Imp, aided by a bounty hunter who's been on your trail for some while, Hand, tracked your journey here, and indeed got here before you. Dark Father is waiting in an anteroom to take you all into custody. Sorry about that – my hands are tied. Not literally. Although they might be literally tied, or at least shackled, if I didn't do precisely what Dark Father demands. He's threatened the existence of the entire City, do you see? So I'm afraid it's a troubled conscience for *me*, and imprisonment, torture and probably a painful death for *you*. Say "Lavie".'

'"Lavie,"' said Hand, too stunned to do anything but respond automatically. His eyes were as wide as saucers, provided we're talking about saucers no more than two centimetres across, such as might be found in a dolls' house, perhaps. But very wide, that's the point.

'You misunderstand,' said Landrove. '*C'est la vie*. Now!' He beamed and rubbed his hands together enthusiastically. 'What do you want to eat? I got herring and matzos – what do you say?'

Chapter Six

Still ꞩwampy ꝺown on ole Swampy Worlꝺ

Luke's training in the ways of the Farce had been proceeding intensively during this interlude. He had learnt how to pratfall, to stumble, to juggle jugs of water in such a way as to spill the water on his own head, to introduce bottles and glasses to one another as if in a social setting, and various other arcane Farcical skills. Yodella had Luke standing on his hands quite a lot. 'Why, master?' asked the young pupil. 'Standing on hands harder is than on legs standing,' said Yodella. 'Students falling over often are. With the Farce get in tune with, they do.'

One day Yodella gave Luke his own lightsword. It was a slender glass tube of a pearly opalescence, with a silvery metal tip in which was contained the power source and the on-off switch. 'A Jobbi's *weapon*, lightsword, is. Take care of it.'

'From my limited experience, master,' said Luke, 'they do tend to, well, break – lightswords, I mean. Is that how they're supposed to operate?'

'Must be used properly,' said Yodella. 'If *improperly*

used, then breakage may occur, for which liable is *not* the company of Yodella Light Bulb Manufacturers Incorporated, no money back, no circulars or unsolicited representation, Board Chairman A. Gonzo.'

'But *how* am I to use it properly?' Luke pressed.

'Turn it on,' Yodella instructed. 'And hold it before you. I mean,' he added hastily, 'you before it hold and.'

Luke did as he was instructed. 'Now, strike me, you will try,' ordered Yodella.

Luke made a pass with the weapon, but Yodella avoided the blow with terrier-like rapidity, and in a moment he had leapt high in the air, and landed on Luke's glowing blade. To Luke's astonishment, the little green man simply stood there, balanced on the lightsword, his eye level with Luke's eye.

'Useless are you,' Yodella said. With a swift backflip he propelled himself into the air, and landed back on the forest floor. 'Now,' he said, 'punch this tree trunk you will – but from a distance of no more than one inch. Put all your energy into the blow – as if to punch through the tree you are trying.'

Luke turned his lightsword off and leant it carefully against a boulder. 'Is this some wonderful trick of the Farce you are about to teach me?' he asked. 'To punch through a massy tree trunk from a distance of no more than an inch?'

'Not really,' responded Yodella. 'Mash up your knuckles, mostly, and make you "ow!" go, it will. But most amusing to watch such a spectacle is. Yodel ay-ippee-ay-*ii*.'

Later that day, Luke was eating his supper with a bandaged hand.

'So let me get this straight,' said Luke. 'You are the supreme Jobbi, the master of all masters, the *capo ∂i capi ∂i jobi*. You have mastered all the Jobbi arts, and possess a higher level of Farcical skill, wisdom, intelligence and power than any other being in the entire Galaxy.'

'True this is,' said Yodella.

'And yet you can't speak even the simplest sentence in Galactic Standard, without mucking the words up.'

Yodella looked sulky. 'Dyslexia have I,' he said. 'Correlate to impaired intellectual ability it does *not*. Many highly intelligent people dyslexia have. Actually.'

'But dyslexia effects the arrangement of letters *within* individual words,' said Luke, genuinely puzzled. 'Not the arrangement of words within sentences.'

'Arse-smart are you,' grumbled Yodella, adding

sulkily, 'Yodel-ay-*i*-*heeee*.' 'Old, am I. Some respect for your elders, you should show. When it was all just fields, used to come here I did, you know. Doctors looking young these days, noticed that have you? Policemen also. Also, this new Imperial coinage, confusing it is; one hundred Imperial cents to one Imperial credit? About what's *that*? What wrong was with the good *old* system of four thousand six hundred and seven zlatps to a pdoing, twenty-seven-and-a-half pdoings to a bdapbamboum, and one-point-one-bdapbamboums to a heebijeebiblubbablubbablubba? Sensible, *that* monetary system was.'

Luke ate in silence for a while, digesting this little speech, whilst also digesting his supper, although in a different sense of 'digesting'. Finally he asked: 'So just how old *are* you, master?'

'I am seventeen centuries old, going on eighteen,' replied Yodella. 'Many changes have I seen.'

'I'm sure,' said Luke, politely.

'Anyway,' said Yodella. 'Way any. Your training over, is.'

'It is?' said Luke, astonished. 'But I feel like I have learnt so little!'

'Did you not attention pay me to? *Un*learn you must. The essence of the Farce is not in learning. Learning, practice, skill, these things run counter to

178

the power of the Farce. The Farce is in *un*prepared-
ness, in ignorance and stupidity, in a jackass readiness
to take absurd risks. No more will I teach you. Go you
must.'

'Go?'

'Yes, go. Your friends in trouble are. Captured by
Dark Father, they have been, yes. Torture and death
he is planning. Hoping to lure you to the Floating City
he is, so that he can embed you within a gigantic solid
block of crystal and thuswise transport you to his
Imperial Emperor as a great prize. Testing, he is, the
machinery that embeds people within the gigantic
solid blocks of crystal on Hand Someman, after
which torture and kill he will, Princess Leper.'

'No!' cried Luke.

'Yes,' returned Yodella. 'Don't interrupt.'

'But how do you know all this, master? Is it the
power of the Farce?'

'That, and a short-short wave radio in my hut.
Informed the entire quadrant of his actions has Dark
Father. All part of his plan to sucker you into trying a
rescue bid it is.'

'But,' said Luke, thinking hard, 'but if Dark Father
is specifically trying to lure me to the Floating City to
ambush and trap me – is it, um, *wholly sensible* for me to
fly right into that trap? I mean, isn't there a danger

179

that Dark Father will do everything you say – will trap me, put me in this machine, embed me in a gigantic lump of crystal and carry me to the Emperor?'

'Idiot you are,' said Yodella. 'Understand the Farce you do not. Think you to harness the enormous power of the Farce by *sensible* being? How would this work, exactly? Nonsense. Put yourself in the way of danger, harm, and comical falling-over you will.'

'Very well, master,' said Luke, casting his face down.

'Take the lightsword I have given you,' said Yodella. 'This spaceship of mine – *borrow*, you may. Damage or dent it do not. Not all the payments have I yet made on it, and very exacting "Crazy Ron's Crazee Prices Spaceship Salesroom" is on the small print of hire-purchase agreements. Fly to the Floating City, rescue your friends, and here return, pronto, with immaculate un-paint-scratched spaceship.'

'Very well,' said Luke getting to his feet. 'I'll not fail you, master.'

'See, we will,' grumbled Yodella, wandering off into the forest, singing as he went 'Don't leave me high-*iiiiii*. Don't leave me dry-*iiiiii*.'

Chapter Seven

The horrible fate prepared for Hand Someman

Everything Yodella told Luke was true: Dark Father did indeed hope to lure Luke to the Floating City, by capturing and torturing his friends, and broadcasting their plight on short-short wave radio to the entire quadrant. He was gambling on Luke Seespotrun being the only person reckless enough to risk everything in a desperate attempt to rescue them.

Yodella was also right about the 'Large-Scale Paper Weight Technology' with which he hoped to immobilise Luke for his journey to the Imperial Emperor. He had brought this with him, and his Sterntroopers had assembled it inside the Floating City. Now, just to make sure it was working properly, he planned to test it on Hand Someman; after which he intended to pass the space pilot's corpse to a certain bounty hunter with which he had made a deal.

'BRING HAND SOMEMAN TO ME,' he

instructed. 'THE TIME HAS COME TO TEST THE MACHINE.'

Two soldiers brought Someman forward. Although each of his arms was being gripped by a burly Sterntrooper, he was struggling. 'Get your paws offa me,' he bellowed, 'you damn dirty Imp-Emp-Imps.'

'COME, COME, MISTER SOMEMAN,' said Dark Father doomily. 'RESISTANCE IS FUTILE.'

'What do you want from me, Dark Father?' demanded Hand. 'Do you expect me to *talk*?'

'NO, MR SOMEMAN – I EXPECT YOU TO BECOME TRANSFORMED INTO A GIANT PAPERWEIGHT.'

This was not what Hand Someman had been expecting to hear at all. 'Oh,' he said.

'THROW HIM INTO THE DEVICE,' Dark Father commanded. The Sterntroopers dragged their prisoner to the brink of the machine.

'Wait!' Someman cried. He twisted his head around his shoulder. 'I love you!' he cried. 'I just wanted you to know before I am cast into this infernal device – I *love* you!'

'Well, that's very flattering,' replied the Sterntrooper holding his left arm. 'If a little sudden. I mean, you didn't prepare the ground at all. Shouldn't we get to know one another a little more before—'

'Not *you*,' snapped Someman, 'you idiot. Not *you*.'

'Well,' said the Sterntrooper, looking behind himself, 'there's nobody else back here.'

'Isn't there? Oh. I thought a second group of soldiers had brought Princess Leper along to watch me meet my grisly fate? Isn't the Princess just back there?'

'Nope.'

'Oh.'

'There was no need to bring the Princess along,' explained the Sterntrooper. 'We decided to leave her back in her cell.'

'I could have sworn I saw something out of the corner of my eye, as I was being dragged along the corridor. Something that looked like two further Sterntroopers hauling along a second prisoner.'

'Nope.'

'Ah well,' said Hand. 'My mistake. Of course, I didn't get a proper look, what with you gripping me so roughly.'

'ENOUGH!' boomed Dark Father. 'THROW HIM IN!'

'Nooo!' cried Hand, but it was too late. He was shoved over the lip of the device. Gouts of steam dashed upwards. The monstrous levers began to heave and pump. There was a colossal clattering and banging noise, and, as if reluctantly, the great wheel on the side turned. Finally, at the far side of the machine, an industrial-grade conveyer belt rolled. Through the half dozen leather flaps that hung down as a rudimentary curtain emerged a gigantic hemisphere of crystal, ten feet in diameter and eight feet tall. And in its very centre, captured in a position of surprise and alarm, and positioned next to a three-foot sea-horse and a patch of imitation seaweed, was Hand Someman. Motionless.

'EXCELLENT,' said Dark Father. 'THIS IS CERTAINLY CAPABLE OF PREVENTING A *GREAT* QUANTITY OF PAPER FROM FLAPPING OR FLYING OFF IN A STIFF BREEZE.'

From the shadows behind Dark Father emerged a crash helmet-clad figure: it was (rather unexpectedly, since we haven't heard of this character before, but that's sometimes how life is, people turn up abruptly and unexpectedly) Cheesa Fetta, the notorious bounty hunter.

'Have you finished your games with Someman?' he asked.

'FETTA,' said Dark Father, 'SOMEMAN IS YOURS. TAKE HIM BACK TO PIZZA THE HUTT.'

'How did you know?' asked Fetta, amazed at Dark Father's prescience, 'that I have been contracted by Pizza the Hutt?'

'ALL PIZZA THE HUTT'S BOUNTY HUNTERS HAVE NAMES DERIVED EITHER FROM CHEESE, MEAT OR SMALL PICKLED FISH,' said Dark Father. 'EVERYONE KNOWS THAT.'

'That's true of course,' conceded Fetta. 'Ah well, I'd love to chat, but I have to fly.' He slapped an anti-gravitational button to the side of the enormous paperweight, and kicked the whole thing easily along the floor and out through the main exit.

'AND NOW,' said Dark Father, smugly, 'THAT WE KNOW THE EQUIPMENT FUNCTIONS TO OUR SATISFACTION, IT IS TIME FOR ME TO CONFRONT LUKE SEESPOTRUN. HAS HE ARRIVED?'

'Sensors confirm,' said the first Sterntrooper, 'that his ship has landed.'

'EXCELLENT. I SHALL MEET HIM IN BATTLE. HE THINKS HIS FATHER IS DEAD, BUT I SHALL SHOCK HIM WITH A REVELATION ABOUT THE TRUE NATURE OF HIS PARENTAGE.' Dark Father looked down at the Sterntrooper standing beside him. 'WHY AM

I TELLING *YOU* THIS? YOU'RE ONLY A LOWLY STERNTROOPER. WHY WOULD I WANT TO CONFIDE IN *YOU*?'

'I don't know, my Lord,' replied the soldier, somewhat nervously.

'NEVER MIND. ONLY – BE SURE AND HAVE THE PAPERWEIGHT-MAKING DEVICE READY FOR MY RETURN.' Dark Father strode out of the room, his black cape swirling impressively.

Chapter Ten

A duel, and a surprising revelation about Luke's parentage

Luke landed Yodella's spare spacecraft on a deserted landing pad. There was nobody about. 'It's quiet,' he said to RC-DU^2. 'Too quiet . . .'

'Eek!' squealed RC, making a dash to get away from Luke, trundling rapidly through an open door and inside.

Cautiously, Luke followed the droid, and made his way through the corridors. Somebody had taped a piece of A4 to the wall, on which in scrawly Sterntrooper handwriting was written: 'Showdown Duel with Dark Father, this way →'

'That's helpful,' said Luke. Clearly he needed to have his wits about him. He pulled out the lightsword that Yodella had given him, and fumbled with the switch at the base. After a couple of spastic flickers, the whole blade lit up gleaming white. He had to concede it looked pretty impressive.

'Right,' said Luke. 'I'm ready for you now, Dark

Father. I shall avenge my own father! – who was killed by Dark Father, or so I am told.' He took a step towards the doorway beyond which waited his nemesis, the greatest test of his nascent Farcical powers. At that precise moment, the floor tilted more rapidly and more severely than usual, and Luke stumbled, hopped for six steps on his left foot, and banged into the wall, thwacking his lightsword against the side. Its light died.

Examining it, Luke could see that he had cracked the glass of the device, thereby compromising its inner fluorescent gases. 'Oh, bother,' he said.

He havered. What was it that Old Bony had done, back on the Death Spa, just before he had faced Dark Father? He had pulled a regular light-tube from its fitting in the wall. Luke looked at the strip lighting in the ceiling of this corridor. On the other hand, he thought to himself, that hadn't done Bony much good. Perhaps it would be better to stick with the weapon he already had. Did it matter that its light was non-functional? Luke was guessing no.

He stepped through the doorway, entering a dimly lit cavernous space.

Inside Dark Father was waiting for him. 'AT LAST WE MEET,' he boomed.

'Evil Dark Father,' said Luke, raising his dim

weapon before him. 'I have come to avenge my father, who, apparently, you murdered.'

'YOU HAVE MUCH TO LEARN, YOUNG SEESPOTRUN. YOU DO NOT UNDER-STAND THE POWER OF THE DARK SIDE OF THE FARCE.'

'You shall never turn me to the Dark Side!'

'BUT YOU HAVEN'T HEARD ANY DETAILS YET. YOU DON'T KNOW ANY-THING ABOUT THE DARK SIDE. THE REMUNERATION, THE BENEFITS PACK-AGE, THE UNIFORM, *ANYTHING*.'

'I don't care.'

'THAT'S A PRETTY CLOSE-MINDED ATTITUDE.'

'Maybe it is. But you'll never persuade me to join *you*!'

'NOT WITH WORDS, PERHAPS,' said Dark Father. 'BUT MAYBE WITH MY LIGHT-SWORD! HAVE *AT* YOU AH WAIT A MINUTE. WHAT'S WRONG WITH YOUR WEAPON?'

'Oh,' said Luke, a little embarrassed. 'It got a crack. It's still structurally pretty much sound. It's just that the light won't come on any more.'

'FOOLISH TO COME TO FIGHT ME

WITH A DAMAGED WEAPON, DON'T YOU THINK?'

'Nonsense! The light part clearly has nothing to do with the effectiveness of this tube as a weapon. I saw how you killed Old Bony K'nobbli – that wasn't light, that was just the jagged edges of broken glass.'

'POOR K'NOBBLI,' mused Dark Father. 'HE TRAINED ME, YOU KNOW. BEFORE YOU WERE BORN. AH – HAPPY DAYS. PEOPLE SHOWED *RESPECT* IN THOSE DAYS. NOT ALL RUSHING AROUND LIKE TODAY. AND THE CURRENCY MADE A LOT MORE SENSE. I'VE TALKED TO THE IMPERIAL EMPEROR ABOUT THESE RIDICULOUS IMPERIAL CENTS AND IM-PERIAL CREDITS, BUT HE JUST WON'T LISTEN. ANYWAY, MUSTN'T GET SIDE-TRACKED – HAVE *AT* YOU!'

The Dark Lord of the Psmyth lurched towards Luke, his own red-glowing lightsword sweeping through a series of precise arcs. Luke moved to parry, stepped back and tripped over a low-set table that happened to be in his way. He fell heavily. In a trice – indeed faster than that, in about two-thirds of a trice, or a 'twice' (not to be confused with the word 'twice' meaning 'once and then again once' which has no relevance here) – Dark Father was on him. He grabbed the end of Luke's unlit lightsword and yanked it from his hands. Then, armed with two lightswords, he bore down on Luke.

Luke got, rapidly scrabbling, to his feet and backed away from Dark Father. Or, to be accurate, *hurried* away from Dark Father. In fact, since absolute accuracy is required, he *turned* his back and *ran* away from Dark Father as fast as his long legs could carry him. But Dark Father was a master of the Farce. With a sweep of his hand he made it so that Luke was running directly into the path of a garden rake, lying innocuously on the floor. Luke's right foot struck the prongs of the rake, and the downward pressure of his stride caused it to rotate very rapidly against its hinge-point, swinging the long wooden pole into a vertical position. This pole smacked Luke in the face, the sort of impact for which the word 'thwacko' was coined back in the 1930s. Luke reeled back, clutching his nose, lost his footing and fell again.

'YOU CAN'T WIN, BOY,' boomed Dark Father, advancing on him.

But Luke, in agony though he was, had not lost all his Farcical skill. As he grovelled on the floor he noticed that Dark Father's path towards him lay over a number of trap-doors. With one lurch he scrabbled

over to a lever set in the wall. Dark Father saw what
he was doing, but it was too late: the flaps of the trap-
doors fell away, and the gigantic black-clad figure
dropped like a six-foot black-clad twelve-stone stone.

Breathing a sigh of relief, Luke got to his feet and
went over to the edge of the trap door through which
Dark Father had fallen, to see what his fate might be.
But, carelessly, he trod a second time on the rake
which was lying a few centimetres from the hole in the
floor. A second time the wooden pole flashed upwards
to collide painfully with Luke's sinuses. 'Ow!' he
cried, staggering blindly forward and tumbling down
the hole that had so recently claimed Dark Father.

He tumbled down a service shaft and landed on
the metal floor of a vast underground kitchenette
complex. Away to his right, behind the stainless steel
cupboards and work-surfaces, he saw Dark Father
standing with his lightsword and the lightsword he
had grabbed from Luke, both of them at the ready.

Luke leapt to his feet. He was unarmed! He must
arm himself! Frantically his eyes searched the ceiling
for a likely-looking neon-lightbulb to unscrew from its
mountings. But then he lowered his gaze and saw
what he would have seen sooner if he had not been so
panicked. Between himself and Dark Father was a
broad flat worksurface, perhaps three metres wide

and thirty or forty metres long. And on this surface lay, neatly ordered, hundreds and hundreds of custard pies . . .

Meanwhile, several levels higher up, Princess Leper and See-thru Peep-hol were being held in a medium-security holding cell, immediately below the street level of the city. Leper kept shaking her head and sighing. 'I can't believe that Hand's friend betrayed us.'

'Well don't look at *me*,' said See-thru. 'I've never had any confidence in *Homo sapiens*.'

At that moment the cell door opened. Two Stern-troopers were standing outside, holding Landrove Afreelanda in an unremitting grip. They hurled him into the cell, and slammed the door behind him. The hurl they used was forceful enough to rotate Land-rove through nearly a hundred and eighty degrees, such that when he landed the part of his body first to touch the floor was the crown of his head. He bounced on this, spoke the single word 'aarrrgh' and collapsed on his back. Then for long minutes he lay there groaning.

'Our betrayer,' said Princess Leper, coming to stand over him. 'I can't say I'm pleased to see you. You swineling.'

'Ouch,' said Landrove, getting to his feet gingerly. 'That hurt.'

'If you think *that's* the worst insult at my disposal . . .'

'I was talking about being bounced on my head. But your comments were also fairly hurtful.'

'I don't care,' said the Princess, recklessly. 'You betraying swine. What are you doing in here, anyway? Why were those Sterntroopers handling you so roughly?'

'Well,' said Landrove, rubbing those sore parts of his body, 'I thought I had a neat enough little deal worked out with Dark Father. I betrayed you all, and helped him embed Luke Seespotrun in a gigantic lump of crystal for passage to the Imperial Emperor. And in return Dark Father agreed not to destroy the City, and leave me in power. But it seems he's changed his mind. He's placed the city under direct Imp-Emp-Imp control, and thrown me in with you lot to be tortured and killed.'

'I see,' said the Princess. 'Well, I suppose I must give you credit for honesty. Were you a more mendacious man, you might have claimed that your apparent betrayal of us was actually a complex double bluff, and that in trying to assassinate Dark Father

and free us all you have been captured and imprisoned.'

'Yes!' said Landrove, brightly. 'That's *exactly* what
happened. Hero, me.'

The duel between Dark Father and Luke was continuing on the lower levels of the city. True, much
of the duel involved Dark Father running at Luke,
wielding two lightswords, and Luke running away as
fast as he could. But I'd still describe it as a duel.

Luke had, in the end, come out of the custard-pie
duel rather the worse than his adversary. Dark
Father's cape seemed to be woven from some futuristic fabric that sloughed off dirt. Luke, on the other
hand, was absolutely covered in custard, from the
top of his yellow hairdo to the bottom of his cream-
coloured boots. Its presence did not make running
across constantly swaying stainless-steel floors any
easier.

'SURRENDER, BOY,' bellowed Dark Father.
'COME WITH ME TO THE EMPEROR. IT IS
YOUR DESTINY.'

'Not *likely*,' retorted Luke. He ducked to the right
through a low door and emerged in the Floating City's
Waste Disposal Area – a huge hangar filled with massy
steel waste-skips and heaps of variegated rubbish. In

the centre of this space was the core of the City's waste-disposal technology: a large hole opening onto the sky beneath, through which garbage was chucked when the City's municipal workers could be bothered.

Luke barely had time to take in his new surroundings before Dark Father burst through after him, swinging both lightswords dangerously. Luke shrieked and leapt forward, slipping on an oil-spill and propelling himself, face first, into an enormous pile of fish-heads. He pulled himself out of this, although many of the rotting piscine crania adhered to the sticky custard on his body. He scrambled on.

He turned briefly to see where Dark Father was. Two lightswords swept through the air, missing Luke's face by millimetres. He staggered backwards, stumbling against a stepped wall of what he took to be bricks, but which, on turning, he saw were actually unsold science fiction novels, stacked together in a towering heap, ready for disposal. He scrambled up this stepped and mountainous pile so rapidly and so flailingly it looked rather like footage of somebody falling *down* some stairs being played in reverse.

But the Farce was powerfully with Dark Father. He took a step backwards, tripped against a discarded bicycle frame, staggered, fell mightily, landed on a heap of old mattresses, and was bounced improbably high into the air (the wind, clearly audible through the great open space, briefly whistled with a reverse-swannee-whistle noise) – turning head over heels he landed, on both feet, a few metres from Luke.

'THIS IS YOUR LAST CHANCE, LUKE. JOIN ME OR DIE!'

'Neither!' cried Luke. Exhausted and covered in filth as he was, he staggered backwards until he reached the very edge of the pile of unsold books. Immediately below him was the gap: the wind whistled ominously; Luke, looking down, could see clouds, and a dizzying perspective through many miles to a hazily visible ground. He hooked his arm around a great vacuum-packed pillar of unsold Darkling-Kinderslay's *Episode One Picture Book Tie-In* hardbacks, and leaned out over the void.

'LUKE—' boomed Dark Father. 'K'NOBBLI NEVER TOLD YOU WHAT HAPPENED TO YOUR FATHER.'

'I know plenty about my father,' gasped Luke. 'I know that he was gifted with the Farce. I know that he turned to the Dark Side. I also know that you, Dark Father, gifted with the Dark side of the Farce as you are, you *killed* him!'

'DO WHAT? NO, NO, NO. I THINK YOU MAY HAVE GOTTEN HOLD OF THE

WRONG END OF THE STICK. WHO TOLD
YOU THAT? WAS IT K'NOBBLI?'

'Erm,' said Luke. 'Yes.'

'HOW STRANGE. I WONDER WHY HE'D
SAY THAT? MAYBE HE WAS PULLING
YOUR LEG.'

'Pulling my leg?'

'YES LUKE. YOU SEE – I, DARK FATHER,
HAVE AN IMPORTANT PIECE OF IN-
FORMATION ABOUT YOUR FATHER.'

'Yes?'

'SHALL I TELL YOU?'

'Yes, go on.'

'THE TRUE IDENTITY OF YOUR
FATHER?'

'Yes, yes, get on with it.'

'LUKE. *I AM YOUR FATHER.*' The wind, by a
strange acoustic freak, seemed to resound through the
hall immediately after these words like three crashing
musical chords, *deh deh derrr!*

Luke's flabber was gasted. 'I'm sorry?' he replied.
'I'm not sure I heard you correctly what with the noise
of the wind and everything. *You* are *my* father?'

'YES.'

'*You*, Dark Father, are my *father*? The father who
went over to the Dark side?'

'YES.'

'Well, stone the crows. That's a turn-up for the books. Are you *really* my father?'

'REALLY.'

'Well,' said Luke, scratching his chin. 'I have to say, I didn't see that coming *at all*.'

'THERE'S MORE. YOU KNOW THAT GOLDEN ROBOT, SEE-THRU PEEP-HOL-BRA?'

'Yes.'

'I MADE HIM. BUILT HIM FROM A KIT. IN A SENSE I AM HIS FATHER TOO, AND YOU AND HE ARE THEREFORE BROTHERS.'

'He's my *brother*? But he's a git.'

'NONSENSE. HE'S FAMILY. YOU CAN'T TALK THAT WAY ABOUT FAMILY.'

'You are my *father*?' said Luke, as if it were only just sinking in. 'Well, strike a light. Well, blow me down. Knock me down with a feather – *you* my father? What a grade-one blinding surprise. What a turn-up for the books.'

'YOU SAID THAT ALREADY.'

'What?'

'YOU SAID "WHAT A TURN-UP FOR THE BOOKS" ALREADY.'

'Well, I'm sorry, but this is all quite a lot to take in My *father*? Hum-de-dum-de-dah. Phew. Just – golly That's what: golly. Goll. Ee. Who'd have though it? Sheesh. Never in a million years, would I have guessed this. This is coming to me completely ou of left field. I'm as startled as a starling in a star ship. Well, split my liver with a brass harpoon Well, *gee*.'

'COME,' boomed Father. 'LEAVE THIS NONSENSICAL BABBLING. JOIN ME ANI WE WILL RULE THE GALAXY! WE CAN TREAT IT AS A FATHER AND SON ENTER PRISE, FOR TAX PURPOSES, ALTHOUGH OBVIOUSLY I'LL DO MOST OF THE ACTUAL RULING. BUT IT WILL NEVER THELESS BE A VERY ADVANTAGEOUS POSITION FOR YOU.'

'Oh,' said Luke. 'You think I'd betray my friends do you? Well, let me tell you something . . .'

But it was at that precise point that the tensile strength of the plastic packaging on the pillar o books to which Luke was clinging gave way. H tumbled backwards into the void.

You might think this would have spelled the end of Luke Seespotrun. But no – instead of tumbling several miles to a splattery end, a freak gust blew him sideways, and banged him into a piece of scaffold-like ironmongery with which the underside of the Floating City was littered. Don't ask me why: I suppose they could have built the underside of their city to be a perfectly smooth surface, but instead they built it to have numerous poles, ladders, downward-antennae and other protrusions.

Luke, holding on for dear life, gripped one of these.

Dark Father, peering over the edge of the book-pile, could see his son dangling there. Activating the communicator embedded in his helmet he broadcast an order to the city above him. 'THIS IS DARK FATHER. SEND AN IMP-EMP-IMP SHUTTLE UNDERNEATH THE CITY AT ONCE – COLLECT THE INDIVIDUAL DANGLING THERE AND TAKE HIM PRISONER.'

'What's that?' came the tinny-voiced reply. 'What?'

'SEND AN IMP-EMP-IMP SHUTTLE UNDERNEATH THE CITY *AT ONCE* AND . . .'

'I'm sorry, I think you have the wrong number. This is the reception of Titherley Gribble, Accountants, here.'

'I'M TERRIBLY SORRY, MY MISTAKE.'

'That's quite alright.'

Cursing, Dark Father adjusted the band of his

comm-unit and repeated his order. With the instant obedience for which Imp-Emp-Imp Sterntroopers are so famous, a shuttle was immediately manned and flown out and underneath the city.

The shuttle was a bulky craft, and its pilots not especially skilled. They located the desperate figure of Luke, hanging to his strut, and tried to manoeuvre their craft close enough to be able to grab him. But as they moved underneath the city their tail fin scraped against the City-bottom and snagged hard against one of the many spars and juts. This stopped them: Luke was still several hundred metres away, but no matter how much the shuttle's engines screeched, the craft was stuck fast. Panicking a little, they tried to reverse, but this only snarled their tail fin more comprehensively in amongst the metal paraphernalia of the under-City.

'FOOLS!' cried Dark Father, who could see all this happening through the waste disposal hole. 'IDIOTS!'

Hearing Dark Father's wrath over their own intercoms, the pilots of the shuttle panicked further. They put the craft in its lowest gear and revved the hyperdrive engines. The Imp-Emp-Imp shuttle, a craft capable of hurtling into orbit in seconds and travelling faster than light, strained against its captivity.

Metal buckled and screeched, but the tail fin only became more firmly embedded in the under-City.

And then the inevitable happened. The mighty pole upon which the entire City rested shuddered – it shuddered and then, with a mighty noise of rending, it buckled. The huge bolts (ten metres in diameter) that held the plate at the pole's top to the underside of the City sheared. With a sound like the world ending, the whole City toppled, angling sharply through forty-five degrees.

Dark Father was thrown off his feet. In the City above him buildings collapsed and people were tossed about like dandelion seeds in the wind.

And for a moment that was where the city stayed: broken from its pole, in the process of toppling, now the only thing that stopped it falling off the pole entirely was the Imp-Emp-Imp shuttle, its engines on full blast. But the scream of those engines indicated that they could not maintain this effort for very long.

Princess Leper had been debating between slapping Landrove on the face or kicking him on the shins, and had finally decided to do both, when the City lurched suddenly through forty-five degrees and her ears were filled with the noise of catastrophe. 'What in the name

203

of Thog,' she cried, as she, Landrove and See-thru were smacked hard against the far wall of the cell.

Almost at once the ceiling fell in. The *Rebel Yell He Said More More More IV*, knocked from its moorings by the cityquake, had tumbled through the air and landed on the pavement directly above the cell, bashing it in. The rear-end of the craft pushed easily through the roadway material. When the dust settled, a startled Princess Leper found herself staring straight at the main airlock of the spaceship.

'Well,' she said. 'That's a piece of luck.'

She hauled the 'lock open, and scrambled aboard with Landrove and the droid. Masticatetobacco was still asleep.

The *Rebel Yell He Said More More More IV* took off and circled the heavily tilted city to see what had caused the damage.

'My city!' lamented Landrove. 'My beautiful City! Still – it's probably for the best, seeing as how I had, immediately *prior* to the City's destruction, decided to throw my lot in with the Rebelend.'

'Isn't that Luke?' asked Leper. 'Dangling from that strut?'

She flew the craft in, much more skilfully than the Imp-Emp-Imp pilots had been able to do, and sent

Landrove to the dorsal airlock to collect him. Then she steered the spaceship down and away.

Almost exactly at the moment she cleared the lip of the City, the Imp-Emp-Imp shuttle's engines burnt out. Their screeching whine died away and the craft lost all power. The mighty City above them groaned, shifted, screeched and then toppled past the point of no return. It fell straight down, crashing down upon and carrying the City's many thousands of innocent citizens to their surely certain death many miles below. But, that's the way the cookie crumbles, sometimes. You can't, after all, make an omelette without killing a few thousand people here and there, as Gandhi, I believe it was, once said. Or was it Pol Pot? It was definitely an Asian politician of some stature. But anyway—

'Thank Thog we were able to rescue you,' cried Princess Leper, turning in the pilot's seat to embrace Luke, and then thinking better of it when she smelt the combination of custard and rotting fish that adhered closely to him. 'Urgh!' she said.

'Thank Thog? Thank the *Farce*, rather,' said Luke. 'That was a wholly Farcical episode, I'd say. Now, is this rebel spaceship fitted with a shower, or bath?'

'No,' said Leper.

'Ah,' said Luke as his rank stench began to fill up

the close confines of the cabin. 'Then this may prove
to be a rather long flight.'

As they soared into the aching blackness of space,
Imp-Emp-Imp cruisers converged, their laser bolts
pulsing through the void. With a series of desperate
manoeuvres Leper flung the *Rebel Yell He Said More
More More IV* through a complex trans-spatial vector
of escape, before triggering the hyperspace drive and
removing them from the scene altogether.

Once in hyperspace, Leper was able to relax. She
sat back in her pilot's chair. 'Luke!' she cried. 'The
most important thing of all – perhaps even more
important than our extremely fortuitous escape.'

'Yes?' returned the foully-reeking young Jobbi.
'What?'

'RC-DU^2! Hand said he'd given him to you! That
little droid contains the Great Secret – if we can only
download it I feel sure that victory against the Imp-
Emp-Imp would be assured. But if we lost it, we
would suffer the most appalling setback. Please,' she
pleaded, '*please* tell me that you left the droid on
Swamp World in the custody of the great Jobbi
master Yodella – please *don't* tell me that you brought
it pointlessly back with you to Floating City, and that
it now lies crushed and smashed to smithereens in the
wreck of that unlucky conurbation?'

Luke swallowed. 'The former,' he said.

Princess Leper breathed a sigh of the purest relief, a great shuddery jiggly sigh. 'Thank Thog!' she cried. 'Then let us set co-ordinates for Swamp World . . .'

'Or,' said Luke, his brow furrowing, 'do I mean, "latter"? I'm always getting those two confused. The second one – that's what I meant. Crushed, smithereens, *that* one.'

'Oh,' said Princess Leper.

RETURN OF THE SON
OF JOBBI RIDES AGAIN

THE IMPERIAL EMPIRE OF THE IMPERIUM SUFFERED A
TERRIBLE BLOW WHEN THEIR MIGHTY DEATH SPA WAS
DESTROYED BY REBELEND ACTION. BUT, BEING DETERMINED, AND,
ALSO, RATHER LACKING IN IMAGINATION, THEY HAD IMMEDIATELY
BEGUN CONSTRUCTION OF A *SECOND* DEATH SPA, EVEN MIGHTIER THAN
THE FIRST. THIS MEGAWEAPON WAS TO BE POWERED NOT BY
PRECARIOUS BLACK-HOLE PHOTON-SHEARING TECHNOLOGIES, BUT RATHER
BY A SERIES OF MUCH *MUCH* SAFER CENTRAL NUCLEAR POWER PLANTS.
REALLY VERY MUCH SAFER, HONESTLY. NO CHANCE OF *THAT*
EXPLODING BECAUSE, SAY, THE MAIN REACTOR IS HIT BY A CAREFULLY
AIMED BLAST FROM A SPACESHIP'S MAIN LASER CANNON. OR, INDEED,
BECAUSE THE REACTOR STAFF, BORED ONE AFTERNOON, START
MONKEYING ABOUT WITH THE CONTROLS FOR NO VERY GOOD REASON,
LOSING CONTROL AND THEREBY PRECIPITATING A CATASTROPHIC MELTDOWN
EXPLOSION AND RADIATION POISONING THAT LASTS DECADES. NO, SIR.
DARK FATHER WAS OVERSEEING THIS PROJECT PERSONALLY. BY THE
WAY, I WAS GOING TO MENTION, HE ESCAPED FROM THE TUMBLING CHAOS
OF THE DESTRUCTION OF THE FLOATING CITY. NO ONE ELSE DID, REALLY,
BUT HE MANAGED IT. EVEN THOUGH HE WAS INSIDE THE CITY WHEN IT FELL,
I KNOW, I KNOW; BUT HIS, UM, I DON'T KNOW - POWERS OF THE FARCE
HELPED HIM ESCAPE. NO, I'M SORRY, I CAN'T BE MORE SPECIFIC THAN THAT.
JUST CAN'T I'M SORRY. THE IMPORTANT THING IS THAT HE GOT AWAY.

MEANWHILE, IN A FASTNESS DEEP IN THE DESERTS OF
TATUONWEINER, HAND SOMEMAN'S PAPERWEIGHTED BODY SITS ATOP A
VERY LARGE PILE OF PAPERS BELONGING TO AND OTHERWISE PERTAINING TO
THE BUSINESS INTERESTS OF NOTORIOUS GANGSTER AND LOCAL CELEBRITY, PIZZA THE HUTT.

Chapter One

Tatuonweiner. Remember there?

It was late forenoon on Tatuonweiner. The sun glow-
ered down on the desert sands; light pouring through
the hazy air like molten copper mixed with gold. Mile
after mile of barren desolate waste. Kilometre after
kilometre. Rather more kilometres than miles, indeed,
because kilometres are shorter than miles. There is a
particular proportion that governs the conversion of
one of to the other, but I'm afraid I've forgotten what
it is. I've got a notion that it is the same proportion
as exists between the number of letters in the words
'mile' and the word 'kilometre', which would certainly
be a handy mnemonic, wouldn't it, and which would
mean that four-ninths of a mile make one kilometre
and vice versa. By vice-versa I mean 'nine-fourths',
which makes, unless I've added it up wrong, two-
and-a-quarter kilometres to a mile. Having written
that out it doesn't look quite right. I wouldn't, if my
life depended on it (and who knows it might) *swear*
that there are two-and-a-quarter kilometres to a mile.
Less, I'd say. Or fewer. Perhaps the mnemonic is two

211

completely different words – 'toupee' and 'lawnmower' for instance. But perhaps not. I wonder if it would be possible for the authorities to fix the proportion of 'mile' to 'kilometre' at four-to-nine? That would simplify life a great deal. Don't you think?

Anyway, sun beating down, desert wastes, measuring-unit after measuring-unit of desolation – and then the traveller comes upon the squat stone towers of Pizza the Hutt's lair, deep in the desolatest desolation. These stumpy redstone protrusions are only the uppermost portions of a vast underground complex of echoey caverns, shadowy halls, and dungeons deep. Deep dungeons, I mean.

And at the heart of this lair Pizza the Hutt himself was moving towards his throne – the vast, circular, slug-like, slug-coloured body, a good ten metres across, undulated across the floor leaving a trail of foul hydrogenated slime, before ascending to his special podium. His cronies cackled and laughed. Pizza himself laughed with a noise of bubbles of foulness bursting in a cesspool, a deep-throated huh! huh! huh! huh!, which, I hasten to assure you, is exactly what bubbles of foulness bursting in a cesspool sound like. I wouldn't recommend you try to double-check that piece of information, you could only do so by lowering expensive recording equipment into a cesspool which would probably spoil it, best just to take my word for it.

Pizza the Hutt's body was a towering mass of red and brown pustules, hideous blisters with a vast matted quantity of congealed yellow pus-like slime on top. His eyes were two pepperoni-like circles, positioned somewhere to the fore of his massive fat-loaded body; his mouth a bulbous crack in his glazed yellow-brown skin. Rarely has so foul and disgusting a creature crawled on the surface of any world; a loathsome spotted beast, a self-confessed tax-avoider, a scrounger-parasite and mafiosi worm, slimy refuse and utterly beneath contempt – indeed, beneath even the contempt we feel for things that are beneath contempt. This monster spent his days sliming his way around his endless lair, planning and plotting his gangster projects, imprisoning and murdering, ordering others to be imprisoned and murdered, and generally being loathsomely loathly. Mad drivel streamed endlessly from his disgusting, pudgy cheese-slavering lips. Not that I'd want to prejudice you against this life form before you'd even met him. You'll make up your own mind, of course; judge him by his actions. It would indeed be shallow to judge him merely on his appearance. All Pizzarians looked like him, after all. It wasn't his fault that he looked a certain way. It's the content of his character, not the pustulated nature of his skin that is important here. Honestly.

And in the midst of Pizza's Great Hall, in which he sat in state with his back to the warren-like complex of ovens at the heart of his evil complex – in this hall, perched atop an absolutely enormous pile of papers, tax demands, fan-letters, junk-mail and the like, sat Hand Someman, encased as he was in a huge hemisphere of crystal – Pizza the Hutt's trophy!

But Hand's friends had not given up on him. One by one they had come, to parley with Pizza, to beg or negotiate, and finally to attempt to bribe. They might have had more chance of success had they all come at once; but that thought only occurred to them after they were all incarcerated in Pizza's foulest dungeon.

First came Landrove Afreelanda to beg for Hand's release, and for anything else that occurred to him. Well, I say 'came'. In fact he was delivered to Pizza's door, trussed up like a chicken, because nobody really liked him, treacherous little git. But Landrove certainly did a great deal of begging, on a variety of fronts, mostly to do with himself, before finally Pizza chucked him in a dungeon.

Then came See-thru Peep-hol-bra, the robot, to negotiate for Hand's release, and for Landrove's too, since his friends now felt bad about the whole chicken-trussing manoeuvre. 'Great Pizza,' announced C3U-πP, standing in the gangster's Great Hall, 'I have come to negotiate with you for the release of Hand Someman.'

Pizza paid no attention to his negotiating, but instead appropriated the robot as his own property, using him as a translator (since Pizza could not speak English, but only Pizzalingua, whereas most of his underworld contacts spoke only Galactic Standard, not Pizzalingua). This arrangement worked well for a while, until Pizza discovered that, rather than faithfully translating his words, See-thru was in fact altering the gist of what Pizza intended to communicate.

So, for example, when the head of the terrifying GLC (the Gangster Lovegrub Clan) sent representatives to Pizza's fastness to negotiate mutually advantageous terms for the divvying up of gambling earnings from the Mountain Casino of Monte Casino, Pizza told them: '[I accept your proposals. Let us not quarrel, your family and mine; let us come to an honourable understanding. We will share the money on a fifty-fifty basis, deducting all expenses according to the same ratio]', See-thru translated this as 'I have lusts for your shins, your knees and shins. Let us throw chub and bass and herring in the air in great profusion and support the candidacy of only bald women in local elections. Dwarfs are the source of most rivers.' Since he didn't speak Galactic Standard, Pizza was unaware of what was being said in his name. But of course, Little Jimmy Lovegrub was horrified, disturbed and not a little puzzled when his representatives reported back to him. Anxious not to lose face he ordered a tactical nuclear strike against the Casino. What with the many deaths, and the radioactive fallout, casino receipts were down that year.

On another occasion, instead of giving a particular Galactic policeman instructions of how to collect his bribe, See-thru gave him instructions to 'open a tin of peaches using only his forehead or Pizza the Hutt will send vagabonds and, um, camels I think it is, to replace all your clothes with dogfood'. Finally, Pizza received a Universal Translator for his birthday, and when he played back his security tapes via the device he understood the deception that had been practised. '[Why?]' he bellowed, through the U.T. '[Why did you do these terrible things? Did you not realise it would rouse my ire?]' 'I didn't do it on purpose,' replied a terrified See-thru, throwing himself face down on the floor before his rageful master. 'Please don't disassemble me! I'm not a translator. I'm a *dictionary* and a *thesaurus*. There's a difference. I think I understood about one in seven of your words. I did my best.'

See-thru joined Landrove in the dungeon, whilst Pizza the Hutt wracked his evil brain for the most painful death he could inflict on his metal prisoner.

Princess Leper tried next, bringing a modest bribe with her and promising the evil Hutt more if he agreed to release Hand, See-thru and Landrove. Pizza the Hutt laughed in her face '[Huh! huh! huh!]' and made her his prisoner.

Then, evil monster that he was, he confiscated her clothes and dressed her in a metal bikini, although none of the Hutt hangers-on could work out why. After all, Pizza was a wholly alien dough-based life form. Princess Leper was a carbon-based humanoid. Pizza could no more find her sexually alluring than any given human male would find a female Pizzarian sexy. The number of human males who could get sexually aroused by a ten-metre pile of quivering pus and red slime is, let's be honest, small. The number of decent, healthy, red-blooded Pizzarians who could be turned on by a one-and-one-half metre tall clump of arms and legs wrapped in a revoltingly pale, tight, smooth skin was even smaller. Still, for whatever reason, Pizza dressed her in the metal bikini, despite her complaints that it caught under her arms and that she was forced to suck her stomach in to prevent the metal waistband from digging in and chafing. Eventually Pizza threw her in the dungeon, to join Landrove and See-thru.

Finally Luke Seespotrun came in person, a young Jobbi knight of increasing power and ability, to free all his friends in one fell swoop.

'[Huh! huh! huh! huh!]' laughed Pizza the Hutt in his deep-throaty way, as Luke stood calmly before him. '[So, young Jobbi. Have you come to bargain and cajole, as did your unsuccessful colleagues?]'

'I'm assuming,' replied Luke, speaking clearly for the benefit of the U.T., 'that you have grown bored with the crystal-confined Hand Someman, oh Mighty Pizza.'

'[By no means!]' chuckled Pizza the Hutt. '[Here – watch this.]' He nodded to one of his henchmen, Kriss, a thirty-foot tall Muscle Beast from the Planet Woodenring. This mass of alien muscle stepped forward, picked up the crystal hemisphere in his huge claws and shook it, replacing it on the pile of paper afterwards. Around Hand's motionless body, the seahorse and the seaweed, a flurry of artificial snowflakes swirled.

'That's very pretty,' conceded Luke. 'I didn't know it could do that.'

'[Isn't it, though? It combines charm and sparkle, I think.]'

'Yes. It's not *entirely* logical though is it? – I mean, isn't that supposed to be an undersea scene? Why is it snowing under the sea?'

'[Nonsense!]' boomed Pizza. '[Logic has nothing to do with it].'

'I suppose so. Anyway – I think you're going to be impressed with this. This is a Jobbi trick I've picked up. It's called "the Voice" and what it means is that, using the power of the Farce, I can influence you to do as I wish, even though your mind may be set against the idea. It's very good.'

'[Huh! huh! huh! I assume you are referring to the celebrated Jobbi mind-trick known as "the Voice". I warn you. "The Voice" only works on weak-minded fools. I am no weak-minded fool – I am very strong minded indeed. There are more than a *hundred* hot chillies diced and embedded in my skin. And not the piddly green chillies either – chillies so red they're almost purple. That's how strong I am. I *scoff* at your Jobbi "Voice" thuswise by laughing at it: Huh! huh! huh!]'

'We shall see,' said Luke, readying himself. He slipped into the Jobbi Voice. 'Aw *go on* – *pleeeeease*? Please? Pretty please? *Please* let Hand go, go on – will ya? Please? *Please*? Go on. I want Hand, I wanna, I wanna, *I wanna*, I'll *scream* if you don't give him to me, I'll scream and be sick, I *want* it, I-want-it-I-want-it-I-want-it-*pleeeease*? – I should warn you,' said Luke, stopping the "Voice" for a moment to talk normally, 'that I can go on like this for hours.'

Pizza had the gibbering Jobbi thrown into the dungeon with his friends.

'So,' said Princess Leper. 'Here you are.'

'Don't sound so despondent,' said Luke. 'I have a plan.'

'Oh what's the point?' cried Leper, in a miserable tone of voice. 'The Great Secret is lost. Destroyed utterly when the RC unit who carried it was crushed in the destruction of the Floating City! Woe!' she cried, vehemently. 'Woe! Woe!' she added, becoming a little, well, *operatic* to be honest.

'Don't be like that,' said Luke. 'I have good news about the fate of the droid. Well, there's good news and bad news actually.'

Leper's face lit up. 'Can it be true? Is the droid still functioning?'

'That's the good news. The RC unit in question escaped the destruction of the Floating City.'

Leper's face lit up. Not in the sense of her face literally catching fire, that would be silly. But in the sense of suddenly appearing much more cheerful. 'Really?'

'Indeed. Rebelend spies have confirmed that the RC unit escaped. That's the good news.'

'But how did he escape? He's only a motile commode – how could he *possibly* get free from a plummeting mass of steel and concrete?'

'It's quite interesting, actually,' said Luke. 'Turns out that RC-DU^2 can fly. He's got these little rockets, two of them, that pop out of the side of his chassis. Two little sapphire jets of rocket flame and he can lift off the ground.'

'I didn't realise that he could fly!' exclaimed Leper.

'No, it was a surprise to everybody. He'd never done it before. Even when he'd been in very perilous situations, situations where it really would have been advantageous to him to demonstrate his flying abilities, he had not done so. Every person who had ever encountered him would have sworn blind that he was incapable of flight. Even his designer. But it turns out he can. So he flew off and escaped.'

'What's the bad news?'

'Eh?'

'You mentioned some bad news, to go with the good news. What is that bad news?'

'Well, it seems that Dark Father also escaped the destruction of the Floating City. Rode away from the disaster sitting on RC-DU^2 in fact. So he's still at large and, rumours have it, building a second Death Spa, more solidly constructed than the first.'

'Curses!' cried Leper. 'Still – it is good news that the droid has not been dashed to smithereens. We must recover the little machine; for within its data-bases we will find the Great Secret. And I am confident that, if we could only get our hands on the Great Secret, then the defeat of the Imp-Emp-Imp would be within our grasp.'

'I've heard this speech before,' Luke reminded her. 'And Dark Father has the robot now. Presumably he's downloaded the Secret.'

'He's had RC-DU^2 in his clutches before,' Leper pointed out. 'So either he has already downloaded the Great Secret, or he hasn't been able to access it. I believe the latter explanation—'

'Latter?' queried Luke.

'The *second* one. I believe the second explanation is the more likely. The Rebelend had the droid for years, and we weren't able to hack into it. I don't believe that Dark Father will have had any better luck.'

'I could hack it,' said Landrove, speaking from the far side of the cell. 'I can hack anything. I'm a skilled hacker.'

'Besides,' said Leper. 'Let's say Dark Father *has* gleaned the Great Secret stored in the robot's databases: that only makes it more imperative that we also discover the nature of the Great Secret.'

'You're sure this Secret will give us the necessary edge?'

'I'm confident.'

'Well,' said See-thru, 'I was with the little dustbin for years and he never said anything to me about a secret. Besides which, aren't you all forgetting something?'

'What's that?'

'We're presently incarcerated in a dungeon,' said See-thru, lugubriously. 'Pizza the Hutt is plotting to annihilate us in the most painful manner he can manage. We'll probably all be dead or dismantled by this time tomorrow.'

'Don't worry,' said Luke, smiling secretively. 'I have a plan.'

It was impossible to distinguish between day and

night inside the dungeon. For a while the group slept uneasily. Finally, after many hours, the dungeon door was heaved, gratingly, open; and various of the Hutt's henchmen, amongst them the sinister Kri*ss*, hauled Luke, Leper, Landrove and See-thru out of their confinement.

The four of them were brought before Pizza the Hutt in his Grand Hall. '[Now hear this,]' the disgusting slimy cheese-covered beast announced through the U.T. '[I have thought long and hard and have finally decided upon your fate. It is to be death! Huh! huh! huh!]'

The room erupted with laughter and cheering from Pizza's disgusting hangers-on.

'[Huh! huh! huh! We shall fly out in my roll-on-push-off hovercraft to the depths of the desert where the Great Sand Maw is located. This beast devours sand, as perhaps you know. It will make short work of your revoltingly limb-sprawly bodies. You will learn a new definition of pain as he digests you over a thousand years! Of course, you'll be dead after a day or two of thirst and possibly dead of suffocation after a few minutes, but it'll still take the Sand Maw a thousand years to digest you, which fact I'd like you to contemplate over the course of your probably quite rapid deaths. Huh! huh! huh!]'

'I *think not*,' said Luke in a clear voice, stepping forward and holding forth a small metal device in his right hand.

The whole room went 'ooo!'

If Pizza was incommoded he didn't show it. '[Huh! huh! huh!]' he laughed. '[What's that? A bomb? Do you not realise, puny Jobbi, that a forcefield exists around the dais on which I am currently sitting? No bomb can harm me.]'

'It could harm the rest of us, though,' put in See-thru. 'Just thought I'd remind you of that, Luke. If you set off the bomb you'll not kill Pizza the Hutt, but you likely will destroy everybody else, carbon-based life forms such as yourself, Landrove and Princess Leper, and zinc-based life forms like me.'

'I know that,' said Luke, crossly.

'It's just something to bear in mind – how futile a gesture that would be,' See-thru added.

'This isn't a bomb,' said Luke, holding the device out for everybody to see. 'It's a mobile phone.' He pronounced these last two words the American way, as if the phone were manufactured by the petrochemical giant Mobil rather than being, as it actually was, a phone mobile in the sense of being moved around. But everybody understood what he meant.

'[A mobile phone!]' scoffed Pizza. '[Do you hope to

injure me with the weak microwave radiation? Pah! This is nonsense.]'

'Perhaps it is nonsense,' said Luke. 'Or – perhaps – it's *sense* of a *new*, *dangerous* kind.'

'[No, it's nonsense.]'

'I agree with the Hutt,' said Leper. 'Luke – what are you playing at?'

'If I press *this* button,' Luke announced, 'the phone will make a call to a preprogrammed number.' He displayed the button, with his thumb over it.

'[Go ahead!]' laughed Pizza the Hutt. '[Press the button! I am not afeared.]'

'But you don't understand,' said Luke. 'I'm not threatening to press the button. I'm threatening *not* to press the button.'

It took a moment for everybody in the room to work out the distinction that Luke was making.

'You see,' said Luke, coming a little closer to Pizza the Hut's forcefield-protected throne, 'before coming here I paid a little visit to a certain office building in Moz Isleybrothers. Yes I did – and in that building I pretended to be a henchman of you yourself, Pizza the Hutt. I did indeed. Which building, you ask? Why, the Credit Card Corporation local headquarters, that's which building. The home of Masterfromdoctorwho

Card and Jambarclaycard and many other cards of a creditable nature. And I told the officials in that building that the great Pizza's credit cards had all been stolen. Do you know what they did? They cancelled all the cards, prior to sending you out replacement cards in two weeks' time.'

Pizza the Hutt had fallen silent '[Scum!]' he muttered. '[You shall pay with your life for the mild inconvenience you have caused me!]'

'Oh it's worse than that, Pizza,' said Luke. 'The number preprogrammed into this phone? It's the customer hotline to the Moz Isleybrothers Electrical Power Corporation. I informed them that the old credit card numbers were no longer valid, and gave them a new credit card account. But they have been waiting for me to ring them with the confirmation security code, and we are approaching their deadline. Unless I ring this number *in the next five minutes* and give them it, they will cut off all power to your remote fastness, Pizza. And you know what that means?'

Pizza the Hutt had gone doughy with fear. '[No!]' he cried. '[You wouldn't!]'

'That's right, Pizza – your children! You see,' said Luke, turning to face the room, 'I happen to know that Pizzarians, in common with other wheat-based forms of life, are not warm-blooded as we are. They require an external source of heat to survive. Now, a fully grown Pizzarian like the Hutt here might be able to survive by crawling to the surface and lying in the hot Tatuonweiner sun. But his children are a different matter – isn't that so, Pizza?'

'[My secret is out,]' said the giant alien, mournfully. '[I came to this backwater world because it was time for me to breed. We Pizzarians do not carry our young inside our bodies as is the frankly disgusting habit with you carbon-based life forms . . .]'

'I hope you're not including me in that sweeping statement,' said See-thru.

'[We form our young in special uterine ovens. Over many years they are baked at temperatures far higher even than is found in the hottest portion of this planet, growing slowly, yeasting and expanding, until their cheese bubbles with maturity and they emerge to slime and oil their way about the world. My own ovens are in the heart of my fastness here, and four hundred of my youngsters are currently cooking there. To have my power supply cut off would be disastrous! They would all die! All my pretty ones!]'

'Let us go, Pizza, and I shall press the button and pass on the code. But if you do *not*, you will have to wait for another fortnight until your new credit cards arrive. Which is it to be, Pizza? Can your offspring survive two weeks in those ovens without power?'

'[You already know the answer to that question,]' said Pizza, in a broken voice. '[Guards! Release them all. Put Hand Someman's paperweight in the back of a speeder and give young Seespotrun here the keys. I know when I am beaten . . .]'

Half an hour later, as they sped over the dunes towards Moz Isleybrothers, Leper kept repeating 'I can't believe it. I can't believe we escaped from there.'

'It was a close call,' agreed Landrove. 'What I don't understand is why Pizza's henchmen didn't just shoot Luke and make the phone call themselves?'

'I suppose,' said Luke slowly, 'that it didn't occur to them.'

'That's especially lucky.'

'I have learnt to trust the Farce in these matters,' said Luke.

'Strikes me as something of an anticlimax, actually,' said See-thru. 'I was expecting you to come in and rescue us with your lightsword flashing, and sweeping and chopping the evil Pizza into a dozen wedge-shaped pieces.'

'Another thing I have learned,' said Luke, 'is that

sometimes the Farce takes the form of anticlimax. Bathos and pathos and something else ending in –athos.'

Chapter Two

On the Death Spa Mark Two

Aboard the still-under-construction Death Spa Mark Two there was an air of nervous anticipation. Ranks of Sterntroopers stood in serried ranks in the main entrance hangar, their white armour polished and gleaming like porcelain. A row of senior military officers stood before them. All were awaiting a very high-profile visitor indeed. All were anxious; particularly the senior staff.

A shuttle approached, breached the forcefield and settled on the landing pad. The ranks of Sterntroopers came smartly to attention.

The shuttle bay doors opened and the long black-clad legs of Dark Father strode down the gangplank. The Dark Lord of the Psmyth marched through the massive hallway, followed by his red-robed functionaries, individuals whose precise function was never very clear, although Dark Father rarely went anywhere without them. General (formerly Commander) Regla Onzedcars took a deep breath, adjusted his collar, and stepped forward to meet his superior officer.

'Lord Father,' he said, falling into step beside the towering black figure. 'This is indeed an unexpected pleasure.'

'GENERAL,' boomed Father. 'YOU MAY DISPENSE WITH THE PLEASANTRIES. I HAVE COME TO ENSURE THAT *THIS* DEATH SPA IS READY ON SCHEDULE.'

'My men are working at double shifts,' said General Onzedcars, 'but they shall work triple. Everything will be in place and operational by the deadline.'

'I HOPE SO FOR YOUR SAKE, GENERAL. WHEN THE IMPERIAL EMPEROR ARRIVES NEXT WEEK, HE WILL EXPECT THE DEATH SPA TO BE FULLY OPERATIONAL.'

'The Imperial Emperor is coming here?' Onzedcars said, alarmed.

'DIDN'T I JUST SAY THAT?'

'Yes, my Lord.'

'DO TRY TO KEEP UP.'

'Yes, my Lord. We shall work quadruple shifts!'

'EXCELLENT, AND GENERAL—'

'Yes, my Lord?'

'THERE IS ONE MORE THING.' Dark Father stopped and turned to face the General.

'My Lord?'

'I HAVE BEEN WORKING ON SOME STAND-UP MATERIAL.'

Onzedcars blinked. 'You – you've been – um. My Lord?'

'JUST A SHORT ROUTINE. I WAS THINKING OF MAYBE TEN MINUTES OF OBSERVATIONAL. PERHAPS A COMIC SONG. THIS WOULD BE A *SMALL-SCALE* PARTY FOR THE IMPERIAL EMPEROR, BY INVITATION ONLY, IN ONE OF THE SMALLER MUSTER HALLS HERE ON THE DEATH SPA.'

'Ah – of course, my Lord.'

'THE THING IS . . .' doomed Father, trailing off.

Onzedcars glanced nervously over his shoulder at the serried ranks of Imp-Emp-Imp Sterntroopers. God how he wished he were somewhere else. Anywhere else. 'Yes, my Lord?'

'I COULD REALLY USE SOME FEED-BACK. ON MY MATERIAL, YOU SEE.' He leaned in closer and jabbed at Onzedcars' chest with his black-gloved forefinger. 'FOR INSTANCE – THIS IS ONE OF MY FAVOURITES – OK –

AHEM, DON'T YOU FIND THAT WHEN
YOU'VE FINISHED TORTURING A SUS-
PECT WITH THE CARELLIAN MIND-
PROBE YOU ALWAYS MISPLACE ONE OF
THE TWO INSERT-ELECTRODES? LIKE,
ALWAYS? I MEAN, WHAT'S *THAT* ALL
ABOUT? LIKE – IS THERE SOME KIND OF
MIND-PROBE INSERT-ELECTRODE *FAIRY*
WHISKING THEM AWAY TO THE MAGIC
LAND OF TORTURE-EQUIPMENT *PARA-
PHERNALIA*? YEAH? YOU DIG WHAT I'M
SAYING? THAT EVER HAPPEN TO YOU?
HEY YOU'VE BEEN A FANTASTIC AUDI-
ENCE, GOOD NIGHT.'

Dark Father straightened up, his face wholly
unreadable behind his black faceplate. Onzedcars
had to exercise conscious muscular control to prevent
his eyes from popping open in naked terror. 'That's
very good – ah, er ha-ha. Ha. Ha ha ha. Excellent, my
Lord. Very funny.'

It was impossible to tell the Dark Father's reaction.
Silently he turned, and swept from the hangar.

Onzedcars' body slumped visibly with relief.

Chapter Three

♪ *Swampy Swampy World – paint my palate green and green.* ♫ *Add some green and then some green – you're the swampiest place I've ever ever seen . . .* ♪ ♫

Luke flew back to Swamp World, just as he had promised his master he would do. Sadly, he wasn't able to return Yodella's spaceship, since that had been smashed up in the destruction of Floating City. But, ever trusting, the Rebelend had given Luke yet another spaceship, and it was in this craft he touched down on Swamp World, not far from the tiny Jobbi's hut.

'Yodella?' he cried, bending down and squeezing through the miniature door. ' Yodella, are you here?'

'Here through,' came a weak voice. 'The bedroom, in.'

On all fours Luke made his way to the bedroom to find the miniature Jobbi Master sitting up in his bed; a very large bed, unusually deep, big enough for a full-sized man to be stored beneath its mattress, in fact, although obviously there was no full-sized man inside it. That was just the way the bed was made.

'Returned you have,' said Yodella, coughing pathetically.

' Yodella! Master! Are you ill?'

'Dying, I am.'

'No! This is terrible news! You can't die?'

'Oh can't I?' Yodella replied, briefly feisty, as if Luke had laid down a challenge. 'Just watch me, you shall.'

'But – there are so many questions I want answered. Dark Father – is he truly my father?'

'Your father he is. Not only that, but Leper your sister is. And Bony K'nobbli was a distant cousin, or uncle, forget the precise details I do.'

Luke's mind reeled. It jigged. 'This is incredible!' he cried. 'Leper is my *sister*?'

'Luke,' Yodella said. 'Dying, I am. Alone have I lived for many years, with nobody to talk to. My life history unrecorded is. To you I wish to tell the whole story. Also, my sole beneficiary you will be; inherit both of my suits of tiny lederhosen you will.'

'Thanks,' said Luke, dubiously.

'The last of my race, am I . . .' murmured Yodella. 'When I die, that race will pass out of all knowledge. A sad thought this is.'

'Yes, I've been meaning to ask you – what race *are* you, master?'

'According to the mythology of my people, the first of us were created when a divine Mop fell in love with a certain god-like living Puppet; their strange cloth-skinned offspring of that union we were. Once we were populous, and successful. When a young person I was – not as you see me now, but young and handsome and smooth-skinned – when young I was, a *theatre* I ran – very successful it was. But one by one my fellows died, they did. I had the chance to continue our species; opportunities there were to mate with others such as myself, small, it's-not-easy-being-greenskinned beings. But love a dangerous drug is! I fell in love with a being from a wholly different species. Porcine. No chance of genetic combination from that union, there was.' He shook his head. 'And so here I am, having devoted my life to the Farce instead.' His voice was barely a whisper.

'What a sad story!' said Luke. 'And, obviously, very interesting. Really very interesting indeed. I'm very much interested to hear more along those lines, really I am . . . but I wonder, since you may only have a few moments of life left to you, whether you might first just say *a little bit more* about the Dark Father being my father, Leper my sister and K'nobbli also related to me in some obscure way stuff?'

'Tell you why my words in my sentences all disarranged are. Why I tend my verbs at the end of sentences to be putting. Tell you, I will.'

'. . . which is very interesting, of course,' said Luke. 'Only I was hoping that you might give me more by way of *family* information. Of my own family, I mean. You see, Dark Father said that . . .'

'The truth to you I shall be imparting. Important it is that you listening are. The fact is, German I am.'

'German – right, lovely. Only I was wondering . . .'

'Not all Germans are beautiful, tall and fair, though the Galaxy in this manner is of them thinking. Some Germans small and froggish are. Difficult to believe it is, I know, but nevertheless, true it is.'

'Well I'd sort of assumed,' said Luke. 'What with the lederhosen and the yodelling. The odd syntax was also a clue, of course.'

'Ah,' said Yodella. 'Observant are you.'

'Yes. But if I could prevail upon you, master, for a moment – I know time is pressing, and, what with dying and everything, you may be disinclined to chat for long. But if you could, *briefly*, you know, briefly, just *sketch in* the true story behind Dark Father being

238

my father, Leper my sister and so on, then I'd be very . . . very grateful if you . . . you could . . .'

But Yodella had passed away.

'Oh bother,' said Luke.

He buried the tiny corpse, and cleared out Yodella's hut, taking the two pairs of miniature lederhosen that were his birthright. These he folded and tucked in his pocket. Then he sat down on a log outside to think things through. 'What do I do now?' he wondered, aloud.

'Hello?' said a familiar voice. 'Hello? Is this on? Hello, can you hear me?'

'Bony?'

Luke turned to see a gleaming spectre dressed in the familiar Jobbi cream and brown. The apparition, or hallucination, or whatever it was, looked very real-istic: it was Old Bony K'nobbli to the last detail, except that this being was shining with a bright inner light.

'Hello Luke,' said Bony's ghost. ' Yodella died, has he? Well, he was very old.'

'Bony!' reproached Luke.

'Hello!' said the spectre, brightly. In several senses.

'Bony,' said Luke, his brow darkening. 'How *could* you? You told me that Dark Father *killed* my father.'

'Did I?' said K'nobbli. 'Really? Um—' He looked over his shoulder, as if he had some urgent business behind him to which he really needed to attend.

'But now I discover,' Luke pressed on, 'that, far from having *killed* my father, Dark Father *is* my father. I mean, how was I supposed to guess that?'

'That is indeed something of a turn-up for the books,' agreed K'nobbli.

'How could you mislead me that way? *Why* did you tell me my father was dead?'

The ghost of K'nobbli sat down heavily on a tree stump. 'Jane Seespotrun,' he said, slowly, as if feeling his way, 'was a fine, upstanding Jobbi knight, gifted with the Farce. But, you see, when . . . um, when he turned to the Dark side, he became Dark Father. On that day, well . . . ah, yes that's it, on that day he "died". In a manner of speaking. *That's* it, yes – yes, I've got it. Jane Seespotrun died, and Dark Father was born. So metaphorically speaking, as it were, Dark Father killed Jane Seespotrun. That's right – that's it.' He looked up at Luke. 'Do you see?'

'So when you told me that Dark Father had killed my father, what you actually meant was that he hadn't killed him.'

'Exactly.'

'So, in fact, you meant "killed" in the rather unusual

sense of "not in fact killed but instead altered his own interior moral compass".'

'I did.'

Luke stared hard at the apparition. 'That's not the usual meaning of the word "killed", though, is it? I mean, not strictly speaking.'

'It's a common enough idiom,' said K'nobbli, evasively.

'I happen to have a dictionary here,' said Luke, pulling a small volume out of his sleeve. 'If I just read you the definition of the word "to kill" . . .'

'Is this really necessary?' asked K'nobbli, shifting his weight from spectral buttock to spectral buttock.

'To deprive of life or vitality,' Luke read out. 'To cause to die, to put to death or otherwise to end a life.'

'Well, when a Jobbi uses a word . . .' said K'nobbli, as if he were about to launch into a long disquisition by way of justifying his usage. But in fact he said nothing further.

Luke tucked his little dictionary away inside his sleeve. 'So it turns out that Dark Father is my father,' said Luke. 'And Yodella tells me that Leper is my sister, despite the rather creepy fact that I've had the hots for her ever since I've met her. And that *you* are a sort of uncle figure. What's Hand Someman? My long-lost brother?'

'Well, clearly,' said Old Bony, 'that would just be silly.'

Luke meditated for a long time. 'What shall I do?'

'You must trust your feelings, and so on,' said Bony. 'If I were you I'd go to the Forest Moon of Endors-Gaim. I have it on very good spectral authority that Dark Father is supervising the construction of another Death Spa there, one built without the fatal weakness of the last one.'

'That's good advice,' said Luke, leaping to his feet. 'Thanks!'

'Oh don't mention it. Just beware the Dalek Side of the Farce.'

'The what?'

'The *Dark* Side of the Farce. The *Dark* Side.'

'Sorry, I thought you said something else.'

Luke was packing up his spaceship, prepping it for take off and so on, whilst the spectre of Bony K'nobbli sat on a tree trunk and watched with an air of detachment – something to which, I suppose, he was entitled, really. He was dead, after all. Which is about as detached as it's possible to get.

'So how does it work, exactly?' Luke asked. 'This ghostly apparition stuff? Do all Jobbi come back as ghosts once they've been killed?'

'Well that's an interesting question,' said K'nobbli, his face creasing into puzzlement. 'Now that you mention it, I can't actually think of a prior example. Ever. In the whole history of the Jobbi order. Lots of Jobbis have died, of course. Indeed, to be strictly accurate, every one of the millions of Jobbi who have ever lived are now dead, with the exceptions of Dark Father and yourself.'

'And Princess Leper,' put in Luke. 'Who turns out to be my sister.'

'She doesn't count. She's a girl. But I'm racking my brains – racking them, I am – to work out if there's ever been a recorded case of a Jobbi hanging about spectrally after death. Perhaps it's for the best it doesn't happen. That would make things pretty crowded! So, no, as far as I'm aware no Jobbi is so powerful in the Farce as to get turned into a spectre of himself after death.'

'Not even Yodella?'

'Ah, of course, he could be the exception that proves the rule. I daresay he'll be back. Probably come back a damn sight quicker than I did.'

'So,' said Luke. 'How is it that *you* are allowed to make this spectral visitation, where no other Jobbi in the history of Jobbi has ever done it before?'

Old K'nobbli's shrug was an elegant, fluid gesture.

'Search me. Maybe things are finally looking up for the Jobbi. I sometimes think – and don't take this the wrong way, Luke, since you are the last hope for Good in the cosmos and so on – but I *sometimes* think that the Jobbi must have handled things very poorly in the past. Look at it this way: once there were millions of us. Now there are two. If you presented the same figures for any other group or species . . . lemmings, say, or cod . . . well there's only one conclusion you'd arrive at.'

'I'm finding this rather hard to follow,' conceded Luke. 'And since I'm in something of a hurry, I think I'll just go. Farewell!'

'We shall meet again,' said K'nobbli. 'Bye bye, now.'

Chapter Four

On the Forest Moon of Endors-Gaim

It didn't take Luke long to convince the Rebelend to concentrate all their forces on the Death Spa being constructed in orbit around the Forest Moon of Endors-Gaim. The Rebelend top commander, General Fishedd Onaslab, fresh from his successes on Brathmonki, had concocted a strategy. The entire fleet, including every single Rebelend spaceship and soldier, would attack the Death Spa, blowing it up before it could be finished. Meanwhile, a special detachment of troops would land on the moon itself to disable the Protective Cordon Sanitaire Machine that was generating a defensive forcefield around the Death Spa during its construction.

'Seems watertight to me,' said General Fishedd Onaslab.

'How many troops will we actually be sending down to the Moon?' asked Leper.

'Forty thousand,' said the General immediately.

'Sir!' squeaked Tutter, his second-in-command. 'We can't possibly spare so many soldiers—'

'I see. How many can we spare, Captain Tutter?'

'Two.'

'Two it is, then. You, Princess and Captain Some-man. That should do it.'

'Let me see if I understand you,' said Leper. 'You want me to attack a concentration of Imp-Emp-Imp forces and droids, amounting to at least twenty thousand crack troops . . . with two people.'

'Well,' said the General, spreading his gill flaps expansively, 'if the troops are already cracked, that should make your job easier, don't you think?'

'Crack,' said Leper, with brittle precision. 'I said *crack.*'

'I do apologise,' said the General. 'My hearing is poor in this airy medium. I see: so you don't think two people is enough? Alright; take young Seespotrun with you as well. Other than that – I don't know. Can't you rally the indigenous population to our cause? What are the moon's indigenous population?'

'A race called,' replied Tutter, consulting an info-flimsy, 'the Tedibehrs.'

'Excellent!' beamed General Fishedd. 'That's sorted, then. You'll pop down there and inspire the hordes of ferocious, probably highly-armed, maybe seven-foot-tall-with-giant-claws-for-all-we-know *Tedibehrs* to attack the forcefield generator. Once it's down, we'll destroy the Death Spa. Then we'll all meet for a debrief at, what do you reckon, Tutter? Twenty-hundred hours?'

'Better make it twenty-thirty, sir. Be on the safe side.'

'Quite right.'

'We want to leave a margin for error, don't we, sir?'

'We certainly do. Well, there you are: meet at co-ordinates delta zero four at twenty-thirty, alright? Will there be . . . ? Hm, I wonder if . . . ah Tutter, before you go, just one more question . . .'

'Sir?'

'Will there be sandwiches at the debrief?'

'Sandwiches? I hadn't ordered any, sir. Do you want me to order some sandwiches?'

'If it wouldn't be too much bother. Some meat, some cheese, so everybody's taste is catered for. And a few cartons of juice. Then we can all have a jolly good debrief, and work out what we want to do with the cosmos after the utter defeat of the Imp-Emp-Imp. Alright! Bye bye, everyone! Let's go!'

It was a somewhat gloomy party of three that left on a cloaked Rebelend shuttle for the Forest Moon circling the planet of Gaim. Princess Leper piloted in silence; Hand and Luke sat looking glum.

Glumness increased when they made contact with the natives of the moon; and were taken to the chief Tedibehr village, a clearing in the woods in which a number of cupboard-shaped halls and boxy houses huddled together.

It turned out that the average Tedibehrs, far from being seven feet tall, stood a little over twelve inches in their bare bear feet. They lacked claws and teeth, although their eyes were flat-edged and hard and could, theoretically, have injured an unwary Sterntrooper had he been so foolish as to inhale one of them.

They seemed bellicose, however. The chief Tedibehr called a village meeting (known as a peec-neec), where discussion amongst the various Tedibehrs demonstrated that they were more than happy to attack the Sterntrooper encampment under the leadership of these offworlders. 'Bad men!' announced the Tedibehr chieftain, Danni, gesturing towards the Imp-Emp-Imp encampment. 'They *very* noisy! They stay up past bedtime! They must pay with their lives!'

A great crowd of Tedibehrs cheered this speech; a sound like a choir of sopranos practising vibrato.

'I don't wish to dampen your battle ardour,' said Princess Leper. 'But you do realise, don't you, that these Sterntroopers are armed to the teeth with devastating state-of-the-art weaponry?'

'They no got teeth!' squealed Danni. 'They faces all white plastic!'

'You misunderstand me,' said Leper. 'I was not referring literally to their teeth. I only intended to draw your attention to the fact that they have laser cannons, laser rifles and pistols, and all manner of automatic death-dealing equipment.'

'We not scared!' cried Danni. 'We have carefully worked out *log*-based military strategy.'

'Did you say *log*-based?'

'I did.'

'I just wanted to make sure I hadn't misheard. *Log*-based, yes?'

'Yes.'

'Not guns? Or bows and arrows?'

'No – no – logs. Logs, fearful logs! Ya-haaah!'

The high levels of Tedibehr excitement rose higher with this last cry, and soon the mass of them were dancing and celebrating around Leper's and Hand's knees.

Soon, though, it was time for bed – a religious observance for the Tedibehr peoples, and thus not one lightly flouted. In minutes the whole village cleared and peace fell.

By the light of the still-glowing evening fires, Luke

sought out Leper. 'I've got news,' he said. 'We've overheard Imp-Emp-Imp transmissions to the effect that Dark Father himself has landed aboard the Death Spa. He has the droid with him.'

'I see,' said Leper, her eyes lighting up. 'That means everything is not lost – we can recover the droid!'

'I guess so,' said Luke. 'I was thinking – whilst you're leading the Tedibehrs to military glory, why don't I go up to the Death Spa and confront Dark Father, even though it is almost certain to mean my painful and premature death.'

'What an excellent idea,' said Leper excitedly, presumably referring to the first rather than the last part of Luke's speech.

Luke nodded. 'I'll do it then. Even though it is almost certain to mean my painful and premature death?'

'Tush,' said Princess Leper. 'Pish. We absolutely *must* retrieve that droid – the RC unit. Once we've got it we can take it back to Landrove, and he'll be able to download the Great Secret from its databases. Then we will truly be victorious! Dark Father has the droid; so you have to confront him.'

'There's a space elevator at the Imp-Emp-Imp base.'

'Then that's how you must go.'

'Leper – before I go. There's something I need to tell you.'

'What?'

Luke looked into her liquid eyes, but then shook his head. 'No – it would be too much of a shock for you. It would distract you from your mission to rally the Tedibehrs. I'll tell you when I get back. *If*,' he added, with melodramatic emphasis, 'I get back.'

'Righto,' replied Leper. 'Well, shouldn't you be on your way? It's a long ride from the Imp-Emp-Imp base up to the Death Spa. And we've got to get to bed. These natives are pretty strict about their night-time curfew. We don't want to antagonise them before tomorrow's war.'

Chapter Five

Yet another showdown lightsword duel. You're probably getting a little tired of all these showdown lightsword duels, I know, but this is the last one. For now. Although I probably should warn you that there are several more to come in the later (by which I mean actually **earlier***) chapters*

Using the Farce, Luke was able to evade the perimeter guards, to fall through a window, trip *up* some stairs (that took some doing, but he managed it) and finally to stumble into the Transit Centre unnoticed.

From there he rode the Great Glass Space Elevator car up from the ground base to the half-built Death Spa. His Jobbi powers enabled his ascent: by closing his eyes, he was able to bang the control panel with his elbow, cry out 'yow!' and accidentally hit the right combination of keys.

The wooded moon of Endors fell away beneath him into a complex stubbling of greens and blues. Beyond it the planet of Gaim loomed over the foreshortened horizon, red and brown in the white light of its sun. Looking down, Luke could see the stumbling and staggering Mono- and Duo-pod craft of the Imp-Emp-Imp patrolling the woods around the ground base. White-armoured Sterntroopers, looking from this height like lice, inched between the trees. He turned his gaze around at the half-built Death Spa above him. It dominated the sky; like a meccano-kit model of a literal-minded vision of a crescent moon, its huge circle bitten into by a great jagged blocky semi-circle.

He made his way through empty corridors and dimly-lit rooms. Everywhere he went he saw unpainted plaster, wires poking through square holes in the walls like plastic spaghetti, hundreds of paint pots with dribbles down the side like icing, lightbulbs dangling, bereft of lampshades, like hanged men, planks and dustsheets in every space.

Luke heard voices. He moved towards the sound, inadvertently tripping over a portable radio, a half-empty mug of cold coffee and a folded-up copy of a popular Imp-Emp-Imp tabloid news-flimsy *The Four Hundred Million Suns* (its headline read: GALACTIC COR! GAS GIANTESS TOPLESS, PAGES 2–

14 INSIDE!). He regained his balance, and moved more stealthily.

Round a corner and creeping along the wall of a corridor, Luke was soon able to make out two voices engaged in discussion. One of them was clearly Dark Father's; the other voice Luke did not recognise, although its identity was soon revealed.

'All I'm saying,' said the second voice, 'is that it weren't forcefield airlock beam modifiers, what was written down on the *order*. That's all I'm saying.'

'AND WHAT *WAS* WRITTEN DOWN ON THE ORDER, MR BOBA?'

'*Forty field* airlock beam modifiers,' replied Boba. 'Which, I need hardly tell you, is not the same thing at all. Nothing to do with me. Seems my supplier can't read the handwriting of your chief architect.'

'I SHALL CRUSH HIS THROAT RE-MOTELY IN THE MORNING, DO NOT WORRY.'

'Oh *I'm* not worried,' said Boba. 'It's just that, what with the ordering cock-up, I can't have the forcefield airlock beam modifiers fitted by Tuesday like I said I would.'

'THEN WHEN? WEDNESDAY?'

'Ooooo,' said Boba, as if Dark Father had said something palpably absurd. 'Dearie me no. Even

assuming the proper parts are delivered by, let's
say, Friday – which is being optimistic – even assuming *that*, well I gotta tell you, Mr Father, that my
lad Wayne has gotta take the first half of next week
off.'

'HAS HE? WHY, EXACTLY?'

'It's his driving test. Landcraft Monday–Tuesday,
spacecraft Wednesday–Thursday. It's no good com-
plaining, Mr Father, I already promised the time off.
I need him to drive the van. What with the wiring
problems, and the re-ordering, not to *mention* the
colour chart – the colour chart *misunderstanding*, shall
we say?'

'I TELL YOU IT'S NOT MY FAULT,' said
Dark Father. It sounded, from his voice, as if they
had been over this ground before. 'MY HELMET
VISUAL INPUT SOFTWARE SOMETIMES
INTERPRETS NAVY BLUE AS FLAMINGO
PINK. I CAN'T HELP THAT.'

'It don't matter whose fault it is,' said Boba,
smoothly. 'Unless you're prepared to leave the walls
pink, we'll have to repaint. And Derek's taken the
paint gun off to another job – won't be back for
another seven days. 'Course, if you *was* prepared to
leave the walls pink . . . ?'

'ON A TERRIFYING DEATH SPA? I

DON'T THINK SO. IT WOULD HARDLY INSPIRE TERROR, NOW, WOULD IT?'

'It is quite a *shocking* pink . . .' Boba said, hopefully, as if trying to persuade Dark Father.

'HARDLY THE SAME THING.'

'They are related terms, though, aren't they though? Shock and awe, and all that?'

'I'M SORRY MR BOBA, I'M NOT BUDGING ON THIS ONE.'

'Well, it's up to you. It's your Death Spa, Mr Father. You're paying for it. I'm only saying it'll add time to the schedule.'

Luke had heard enough of this. He came round the corner, and saw the man with whom his father was conversing: a jowly, tubby humanoid, who was writing on an interactive scrawl pad with a stumpy pencil.

'Father,' said Luke, stepping from the shadows. 'We meet again.' With a flick of his thumb he lit up his lightsword, a searing white light.

Dark Father, wordless, pulled his own lightsword from his belt and pressed the 'on' button at its base. Its red light glowed malign and fierce.

The two Jobbi knights, father and son, squared off, legs a little apart, weapons before them, circling one another.

'Right' said Boba the Builder, looking from one to the other. 'I can see you're busy right now, Dark Father, so if it's all the same with you I'll just take a quick – tea break.' He spoke these last two words at a higher pitch than the rest of the sentence, and drew the vowels out rather after this fashion, 'teee breeeaak', because he was running as fast as he could towards an exit as he spoke and the effort distorted his words rather.

Father and son were left alone.

'I'm sorry to interrupt your conversation, Father,' said Luke. 'But you and I have some unfinished business.'

'YOU HAVE COME FOR THE DROID,' said Dark Father in his usual menacing way. 'THE EMPEROR HAS FORESEEN IT.'

'I may, or may not, have come for the droid,' said Luke, circling Dark Father with his lightsword before him.

'NONSENSE,' replied his Da. 'YOU BELIEVE THERE TO BE A GREAT SECRET HIDDEN INSIDE THE DROID. THAT IS WHY YOU HAVE RISKED EVERYTHING TO TRY AND RETRIEVE IT.'

'Well,' said Luke. 'Maybe. *Or* maybe not. Or maybe. You'll get no clues from me. Maybe – or maybe *not*. But, let's, for the sake of argument, go with maybe for a minute. You know about this Great Secret?'

'OF COURSE.'

'Ah. I suppose it terrifies you – the thought that I might recover the Great Secret and carry it back to the Rebelend. Then we would be able to defeat the Imp-Emp-Imp utterly and rid the cosmos of your tyranny.'

'OR NOT,' said Dark Father.

He swiped at Luke, his red-gleaming lightsword cutting through the darkness. Luke responded by making three 'S' shapes and three 'Z' shapes in the air with the tip of his blade. The two men danced around one another, angling and swivelling to keep their swords between them and their adversary. Dark Father waggled his lightsword over his head so rapidly that, for an eyeblink, it looked as though there were half-a-dozen blades there. Luke backed up a flight of metal stairs, with Dark Father cautiously following, until they were both on a raised platform. A balustrade ran round this, with regularly-spaced giant metal petals sprouting up from it.

'You don't fool me, Father,' said Luke. 'I mean, father,' he added. 'I know that if you had *truly* downloaded the Great Secret from the droid then you would have used it to crush the rebellion. Ergo, you do not know the Great Secret.'

'ERGO?' queried Dark Father. 'THAT'S FANCY TALK.'

'Since studying with Yodella I have learned many things.'

'AND YET YOU HAVE NOT LEARNED THE NATURE OF THE GREAT SECRET?'

'Well, maybe I haven't. But it's not as if *you* know it either.'

'BOY, I HAVE KNOWN THE NATURE OF THE SECRET SINCE BEFORE YOU WERE BORN!'

'Vain boasting and idle words,' scoffed Luke. He leapt forward, swinging the blade before him. Dark Father, unflinching, stood his ground, holding his lightsword up to intercept Luke's blow. The two 'swords met with a great clash. Their two lights extinguished simultaneously as shards of glass flew in various directions.

Luke, wary of getting glass in his eye, darted backwards. His lightsword was now less like a gleaming shaft of hard light, and more like a narrow broken bottle. Naturally, the weapon was now more dangerous than before, but it required a different style of fighting to wield it. In place of the former elegant swordsmanship, the two warriors now circled one another more warily, occasionally jabbing the sharp ends of their jagged weapons forward.

'You seem to be wheezing and panting, father.'

'WHEEZING?' gasped Dark Father. 'AND PANTING?'

'And panting, yes.'

'I'M JUST REALLY EXCITED BY THE DARK SIDE OF THE FARCE,' said Dark Father. 'SO EXCITED THAT I GET A LITTLE BREATHLESS, ACTUALLY.'

'If you truly knew the nature of the Secret, then why would we even be fighting in this manner? You would surely just use the Secret to destroy me?'

'YOU REALLY HAVEN'T A CLUE AS TO WHAT SORT OF SECRET IT IS, DO YOU?'

'I do!' said Luke, his pride stung. 'I mean, I can imagine the sort of thing it's likely to be.'

'REALLY? WHAT SORT OF THING DO YOU THINK THE SECRET TO BE?'

'I don't know. The key to some tremendous, Galaxy-destroying power, maybe? The square root of minus one? The magic word that summons a powerful genie to do your bidding?'

'IT'S NOTHING LIKE THAT,' said Dark Father.

'Like you'd know,' scoffed Luke. But his scoffing was a little less scoff-ful now. Could Dark Father be speaking the truth?

'DID YOU EVER WONDER, SON,' he boomed, 'WHY I CONVERTED TO THE DARK SIDE OF THE FARCE?'

'Not really,' said Luke.

'DID YOU, PERHAPS, THINK IT WAS CONNECTED TO THE SECRET OF WHICH YOU SPEAK?'

'Pah,' said Luke. 'We're talking about a secret that was hidden inside the databases of a toilet droid. How could that provoke a young Jobbi knight to convert to the Dark side?'

'DO YOU KNOW WHO HID IT?'

'No.'

'YOUR MOTHER.'

'*Again* with the family-related revelations? They've lost the power to shock me on that front, I can tell you that right now.'

'THERE WAS A REASON WHY SHE HID IT, YOU KNOW.'

'Alright, then,' Luke challenged. 'Why not tell me what the secret it? If you know it, why not just come out with it? Tell me what it is!'

'ALL IN GOOD TIME. WHEN YOU HAVE

ACCEPTED YOUR DESTINY. THEN I
SHALL BRING YOU BEFORE THE EM-
PEROR AND HE SHALL TELL YOU.'

'Yah,' said Luke in tones of mockage and jibery.
'That's just another way of saying that you don't
know.'

'NO, IT'S NOT.'

'Oh yes it is.'

'OH NO IT'S . . . LOOK, SON, I DON'T
WANT TO GET INTO A SLANGING
MATCH WITH YOU. SURRENDER YOUR
WEAPON AND COME WITH ME TO THE
IMPERIAL EMPEROR. HE WILL EXPLAIN
THINGS MORE FLUENTLY THAN I AM
ABLE.'

'Or, alternatively,' said Luke, sprinting forward, his
jagged-edged shaft of broken glass at arm's length in
front of him, 'why don't I – *not*.'

Dark Father sidestepped. Luke collided at speed
with the waist-high railing that circled the platform.
All the breath went out of his lungs with a noise that
was an exactly halfway between an *oufff!* and an *urgh!*
He swivelled forward, dropping his lightsword and
only a desperate scrabbly grabbing at the balustrade
prevented him toppling after it. He was dangling over
the edge, looking nervously down. He seemed, perhaps

by the power of the Farce, to be hanging over a deep well-shaft, leading down into the distance. To fall or relinquish his hold would mean certain death.

'IT SEEMS YOU ARE AT MY MERCY,' said Dark Father sinisterly, peering down at him. 'SURRENDER OR DIE!'

'Surrender to you? To become your *slave*?'

'IT IS YOUR DESTINY.'

'My destiny to become your slave? Never!'

'THE IMPERIAL EMPEROR HAS FORESEEN IT.'

'You keep saying that.'

'IT KEEPS BEING TRUE.'

'Yeah, well. So, anyway,' Luke asked, conversationally changing the subject, 'I've a question for you. Is it true that your name used to be Jane Seespotrun?' He was trying to scrabble his legs up approximately to the level of his armpits and use them to lever himself along the balustrade to move himself away from the shaft directly below him.

'THAT NAME NO LONGER MEANS . . .'

'Kind of a *girl's* name, isn't it?'

Dark Father's breathing seemed to have become even more audible. 'WHAT DID YOU SAY?'

'I'm just wondering why my Dad was named after a little girl, that's all.'

'THAT'S *IT*,' boomed Father. 'I'VE HAD ENOUGH OF YOUR INSOLENCE. YOU ARE *GROUNDED*.'

'Grounded?' asked Luke. 'In the sense of . . . ?'

'IN THE SENSE,' said Dark Father, 'OF THE GROUND WHICH WILL SHORTLY BE RUSHING UP TOWARDS YOU WITH LETHAL SPEED.' He brought the jagged edge of his lightsword sharply down onto Luke's knuckles. With a sharp 'yow!' Luke let go his grip, and instantly he was falling through nothingness. The ground, though distant, was rapidly coming closer. As he tumbled away he screamed up at his father's diminishing figure 'I hate you! I'm *not your slave*! I *hate* you . . .'

Chapter Six

So: how was the battle going, down on the moon?

The battle was not going well down on the moon.

The Sterntroopers, to be frank were making short work of the Tedibehrs. Their laser rifles and pistols tore through the diminutive ranks, ripping stitching and tearing limb from tiny limb. The Tedibehrs tried to retaliate, but their weapons were largely log-based in concept. They tried rolling logs down slopes at the Imp-Emp-Imp battlecraft. The flaw in this thinking was that rolling logs move relatively slowly and make a lot of noise; the Imp-Emp-Imp Multipods were fitted with automatic laser cannons designed to shoot down shells and missiles travelling very much more rapidly and quietly. They made short work of the logs.

Other log-based attack strategies included: log-guns, in which a slightly smaller log was loaded into a hollowed-out bigger log, and fired by setting fire to a third log located at the base of the bore. This cannon was, as perhaps you can intuit from this brief description, perhaps the most useless weapon ever used in warfare. The Tedibehrs also tried using logs suspended, pendulum-like, on jungle creepers, which might have been more effective had the Tedibehrs had more strength in their stubby limbs to pull them back far enough such that releasing them gave them a crushing momentum. I'd say, talking roughly, that pulling back the logs to an angle of at least fifty degrees would do it. The Tedibehrs managed four degrees.

They did not give up on their master strategy of a log-based assault. They carved the ends of logs into sharpened points and tried ramming the Imp-Emp-Imp Multipods; but even with a hundred Tedibehrs carrying these logs it was hard to get up any speed.

Meanwhile the Tedibehrs were suffering horrendous casualties. Little lifeless Tedi bodies littered the forest. There was stuffing *all over* the ground, pouring out of many gaping wounds. A few survivors were trying, though fatally wounded, to crawl away, several with limbs attached to their torsos by only a few stitches. There was widespread scuffing and baldness. One tiny Tedi crouched over the body of a fallen comrade, his paws covered in sawdust, his stumpy arms raised to the skies as he cried 'Why?'

From their position at the rear of the assault Princess Leper and Hand Someman watched the utter catastrophe of the Tedis' frontal assault. 'Well,' said Leper, 'I'd say that was about as complete a military failure as it's possible to imagine.'

'Agreed,' said Someman. 'So what do we do now?'

Sixty Imp-Emp-Imp Octopods, each of them twelve metres high and hideously beweaponed, were smashing through the woods on all sides. Ground troops rushed from cover to cover, spraying the area with high-power laser fire. The last of the Tedibehr army was fleeing through the undergrowth, often becoming immolated by pursuing troops, and giving off noxious smoke as they died.

'What do we do now?' echoed Leper. 'We run away.'

'Agreed,' said Someman.

Chapter Seven

The final *final showdown between Dark Father and Luke Seespotrun*

Luke fell perhaps hundreds of metres, fully expecting to die. But at the base of the shaft he encountered not hard floor, but something rather different.

The shaft opened up into a large half-plastered room in which four of Boba the Builder's workers were just sitting down to a nice cup of tea, some digestives, to be followed by a quick, relaxing bounce on a trampoline – after which, of course, they were planning on going back to work. They had set up the trampoline in readiness, and were now settling themselves down onto a few packing crates with their tea mugs in their hands. They were as surprised as anybody would be to hear the sound of a swiftly crescendoing yell of 'arrrghh!' as Luke's falling body tumbled through an open trapdoor in the ceiling, boinged into the trampoline and reboinged up. He vanished as rapidly as he had come, his 'arrrghh!' now receding into the background.

The builders stared at the space where, briefly, Luke had appeared.

He hurtled upwards, his yell now more surprised than despairing, and in a trice he popped back up to the podium upon which he had previously been hanging. Desperately he scrabbled at the railing, caught hold, and held on.

'YOU AGAIN?' boomed Dark Father. He reached over, grabbed his son by the back of his shirt, and hauled him over onto the raised platform.

As he grovelled on the floor, Luke looked up to see a figure coming slowly up the steps.

'NOW,' said Dark Father. 'MEET YOUR NEW MASTER . . . THE IMPERIAL EMPEROR OF THE IMPERIAL EMPIRE OF THE IMPERIUM.'

Luke gasped and looked up. He had, perhaps, been expecting a towering, intimidating figure, dressed in purple and gold and flanked by dozens of Praetorian Sterntroopers. But the thing that most struck him about the Imperial Emperor was how diminutive a figure he was – only a little over five foot tall. He walked steadily forward, supporting himself with a walking stick, although there were occasional blips in his movement, such as that he might twitch instantly forward by several inches, or his hand might leap without movement from his side to his chin – as if time itself were strained and cracked around him by his command of the Farce.

'O GREAT ONE,' said Dark Father, dropping to one knee. Luke was astonished; he had never before seen his father abase himself.

The Imperial Emperor was standing only a few feet from him. And, now that he was this close, Luke was amazed by how tatty his Imperial costume was: a worn black coat, a junk-shop bowler hat, trousers that were patently too big for him. Surely, Luke thought to himself, the most powerful being in the cosmos could command tailors to make him a better outfit? And surely a figure of such terror would carry a gold-topped ivory cane, perhaps carved from the thigh bone of a defeated enemy? But the Imperial Emperor's cane was a skinny bamboo object that bent prodigiously whenever he put weight upon it.

Looking down at the kneeling figure of Dark Father, the Imperial Emperor adjusted the angle of his bowler hat by poking it with his cane. Then he whipped out a black rectangle, bordered neatly with an embossed repeating leaf pattern. In the middle words appeared, silver against the dark background:

RISE, MY FRIEND
YOU HAVE DONE WELL
IN CAPTURING YOUNG SEESPOTRUN

Distantly, perhaps from some other room in the unfinished Death Spa, Luke thought he could hear the sound of jolly piano music.

'I'll never join you!' he cried, mustering his dignity.

The Imperial Emperor put his head on one side, and spun the black rectangle he was holding right around. When the front was facing Luke again, he saw that the words had changed:

YOU WILL JOIN US
YOUNG JOBBI
OR YOU WILL DIE!

The Emperor flipped the rectangle again:

HA HA HA HA!
HA HA HA HA HA!

There was no time to waste. Luke leapt up, snatched the lightsword from the kneeling figure of his father, and rushed at the Imperial Emperor. With a devastating rapidity and grace the rectangle disappeared, and as Luke thrust the jagged glass as hard as he could at the Imperial chest the thin bamboo cane whipped up. Somehow it not only deflected the blow, but flipped the lightsword spinning into the air. Then, with astonishing speed and grace, the Emperor darted round behind Luke, kicked him hard in the behind, did a little dance, slid across the floor, and regained his original position.

Luke was slack-jawed with amazement.

Dark Father stepped up and snatched the spinning lightsword from the air. The expression on the Imperial Emperor's face had become stern:

KILL HIM, DARK FATHER
IF HE WILL NOT BE TURNED
TO THE DARK SIDE OF THE . . . [CONT]

Both Luke and Dark Father read the words quickly, but had to wait for several long seconds before the Emperor flipped the card:

. . . FARCE. THE TIME HAS COME
TO PUT AN END TO THIS
PUNY REBELLION ONCE AND FOR ALL

'No!' cried Luke.

Chapter Eight

Events take a dark turn down on the moon

Leper and Hand, down on the moon, were in the process of running away. Unfortunately for them, they weren't very accomplished running-awayers. Within minutes the forces of the Imp-Emp-Imp had cornered them, disarmed them, and captured them.

With their hands on their heads, Leper and Hand were led back to the Sterntrooper compound. All around them they could see the white-armoured troops, gathering together the dead bodies of Tedibehrs in great heaps, or marching in order through the woods to seek out the last survivors.

Leper and Hand were taken inside the base. 'Our orders are to take you up in the Great Glass Elevator to the Death Spa,' the Sterntrooper captain said. 'Dark Father wants to have a word with the both of you.'

'Why?' demanded Leper. 'What does he want?'

'*I* don't know. Probably wants to know which way up you want to be tortured.' The Sterntrooper chuckled at his own words.

The line sounded vaguely familiar to Leper; but she couldn't place it.

She and Hand were made to stand to one side, still with their hands on their heads, whilst the victorious Sterntroopers secured the area, and reported back to their commanders.

'Looks like this is it, kiddo,' said Hand.

'The end,' agreed Leper.

'Since we're going to die,' said Hand, a lump visible in his well-proportioned throat, 'there's something I've been wanting to say to you for the longest time . . .'

'Wait,' said Leper.

'No, that's not it. It's —'

'No,' said Leper. 'I was saying wait. I've had an idea – a brilliant idea!'

'Can't you just hold on for a sec with your idea?' Hand replied, peevishly. 'This thing I've been waiting to say to you for the longest time . . . it won't take long . . . and it's not easy for me to put it in words . . .'

'But this may save us, and save the whole Rebel-end . . .'

'You see, I've been summoning the courage, and now I think I . . .'

'*Behind* us!' hissed Princess Leper. 'There's a control panel, within reach . . .'

275

'. . . it's only three little words,' Hand went on. 'But they're the three most important . . .'

'. . . out of the corner of my eye,' said Leper, turning her head a fraction, '. . . I can see the forcefield regular control toggle . . .'

'. . . the truth is, I've felt this way for a long time now . . .'

'. . . I think, if I wait until the Sterntroopers are looking the other way . . .'

'. . . since we're going to die now for sure, there's no point in keeping it to myself any longer . . .'

'. . . I could turn the traction beam intensity toggle to *full* . . .'

'. . . and I know there's no guarantee that you feel the same way, but . . .'

'. . . which would effectively *quadruple* tractor beam strength . . .'

'. . . if there's even a tiny chance, then I could never forgive myself for not saying something . . .'

'. . . bringing the Death Spa *crashing down* . . .'

'. . . frankly I love . . .'

'. . . into the moon of Endors-Gaim . . .'

'. . . you, and I always will, I yearn to embrace you and cover you with kisses . . .'

'. . . destroying it! What do you think? . . .'

'. . . Eh? I'm sorry,' said Hand. 'I wasn't really paying attention. What were you saying?'

'Honestly,' said Leper, crossly. 'Do you think it's *worth a chance*?'

'Of course I do!' said Hand, his heart leaping up and a big beaming smile lighting his attractively proportioned face. 'I'm so glad you feel the same way!'

'You do? But it might provoke a Sterntrooper to shoot us *both* dead.'

Hand looked at the soldiers. 'Could they be so mean-spirited? We've only got a few hours to live anyway.'

'Mean-spirited? What do you mean?'

'I think they'd understand,' said Hand.

'Understand? I don't think so.'

'I'm sure they've been in love,' said Hand. 'I'm sure they know what it means to hold a beautiful woman in their arms . . .'

'What *are* you on about? Stop babbling, Hand, and tell me what you think: shall I make a grab for the toggle?'

'Fan*tastic* idea,' said Hand, immediately, his eyes wide with astonished delight and gratitude. 'Go for it! Boy, I had no idea you were so *keen* . . .'

Leper shimmied left and, to Hand's puzzled disappointment grabbed the forcefield regulator control button on the panel behind her, yanking it to the 'maximum' position.

The two nearest Sterntroopers spun round, but it was too late: the damage was done. As Leper and Hand leapt left, they opened fire; but the laser bolts missed their targets and instead collided with the control panel, exploding it and – by a freakish chance only possible in a parody of life (you might say) – locking the tractor beam in 'maximum' position.

With a mighty shuddering groan, the giant equipment began tugging the half-built Death Spa to its destruction.

Chapter Nine

The very last and final *final* showdown between Luke Seespotrun and Dark Father, honestly. I know I've said it before, but this really is the last of it, at least as far as those two are concerned

Luke ran down the steps, and picked up a two-by-four from a pile of as yet unused timber. Dark Father, only strides behind him, tried a cutting blow with his lightsword, but Luke's parrying blow shivered the blade into innumerable fragments. 'Ha!' cried Luke, swinging a blow of his own that caught Dark Father on the side of his black helmet. It made a curiously bell-like sound.

The Emperor had also come down, carrying his black rectangle before him:

EXCELLENT! FIGHT!
THE WINNER WILL SERVE ME!
HA! HA!

Luke read this, and turned to look at his father again just in time to see that he too had picked up a plank of wood. The next thing he knew was the crushing pain of this piece of wood as it impacted with his face. The force of the blow pushed his lips back into the rictus of a grin. Light dazzled his eyes. There was a ringing sound in his ears. One after the other, his front teeth disengaged from his gums and clattered to the floor like Scrabble tiles.

The Farce saved him. He swayed back just as Dark Father swung round with a second, killer blow: he felt the swish of wind as it missed his nose by millimetres. Used to a less weighty lightsword, Father was himself unbalanced and staggered. This gave Luke just enough time to shake his stunned, mostly toothless head, and swing his own two-by-four.

Luke and Dark Father fought through room after room, all unfinished, unplastered or unpainted. They fought past piles of bricks, and stacks of timber; past cardboard boxes filled with tins of paint and great cartwheels of wound cable. All the way they were followed by the grinning form of the Imperial Emperor, whose boards indicated that he was enjoying the spectacle very much.

They passed from residential and office spaces deeper into the Death Spa. Here, similarly in various states of unreadiness, were the gigantic machinery and complicated devices of the giant artefact. They fought, thwacking one another with planks, against a background of a number of huge cogged gearwheels – twenty feet in diameter, turning slowly in the process of some unimaginable operation.

Luke paused, to catch his breath. He looked from the grinning face of the Imperial Emperor to the dark mask of his master.

'IF YOU DO NOT SERVE US,' said Dark Father. 'YOU WILL DIE'

'You would kill your own son?'

'YOU MUST UNDERSTAND THE POWER OF THE DARK SIDE.'

'Threatening my life will not make me betray my friends,' said Luke hotly, and indeed a little priggishly, if we're honest.

'VERY WELL. PERHAPS I NEED TO USE A *DIFFERENT* SORT OF PERSUASION. JOIN US OR – I WILL KILL NOT YOU BUT *YOUR SISTER.*'

'You monster!' cried Luke. He rushed forward, but Dark Father used the power of the Farce to have his right foot skid on a small pool of spilled paint, slip sharply forward whilst his left foot snagged and slipped back, such that he hit the ground very painfully, unwillingly adopting that position known as 'the splits'. The pain was excruciating. Luke dropped his plank.

'YES—' said Dark Father. 'YOUR SISTER. PERHAPS I SHALL CUT HER IN TWO WITH THE JAGGED EDGE OF MY LIGHT-SWORD – WHAT DO YOU THINK? YES – THEN YOU WOULD HAVE NOT SO MUCH A SISTER AS *TWO HALF SISTERS*. HA! YES . . .'

Luke groaned, picking himself up with some caution. 'Is that the best you can do?'

Dark Father stopped. 'WHAT DO YOU MEAN?'

'That joke. That was *terrible*.'

'NO IT WASN'T. IT WAS WITTY AND POINTED.'

'Oh, come on, Dad,' said Luke. 'Let's be honest. It really wasn't. That was just rubbish. That's the kind of joke that somebody without a sense of humour thinks is funny.'

'I HAVE AN EXCELLENT SENSE OF HUMOUR,' announced Dark Father, his voice betraying the rising anger in his breast.

'But clearly you *haven't*.'

'SILENCE!' roared Dark Father.

'Look,' said Luke. 'All I'm saying is that the half-sister gag was rubbish. Don't get your knickers in a twist. You still have many skills – lightsword fighting, for instance. Or remote tracheal crushing, I understand you're very good at that.'

'DO YOU *DARE*,' said Father, his voice low and pregnant with terrible menace, 'DO YOU *DARE* TO SUGGEST THAT I LACK A SENSE OF HUMOUR?'

'Frankly,' said Luke, 'Yes. I'm sorry, Dad, but you know it's the truth.'

Dark Father's breathing became increasingly pronounced. He was evidently on the verge of some huge explosion of anger. Luke steeled himself. But when it came the explosion was of a very different sort.

Dark Father drew a shuddering breath into his lungs and bawled 'OH WHAT'S THE USE – IT'S *TRUE*, IT'S TRUE, I KNOW IT'S TRUE.' He dropped his weapon and slumped down to sit cross-legged on the floor. 'I KNOW YOU'RE RIGHT,' he sobbed. 'I'VE GOT THE WORST SENSE OF HUMOUR IN THE UNIVERSE! I'M A FAILURE AT HUMOUR! WOE! WOE! WOE!'

This completely threw Luke. 'Oh,' he said, awkwardly. 'Hey. C'mon Dad, it's not that bad.'

'IT IS!' howled Dark Father.

'Really, it doesn't matter . . . hey, are you actually *crying*?'

'BOO HOO!' cried Dark Father. 'NOBODY UNDERSTANDS HOW MISERABLE I AM! I SPEND HOURS ALONE IN MY SPACIOUS QUARTERS PRACTISING WITTY ONE-LINERS AND THROWAWAY OFF-THE-CUFF REMARKS. I STUDY ALL THE CLAS-SICS . . . TWO RONNIES, FRASIER, CARRY ON . . . BUT IT'S NO GOOD!'

This wrongfooted Luke a little. 'Er,' he said. 'Hey.'

'WAAAH!' cried Dark Father.

'Hey, c'mon,' said Luke, embarrassed. 'There there. Really – it's not the end of the world, is it now?'

'AH, BUT IT IS! LAUGHTER IS EVERY-THING. YOU'VE GOT TO *LAUGH*, HAVEN'T YOU?'

'I don't see that,' said Luke. 'Sometimes – sure. But all the time? There are occasions when laughter is plain inappropriate.'

'BUT . . .' said Dark. 'BUT IF I CAN MAKE PEOPLE LAUGH . . . THEN THEY WILL *LIKE* ME.'

'Oh, piffle. Nobody actually *likes* comedians. People like *regular* people, not clowns. Clowns are fine in performance, but in regular life they're just tiresome.'

'DO YOU THINK SO?' asked Dark Father, tentatively.

'Of course I do. I tell you what else, Dad: you may be ultimate evil, and all that, but I like you.'

'YOU DO?'

'Yeah. You're my Dad aren't you? There you go. Blood thicker than water, and all that.'

The expression on the Imperial Emperor's face made it clear that he was finding all this talk tiresome. He flipped his black rectangle round:

ENOUGH! FINISH HIM
DARK FATHER, AT ONCE.
HE DISAPPOINTS US.

Dark Father looked at his master, and got slowly to his feet. Signs of impatience became more pronounced on the Imperial face. The rectangle flipped:

DO IT NOW! KILL HIM!
AND MAKE IT
FUNNY . . .

Distantly, the sound of the piano music could still be heard. Though the sound was very muffled, it sounded rather like Scott Joplin.

In a trice Dark Father was at the Emperor's side. He grabbed the diminutive figure, lifted him bodily into the air. As the black rectangle fell away, Luke just had time to make out the words:

... UNHAND ME ... TREACHERY!
... INFAMY! ...
... YOU SWINE, YOU ARE DEADING ME ...

Dark Father hurled the Emperor onto a conveyer belt and watched as he moved sharply through a hatchway. The next thing that Luke saw was the Imperial body being crushed and mangled by the giant cogwheels, passed in a sinuous path into the bowels of the machine, carried round the top of the first giant cogwheel, and then underneath the second. In moments he had disappeared from view.

'Where does that go to?' Luke asked.

'INTO THE BOWELS OF THE NUCLEAR REACTOR. THE INSERTION OF A FIGURE

SO PROFOUNDLY POWERFUL WITH THE
FARCE INTO THE POWER SOURCE WILL
BE SURE TO RESULT IN EXPLOSIONS,
DISASTER AND THE DESTRUCTION OF
THIS DEATH SPA. WE MUST LEAVE AT
ONCE!'

'Good idea,' said Luke.

Meanwhile, down on the moon, the Imp-Emp-Imp
base had been thrown into confusion by the quick
thinking of Princess Leper. The control machinery
was exploding under the strain of hauling the Death
Spa.

Darting through the main entrance, Leper led
Hand. They ran together across the runway towards
an Imp-Emp-Imp shuttle parked on the far side.

Hand in hand with Hand, Leper hurried up the
gangway. 'We've got to get off this world,' she gasped
as they made their way to the cockpit. 'The crashing of
that Death Spa will act as a total extinction event.'

'Tough news for the Tedibehrs,' said Hand.

'What? Oh yeah. I'd forgotten about them. Ah well,'
she said, strapping herself in and priming the launch
motor, 'their sacrifice will not be forgotten in the
mighty struggle against tyranny et cetera. Come on!'

❋

Aboard the Death Spa itself, Luke and Dark Father staggered along the shaking corridors, avoiding falling columns and bits of plaster. 'What's happening?' Luke cried.

'THE DESTRUCTION PROCESS HAS BE-GUN,' gasped his father. 'YOU MUST TAKE MY SHUTTLE AND FLY FROM THE MAIN HANGAR'

'You're coming with me!'

'I AM AFRAID NOT, SON. I AM SUS-TAINED ONLY BY THE FARCE, AND MY POWER WAS CLOSELY CAUGHT UP WITH THE MIGHTY FARCICAL POWER OF MY MASTER. WITH HIS DEATH I FEEL MY OWN POWER EBBING.'

'Bummer,' said Luke.

They made it to the hangar before Dark Father collapsed. 'TAKE OFF MY MASK,' gasped the former Dark Lord of the Psmyth.

'I'm not wearing your mask,' replied Luke. But it was a feeble sort of joke, unworthy of the Farce, and they both knew it.

With some difficulty Luke unhitched the black skull-mask, revealing a round, pudgy, white Oliver Hardy-like face inside. 'That's odd,' he said. 'From you stature I was expecting you to be tall and thin.

But it turns out you're short and fat. I guess appearances can be deceptive.'

'I am both together, both short, fat and pompous, and tall, thin and stupid,' gasped Father. 'It is one of the mysteries of the Farce . . .' The hangar was rapidly turning into a fine mess around them.

'*You must go, son . . .*' Father wheezed.

'Quick, before I do . . . can you tell me the Great Secret? Don't let it die with you . . . pass it on to me . . .'

'*The secret is,*' Father said, in a strangulated tone, '. . . *aaaaaaaaaaaahhhhh.*'

'Is what?' pressed Luke. 'What does that mean?'

'It means,' said Father, a touch crossly, 'that I'm dead.' His eyes rolled upwards.

And so he was.

Luke flew the shuttle out of the main hangar just in time. In the rear-view mirror he saw the half-built Death Spa catch flame in a thousand places, even as it veered out of orbit and tumbled towards the surface of the wooded moon of Endors-Gaim. As his spacecraft was buffeted by waves of expanding gas and debris, Luke caught one stunning view of the collision: the Death Spa careering into the flank of the great moon, igniting its atmosphere in an apocalyptic firestorm that spread in a galloping wavefront of destruction away over the visible horizon, immolating everything in its path.

'Phew,' said Luke. 'That was a lucky escape . . .'

Chapter Ten
Conclusive

By the time Luke, Leper and Hand got to the muster point it was nearly twenty-one hundred hours, and all the sandwiches had been eaten, and most of the wine drunk. But the three of them joined the gathering of soldiers and officers in the muster hall of the biggest of the Rebelend space cruisers.

'We have triumphed!' announced General Fishedd Onaslab. 'We have defeated the evil Imp-Emp-Imp!' Everybody cheered.

'The Emperor is dead!'

There was more cheering.

'And Dark Father too! Let us not forget: Dark Father was the most evil dictator in the history of Galactic civilisation,' General Fishedd blustered. 'His name deserves to live in infamy! He was utterly evil.'

'Well,' said Luke. 'It transpires he *wasn't* utterly evil after all.'

'No?'

There was a general sensation in the hall.

'No,' said Luke, stepping up to the podium.

'Granted he was responsible for the death of untold billions. And, yes, he was a torturer, a tyrant, and a military dictator. Yes he crushed the spirits and oppressed the societies of thousands of worlds, grinding all cultural and ethnic diversity beneath the faceless rollers of Imp-Emp-Imp conformity. True he worked with all his might for the ultimate unending triumph of evil. But – and this is the crucial thing – but at the last minute, he *saved the life of his own son.*' There were gasps of astonishment. 'I know, I know,' said Luke. 'It's an almost unbelievably selfless and heroic thing to have done, but let me just reiterate: he saved the life of *his own son.* And that,' Luke concluded, looking about him, 'I think we can agree, means that he merits complete vindication, and can now be regarded, in fact, as something approaching a saint.'

There was a general murmuring and nodding of heads. 'How true,' said Fishedd, 'how very true that is.'

'Let us erect an enormous statue to his honour!' cried another.

'He is a hero of the revolution!' shrieked a third. 'Let anybody who says otherwise be executed by executive revolutionary order!'

And so it was that Dark Father, also known as Jane

Seespotrun, became a shining light of revolutionary brilliance.

Princess Leper, her heart full, slipped away from the hall. Luke saw her go, and followed her, joining her on a balcony looking down over the main hall. The two of them stood and watched the rock and roll celebrations of the victorious Rebelend below: drinking, dancing, eating, vomiting, the full gamut of human enjoyment.

'You realise, of course,' said Luke, speaking gently for fear of upsetting his sister, 'that we may *never* know what the Great Secret is, now? Dark Father told me that he knew the Secret, but he is dead now. And RC-DU^2 has been destroyed in the conflagration that marked the end of the Death Spa.'

'I can't say it bothers me over much,' said Leper. 'The main reason I wanted to know the Secret was to defeat the Imp-Emp-Imp. We've managed that without knowing the Secret, so it doesn't really matter. Of course, I'm still curious . . .'

'Curious, yes. Me too.'

'But I suppose it'll just be one of those things.'

'One of those things, yes.'

'Luke, why are you repeating everything I say?'

'Leper – I have something to tell you. It may be a

shock. You know that Dark Father was my father? Well he was your father too. You and I share the same parents. We are, in fact, brother and sister.'

'I don't think so,' said Leper, matter-of-factly.

'I know it's hard to accept. I refused to believe it at first too . . .'

'It's not that,' said Leper. 'But it's not genetically possible for you and I to be brother and sister. Dark Father can't be my father.'

'You sound very sure.'

Leper turned to look at Luke. 'Come on, Luke. These tentacles, curled at the side of my head? I know you've noticed them, because you've mentioned them several times.'

'Tentacles?' said Luke, uncertainly.

'I'm a Keflapod, from the planet Keflapodia. What did you think my tentacles were, otherwise?'

'I don't know,' Luke mumbled. 'Some kind of fungoid growth . . .'

Leper boggled at Luke, by which I don't mean that she played a letter-dice-based word game with him, but rather that she was astonished by his ignorance of the ways of the universe. 'You're quite astonishingly ignorant about the ways of the universe,' she told him. 'How many humans have you seen walking around with tentacles like these growing out of the side of their heads?'

'None,' conceded Luke.

'Yet you didn't make the obvious logical deduction from that fact?'

'So,' said Luke, thinking slowly. ' —you're not human?'

'No.'

'But you *do* have leprosy?'

'Keflapodic leprosy, yes. It's a disease very similar to human leprosy. But it's under medical control.'

'I'm sorry,' said Luke. 'You look so human – so beautifully human. I just assumed you were human. Despite the curled-up tentacles on either side of your head.'

'I am human*oid*,' she said. 'That oid makes all the difference. It means, for instance, that my people cannot breed with your people; we're genetically incompatible. So I can't be Dark Father's daughter, or your sister.'

'I wonder why he said you were, then,' said Luke.

'Who knows.'

'Bony K'nobbli said it too.'

'Again – my shoulders are shrugging. Perhaps you can see them? There they go – shrug shrug. It means,' she added, 'that I neither know nor care.'

Luke stood in silent thought as the fireworks blossomed like tenuous yet gigantically shining lilies and daffodils of light, filling the dark-purple sky with shuddering brilliance. 'So,' Luke said finally, slowly. 'You're humanoid, are you?'

'That's right.'

'Which is,' Luke continued, carefully, '*very like* human?'

'Yes.'

'Capable—' Luke went on 'of, um, of *interacting* with humans in . . . what? Some ways? Most ways? All ways?'

'Interacting?' said Princess Leper crossly. 'What do you mean "interacting"?' She looked into Luke's face, and her crossness dissolved away. 'Oh,' she said, comprehension dawning. 'Interacting in *that* sense. Well, the answer to that would be . . . yes, actually.'

'Really?' said Luke drawing closer to her and slipping his arm around her shoulder. 'That *is* interesting.'

Away on the far side of the hall Masticatetobacco – who had been slumped in a spare chair and left to slumber on – gave a start, shook his head, and sat up straight. He rubbed his eyes and blinked for several moments. 'Good grief,' he said, in his cut-glass quasi-Etonian accent. 'What a strange dream I've been having . . .'

THE FANS-OF-TRON MENACE

IT WAS THE FOUR HUNDREDTH YEAR OF THE GALACTIC
FEDERAL CONSOLIDATION, AND THE PLANET YA!BOO! HAD BEEN
UNFAVOURABLY AFFECTED BY THE SEVENTEENTH SUB-CLAUSE OF
THE FEDERAL CONSOLIDATION INNER-GALACTIC REVENUE CODE
AMENDMENT ACT, SPECIFYING THE NUMBER OF EXEMPTIONS ALLOW-
ABLE FOR EACH ELIGIBLE AND ACCREDITED CITIZEN-DEPENDENT IN THE
FILING OF INTERSTELLAR TRADE TARIFF AND TAX RETURNS, THE
MINISTER OF ACCOUNTING SOMEHOW, INEXPLICABLY, HAVING FAILED
TO NOTIFY THE CENTRAL TAX PLANET OF A REDESIGNATION OF THE
PLANET FROM ISQ 9000 TO ISQ 9001 (AN UPGRADE IN GENERAL TAX-
LIABILITY CLASSIFICATION THAT, FOR REGISTRATION PURPOSES, MOVED
YA!BOO! FROM LOWER-PRIORITY TO MIDDLE-PRIORITY FIRST QUARTILE
ACCOUNT TRANSPARENCY) UNTIL NEARLY TWO WEEKS AFTER THE
DEADLINE REQUIRED BY THE GALACTIC FEDERAL CONSOLIDATION.
THIS, IN TURN, REQUIRED A REVALIDATION OF THE PLANET'S CENSUS
BUREAU REORGANISATION LAWS, TO BRING THE CENSUS DETAILS OF
CITIZENS UP TO THE LATEST GALACTIC FEDERAL CONSOLIDATION FOR TAX-
ASSESSMENT PURPOSES, WITH PARTICULAR REFERENCE TO MANUFACTURING
AND SERVICE INDUSTRY TAXABLE LIABILITY. DUE TO THE OVERSIGHT ON
BEHALF OF THE MINISTER OF ACCOUNTING, YA!BOO! FACED THE TERRIFYING
PROSPECT OF BEING ELIGIBLE NEITHER FOR THEIR USUAL TRADE TARIFF
REBATE, NOR FOR THE SLIGHTLY LARGER TRADE TARIFF REBATE AVAILABLE
UNDER THE ISQ 9001 SCHEME, TO CLAIM WHICH THE YA!BOO! GOVERNMENT HAD

REDESIGNATED THEMSELVES IN THE FIRST PLACE. WITHOUT
THEIR REBATE, THE YA!BOO! DEMOCRATICALLY ELECTED GOVERN-
MENT FACED HAVING TO HOLD OVER A HALF PERCENTILE OF AN ALREADY
ASSENTED BUDGETARY OVERFALL, WHICH IN TURN COULD IMPACT VERY NEGATIV-
ELY UPON BOTH THE PENDING ARTS' SUPPORT AND WELFARE REORGANISATION LEGISLATION.
BECAUSE OF THIS SITUATION, THE GALACTIC FEDERAL CONSOLIDA-
TION HAD NO CHOICE BUT TO DECLARE WHAT THE GALACTIC FEDERAL
CHIEF ADMINISTRATOR DESCRIBED AS '*KRIEG* OF THE *BLITZ* VARIETY'
UPON YA!BOO!, AND TO 'DROP MORE BATTLE DROIDS ON THEM THAN
HAVE EVER BEFORE BEEN ASSEMBLED IN MILITARY OPERATIONS'.
THINGS LOOK BLEAK FOR THE BEAUTIFUL YOUNG TAX-ASSESSOR PŌKME
AMIDSHIPS.   NOW READ ON . . .

Chapter One

The regrettable situation on Ya!Boo!

Two Jobbi masters alighted from their space ship on the verdant fields of the planet Ya!Boo!: one, Kwai Gone Bridge, had the suave patrician charm of a middle-aged Jack Hawkins. The other was his handsome and eager apprentice, Wobbli Bent K'nobbli. Kwai Gone exuded a calm stateliness. K'nobbli, on the other hand, was in the prime of his youth, or indeed, judging by his face and its lack of resemblance to the face it would become in later years, in the prime of somebody *else*'s youth.

They were met by the young Tax Assessor Pōkme Amidships. 'Good day,' she said, rather stiffly.

Pōkme was nearing the end of her indentured period as a Galactic Federal Consolidation-owned civil servant (with special responsibility to tax affairs). Slavery had, of course, once been widespread amongst human cultures. The invention and mass manufacture of robots had long since obviated the need for *manual* slaves – the demand for a workforce needed to, say, erect a pyramid or harvest tobacco could more

efficiently be met with zinc-based workers than
carbon-based ones. But this was not to say that slavery
had been banished. Far from it. Rather the burden of
slavery shifted from the lowest level of society (who
were granted the freedom to starve, provided only they
did not do it in too public a manner) to the middle
managers. It benefited the wealthy to have a class of
indentured servants to fill in their tax returns, to
address their insurance needs and to sort through
the tangle of the thousands of conflicting legal codes.
This new class of slaves endured all the disadvantages
of previous varieties of slaves, although the cannier
amongst them were sometimes able to work themselves free – by, for instance, taking on extra assignments, particularly dangerous assignments. In this way
Pōkme Amidships (in a state of affairs rare amongst
the peoples of Ya!Boo!) had brought herself to within
spitting distance of her own freedom. Not that she
would spit. She was far too pretty and well-bred to do
that.

'Pleased to meet you,' said Kwai Gone. 'I'm Kwai
Gone.'

'I'm Wobbli Bent K'nobbli,' said K'nobbli puppy-
ishly.

Pōkme did not bother telling them her name; as
with all the indentured she wore a name badge that

said 'Hi! I'm **Pōkme Amidships** How Can I Be Of ☺ Service?'

'At last,' she snapped, 'the Council has sent representatives. You can witness for yourself the damage that has been done to our beautiful planet . . .' She gestured: the green hills and fertile valleys of Ya!Boo! visible from the landing platform were pitted with brown craters. The ruins of several of the larger villages were smoking. Smoking, of course, is as bad a sign in villages as in humans, and almost always indicates a poor state of health.

'We are truly sorry,' said Kwai. 'The entire attack upon your world was a deeply regrettable incident.'

'Regrettable!' said Pōkme, colouring. 'Is that all you can say? Galactic Federal Consolidation Legislation expressly states that no planet shall be bombed until two weeks *after* any appeal committee of independently appointed Revenue Appeal officers has convened and judged with a simple majority in the case of non-payment of account but a *two-thirds majority* in the case of all other rubric infractions . . .'

'You are absolutely correct,' said Kwai Gone, holding up his hand. 'One of the reasons the Council has sent me is to offer our apologies.'

'Apologies?'

'Yes. It is indeed true that the Appeal Committee,

although they did vote for bombing by a simple majority, did not pass the annihilation motion by the required two-thirds majority.'

Pōkme looked from the older Jobbi to the younger. 'So what happened?' she asked.

'We suspect treachery by a secret organisation. Our intelligence talks of a mysterious group called the "Fans-of-Tron" . . . although we are not sure what the name means.'

'Fans-of-Tron,' said Pōkme, trying the phrase out. 'No, that means nothing to me. Wasn't there a film once called *Tron*?'

'Yes; it is a classic from the age of the Twentieth Century, the Golden Age of Disney and Pokemon, as it is sometimes called. But we cannot see why a terrorist organisation would take it as their name. There's worse news too. It may be that the Dark Side of the Farce has infiltrated the Council itself.'

'No!'

'I'm afraid so.'

There was a huge crunching noise high above them. The three of them looked up to see the sleek forms of Mercenary Viral Fighters shrieking through the sky, each of them shedding missiles from the ordnance pores pitted all over its fuselage, like a dog shaking itself dry. 'Quick!' cried Pōkme. 'Into one of the shelters!'

The shelter was huge, but nevertheless filled to capacity. About half the people inside were human; the remainder belonged to the 'Keflapod' race, an indigenous population who lived in and under the water. Keflapods had evolved via a curious symbiosis between a highly intelligent squid creature and a highly stupid ape. The ape, as natural selection worked its magic, had become stupider and stupider, its brain pan shrinking and its head retreating into its shoulders until it had no head at all. At some point in the long ago, the squiddy proto-Keflapods had sunk six of their eight arms through the next stump and into the nervous system of these anthropods, leaving two tentacles, one on each side of their head. This combined life form was more successful than either of its originators, and had spread widely across the world.

Then the humans had arrived.

It is true that the human population shipped into the world had been one of slaves, but they were middle management slaves. Their masters had long ago learnt that one way to keep slaves contented is to give them slaves of their own. So long as a slave has somebody else to cook, clean and skivvy for them, they are much less likely to rise up against their own oppression.

Kwai Gone and Wobbli Bent were squeezed on a long bench, with Amidships on one side and a group of Keflapods on the other. 'Hello,' said Kwai Gone, who prided himself on being open-minded. He shook the hand of the Keflapod sitting on the bench next to him.

'Yassa? Yousa talking to *meee*?' replied the Keflapod, his eyes wide in astonishment. 'Howsa yowsa massa! I speakee howdy-doody. Yousa mesa eata warty-melon, sitsy downsy yowsa! Yassa massa!'

'Of for the love of – just shut *up*, Jam-Jar,' came a voice from further down the bench. It was another Keflapod. 'You'll have to excuse him, I'm afraid.'

'I'm Kwai Gone and this is my apprentice Wobbli Bent K'nobbli,' said Kwai Gone.

'I know, said the Keflapod. 'My mistress told me all about your visit. I'm Psoriasis, her maid.'

'Why does he talk like that?' Wobbli asked.

'Nobody knows,' said Psoriasis, sighing. 'The nearest I can make out, he's just an idiot.'

'Ah,' said Wobbli, nodding. As a Jobbi he knew about idiocy.

'Whosa?' said Jam-Jar. 'Yabba-dabba, yousa say wesa gonna . . .'

'If you don't button it,' said Psoriasis, in a tight but focused voice, 'I am going to hit you so *very* hard . . .'

'Oh *alright* then,' said Jam-Jar, sulkily. He crossed his arms and pouted at the floor.

A siren clanged, gong-like. 'That's the all-clear,' said Pōkme. 'Come on.'

'Miss Amidships? We must put an end to this . . . regrettable destruction. Will you come to Metropolanet with us, and submit a report to a reconvened Tariff Committee?'

'It's not as if I can say no, is it?' said Pōkme, bitterly. 'I'm indentured, aren't I?'

'But you're close to earning yourself free, though, aren't you?' said Wobbli. 'I mean, if I haven't misunderstood. This job would put you one step further towards that goal.'

Pōkme gave him a sour look.

Chapter Two

A pram race on Tatuonweiner

Pōkme boarded the Jobbi spaceship, attended by the Keflapod Psoriasis, who in turn was attended by the Keflapod Jam-Jar Oinks. 'It seems,' said Wobbli, 'that the principle of hierarchical subservience extends all the way down in any slave-based social system.'

'Waa?' replied Jam-Jar. 'Yousa massa talkee-talkee to . . .'

'Oh just put a Galactic *sock* in it, Jam-Jar,' said Pōkme.

'Yes,' agreed Wobbli. 'Shut up. Stop speaking and say nothing more.'

'Well, if everyone's going to be like *that*,' said Jam-Jar, in sulky passion. 'I am going to have a lie-down.' He stomped off.

'We're going to have to make an unscheduled stop on a desert backwater called Tatuonweiner,' announced Kwai Gone. 'To, er, refuel.'

'Refuel?' repeated Pōkme. In frank disbelief. 'What kind of spaceship is this?'

Wobbli K'nobbli blushed deeply. 'Um,' he said. 'My master is trying to spare my feelings,' he admitted to Amidships. 'The truth is that, when my apprenticeship is completed, I am to be banished—'

'Not the "b" word, Wobbli!' warned Kwai Gone.

'—sent on *an important solo mission*,' Wobbli corrected himself, 'to one or another backwater dead-end world. The Jobbi order wants to examine Tatuonweiner as a possible destination. We need to know that it is utterly parochial, miles from anywhere, lacking any indigenous culture, and very far from the trade routes. Ideally it should be the last place in the world you'd want to live. Tatuonweiner may meet these requirements. We just want to check it out.'

'Makes no difference to me what you do,' said Amidships, in a manner at once offhand and sincere.

Tatuonweiner was every bit as dull as Kwai and Wobbli had suspected. Wobbli walked around with a glum face, contemplating the metaphorical septic tank in which he would, probably, spend his future.

'Why are you to be banished?' Pōkme asked.

Wobbli cast a glance in the direction of his master. 'It's complicated,' he said. 'Internal Jobbi politics. Suffice to say that I have . . . annoyed the senior Jobbi Council.'

The three of them came to the top of a long flight of public steps, leading down towards a dusty square and an artefact that would have been a fountain and pond had there been any water in it. A large crowd of excited Tatuonweiner locals had gathered at the top. Bets were being made.

'What's this?' Kwai Gone asked one of the milling locals.

'Weekly pram race,' was the reply. 'You want to make a bet? The shortest odds are on young Jane Seespotrun.' He pointed to a young woman cooing over a large black hooded pram. 'That's his mother, Dick.'

'Did you say – Dick?'

'That's right.'

'Interesting.' Kwai Gone folded his hands inside his robe, and stood watching. Pretty soon a dozen mothers were lined up at the top of the steps, their prams before them. The crowd had formed a semi-circle, and were egging on their favourites. A tall skinny fellow held his arm up, and then sliced it down suddenly, yelling 'go!'

All the mothers shoved their prams forward at once.

A dozen prams rattled over the edge of the top step and started bouncing and careering down the long flight. Kwai Gone kept his eye on the pram in which the favourite, young Jane Seespotrun, was lying. The early stages of the race depended, essentially, on the initial impetus imparted to the pram by the mothers. The lead pram had been pushed by one particularly well-proportioned mother, with forearms like hay bales and a chest that could, fixed to the front of a ship in the Arctic, have cut through the ice sheet: she was able to shove her baby with such vehemence that he was a third of the way down the long flight whilst the rest of them were just cresting the top steps. The pram pushed by Dick Seespotrun was somewhere around last position; not surprising given the scrawny frame and general pastiness of the woman doing the pushing.

But almost at once the power of the Farce began to make itself obvious. The pram carrying Jane Seespotrun hit some sort of snag, perhaps a slight chip in the stone of the steps; but rather than merely rattling over this minor glitch as the laws of physics might suggest, the pram flew high and wide. It soared through the air, vaulting over the intervening prams (again, rather in contravention of the physics governing bodies in effective free fall), bounced on the hood of the lead pram, flipped right over, and landed in the lead position.

The pram whose lead had been usurped jockeyed

for position, lurching forward, swerving to try and pass Seespotrun's chariot. It bounced and jiggled a little faster downhill and pulled alongside young Jane's pram, and swerved violently, trying to run him off the stairs entirely.

Suddenly, two curving blades popped from the hubs of the right-side pram wheels. With another swerve, the whirling metal bit into Jane Seespotrun's pram-wheels. Plastic flew upwards in shreds like sparks, and Jane's pram tipped forward. But, instead of crashing and stopping, the pram body spun through the air, rammed the aggressor pram from behind, shunting it off its own wheels.

The other baby's pram body crashed to the ground, hitting the steps, flipping end over end and finally bashing into the metal balustrade and coming to a full halt. Meanwhile, to enormous cheering, Jane Seespotrun's pram rattled down the last few stairs and rolled smoothly over the finishing line.

The rest of the prams – those ones which had not collided with obstacles or otherwise come to unlucky ends – rolled over the finishing line some time behind them. The adults came trotting down the stairs to recover their prams, and collect their winnings.

'Your young son is very strong in the Farce,' observed Kwai Gone Bridge to Dick Seespotrun.

'Sure he is,' said Dick Seespotrun, lighting a cigarette. 'Farcical – yeah.'

'Waaaaah!' put in Jane Seespotrun.

'I would like to take him away from you, fly him halfway across the Galaxy, and train him as a Jobbi. He would be trained in all the Farcical arts, and would thereafter be expected to devote himself to the Jobbi order forever.'

'Would I ever see him again?'

'Probably not.'

'Ach well,' said Dick taking another drag. 'Easy come, easy go, that's what I always say. Take him, if you like.'

Chapter Three
Before the Jobbi Council

The ship flew on, flew all the way to Metropolanet – the centre of the Galactic Federal Consolidation. Metropolanet was, as I'm sure you know, a world whose entire surface was covered by one enormous city; as far as the eye could see there were buildings, towers, factories, chimneys, steel, concrete and plastic. It was a wonderful place, with more estate agents per head of population than anywhere else in the Galaxy, although precisely how its ecosystem processed enough oxygen into the atmosphere to make the air breathable was something of a mystery. It might have had something to do with all the pot plants on the windowsills. But we can't be sure.

Kwai Gone Bridge brought Jane Seespotrun before the Jobbi Council. Wobbli and Pōkme stood a little way behind him. Yodella sat in a very large chair, a chair whose very spacious body was somewhat at odds with the tiny frame of the person occupying it. Various Jobbi elders sat around him.

'Master Yodella,' said Kwai Gone, holding the

wriggling form of Jane Seespotrun in his arms. 'I seek the Council's permission to train this youngster in the ways of the Farce.'

'Too old, he is!' shrieked Yodella. 'Too old for the training.'

'Too old? He's barely seven months old.'

'Waaa-*aaaaaaah*!' confirmed Jane.

'No! Too old!' said Yodella.

'You didn't say that,' put in Wobbli K'nobbli, stepping forward to support his master, 'when that seventeen-year-old Danish exchange student put herself forward for training last Thursday. What was her name again?'

'Question him, I will,' said Yodella in a loud voice, as if wishing to curtail Wobbli's speech. 'Decide will I whether capable of becoming a Jobbi he is.'

'Waaa-waaa-waaa,' suggested Jane.

'Youngling!' said Yodella, peering intently at the tiny form. 'Much fear I sense in you!'

'Wa-a-ah! Wa-a-ah! Waaaaaaaaaaaah!' countered Jane.

'Fearful is he,' pronounced Yodella.

'I think he may just want his nappy changing,' said Pōkme.

'No! Fear, it is! Fear! A Jobbi must feel no fear! Fear leads to anger,' said Yodella, in a voice fraught with meaning. 'Anger leads to hatred. Hatred leads to suffering. Suffering leads to the Dark Side.'

'So let's say, for example,' said Pōkme in a 'time for a recap' sort of voice, 'that I am afraid of dying. This leads me to be angry at the thought of my dying. Inevitably this leads to hatred of death. Which leads to suffering, because . . . um. How does the suffering come about?'

'No,' said Wobbli. 'A better example would be: let us say that I am afraid of spiders. This leads me to be angry with spiders, which in turn compels me to hate spiders. This then leads to suffering.'

'For the spiders?'

'For me – I think. Is that right, Yodella?'

'No no no. Spiders, *no*, yodel-ay-i-hee-*iiii*,' returned the tiny green fellow. 'Learned nothing you have. Banishment too soon cannot come – important *solo* mission too soon cannot come, I mean.'

'Let us say,' said Kwai Gone, shaking his head indulgently at the ignorance of his apprentice, 'that I encounter an Arcturan tiger in the forest. I am afraid, and run away. So my life is saved? No – because my fear makes me angry with the tiger. And my anger leads me to hate the tiger. So that I then return to the forest to confront the tiger, thereby precipitating suffering.'

'For you? Or the tiger?'

Kwai Gone pondered this question, apparently wavering between one answer and the other. Finally he said, nodding significantly, 'both.'

'So what should you do, when you meet the tiger?' Pōkme asked. 'Not be afraid?'

'Exactly.'

'But then you wouldn't run away.'

'No.'

'Wouldn't that just fast-forward you to the *suffering* part? At least if you run away you get a breather.'

'Getting bogged down in this discussion, we seem to be,' interrupted Yodella. 'Losing ourselves in less important business we are. Councillor Palpating has asked us to meet with him! Important information he says he has about the Fans-of-Tron.'

'And the boy?'

Yodella peered at him again. 'Train him, if like you. Or train him not. Bothered am I,' he concluded, 'not.'

The Jobbi Council, with Kwai Gone, Wobbli and Pōkme in attendance, made their way through the corridors of Metropolanet to the official residence of Councillor Palpating.

Councillor Palpating did not have a very euphonious name. He knew it. Everybody around him knew it. It made people think of a large, ill-defined mass of flesh quivering on a slab. Of course, Councillor Palpating looked nothing like this; looking, in fact, rather fresh-faced and young-looking, with a cheery, round, open face. But the name influenced his destiny. Put it this way: if you had been christened 'Nogbad the Bad', would you have chosen the paths of righteousness? Mind you, nobody *at this time* knew that Palpating was going to become an Emperor of Evil. They couldn't see the future, after all. They all thought he was a jolly decent sort of chap. I mean – perhaps he was. Perhaps he doesn't become an Emperor of Evil. I'd like to preserve some narrative mystery and suspense.

Be honest: you can't be *sure* that Councillor Palpating will become an Emperor of Evil, can you? I mean, *absolutely* sure?

'Thank you for coming to see me,' said Palpating. 'And who is this little chap?' He walked towards the baby in Kwai Gone's arms.

As he reached forward to pet the child, his foot somehow went into a waste-paper bin. Wrongfooted, he lurched forward and landed, head-first, in a second waste-paper bin.

'My,' said Palpating, extricating himself with some difficulty. 'He is extremely strong in the Farce, isn't he?'

'The strongest I've yet seen,' said Kwai Gone.

'Interesting. Is he to be trained as a Jobbi?'

'He is.'

'Interesting,' Palpating repeated. 'Anyway. Let me tell you why I asked to see you. In fact, I have alarming news. It seems that one of the agents of the Psmyth, a senior fan in the Fans-of-Tron, is here – on this very world.'

'No!' exclaimed Yodella.

'Indeed. He is called Dark Mole. You will easily recognise him by his star-shaped nose and the fine covering of black hair over his whole body. But do not be deceived – he is a deadly killer, a vicious monster. Being a mole, and shortsighted, and accordingly liable to bang into things, he has a head start in the business of the Farce.'

'We must confront him!'

'Yes. I shall alert the Metropolanet police force of his description, and hopefully we shall soon know his whereabouts.'

Shortly afterwards the meeting broke up. Yodella and the Jobbi Council returned to their luxury high-rise. Kwai Gone Bridge and his young apprentice took a different path, to a reasonably cheap bed and breakfast.

❋

No sooner was he alone, than Palpating summoned a holographic image of – yes, you guessed it – Dark Mole. The terrifying figure appeared: though small of stature and rather blinky, he emanated evil power. He wore moleskin trousers and a moleskin cloak (the equivalent of a human assassin dressing in humanskin trousers and cape; nasty, yes?). He squinted into the holographic projector.

'Yes my Lord?'

'The Jobbi knights,' said Palpating, 'Kwai Gone Bridge and Wobbli K'nobbli will shortly be passing through sector seventy-eight, on their way to their lodgings. They have with them a young child. You must seize this baby, Dark Mole. Carry him away – it is imperative that he be raised by the Dark Side. He is stronger in the Farce than any child I have seen. He will be a tremendous asset to the Psmyth.'

'Very good, my Lord. And the Jobbi knights?'

'Kill them.'

A smile passed over the furry face. 'Yes, my Lord.'

Chapter Four

Ah, a lightsword duel! We haven't seen one of those in ages, *have we. Excellent. I'm looking forward to this. Let's hope it's an exciting one, long-drawn out, and with graceful stunt-work and exciting music, ∂m-∂m-∂iddle-um, ∂m-∂m-∂iddle-um, DM-DM-DIDDLE-UM* DAH-DAHHH!!

Dark Mole ambushed Kwai Gone and Wobbli as they passed through sector seventy-eight. The battle was fierce. Kwai Gone was stabbed fatally in the chest, but Wobbli managed to kill the sinister Fan-of-Tron.

Chapter Five

Oh. Is that it then?

As he lay dying on the metal floor of sector seventy-eight, Kwai Gone Bridge breathed his last breath. 'My Thog,' he gasped, 'what have I done?'

'Got yourself killed, master,' said Wobbli, rather crossly. 'That's what.'

'Raise the child, Wobbli,' said Kwai. 'Raise him as a Jobbi. He will bring comical unbalance to the Farce.'

'Right,' said Wobbli. 'Anything else?'

'Not that I can think of right now. Oh – I remember. You know that packet of biscuits you bought? Then you couldn't find them? You looked everywhere for them?'

'I remember, master,' said Wobbli. 'You told me that the Dark Lords of the Psmyth had stolen the biscuits, to feed the Fans-of-Tron.'

'No,' rasped Kwai Gone. 'I ate them. I had a sort of piggish moment, I'm afraid.'

'That's alright, master,' said Wobbli. 'I can always just buy another packet of biscuits.'

But it was too late. Kwai Gone Bridge was dead;

and the mystery of the Fans-of-Tron was no nearer solution. Wobbli K'nobbli picked up the sleeping infant, tucked its blanket more tightly about it, and made his way out of sector seventy-eight.

Episode Two:

ATTACK OF
THE CLICHES

JANE SEESPOTRUN HAD BEEN ACCEPTED INTO THE JOBBI
ORDER, TO BE TRAINED BY WOBBLI BENT K'NOBBLI. MEAN-
WHILE, THE ACTIONS OF THE FANS-OF-TRON HAD BECOME MORE
DESPERATE. CO-ORDINATED BY A SHADOWY FIGURE CALLED LORD
TYRANNICAL, THESE OPPONENTS OF THE JOBBI ORDER CLAIMED
TO HAVE ACCESS TO A HIGHER PERCEPTION OF THE NATURE OF
REALITY – THE TRUE NATURE OF REALITY, THEY CALLED IT. IT
WAS, ONE MIGHT SAY, A MIGHTY SECRET. WHICH REMINDS ME
OF SOMETHING . . . WHAT WAS IT? . . . HMM HMM HMM . . .
AH YES, I REMEMBER. THE GREAT SECRET HIDDEN INSIDE THE DROID
AT THE BEGINNING OF THE FIRST PORTION OF THIS WORK. COULD THIS
LATER (ACTUALLY EARLIER) SECRET BE RELATED TO THAT EARLIER
(ACTUALLY LATER) SECRET? COULD THEY IN FACT BE THE *SAME* SECRET?
TIME WILL TELL. WINK WINK. ALRIGHT?
MEANWHILE, JANE SEESPOTRUN HAD GROWN INTO A HANDSOME
YOUTH. HE AND HIS MASTER K'NOBBLI HAD BEEN SUMMONED TO THE
CITY-PLANET METROPOLANET, TO JOIN A JOBBI ARMY THAT YODELLA AND
AND COUNCILLOR PALPATING PLANNED TO SEND TO DESTROY TYRANNICAL . . .

Chapter One

On Metropolanet

Many years passed, and Jane Seespotrun grew to full manhood. At sixteen he stood six feet six tall, which I'm sure you'll agree counts as full manhood, fuller than most and only two inches short of fullest manhood. He was as gangly and loose-limbed as you might expect a sixteen-year-old six-and-a-half-footer to be; but he was gifted with the Farce, such that his physical stupidity approached genius. He would stumble over a doorstep when coming into his house: but instead of falling flat on his nose, he would instead – spontaneously – perform a Level 8 'flailing arm, head down' tap dance across the hallway and into the kitchen. He could juggle four empty crystal vases without even thinking about it. If he put a wooden plank over his right shoulder and walked forty yards with it, turning from time to time, he could produce more devastation than a small neutron grenade.

It was clear that his skill surpassed that of his master, Old Wobbli K'nobbli.

The two Jobbi knights met with Pōkme on

Metropolanet, where she was attending the last of her scheduled Accountancy and Interplanetary Tax Law Seminars.

'Good to see you again, Wobbli,' said Pōkme as she stepped from her spaceplane. 'And you too Janey – how you've grown!'

'Gosh,' said Jane Seespotrun, turning the colour of raspberry sorbet. He clasped his hands tight together behind his back and thrust them as far down as his arms would allow. He turned his right foot through ninety degrees, and looked down at a piece of ground twenty feet away to the north-north-east. 'Gosh,' he said again.

Pōkme and Wobbli walked towards the conference hall. Jane fell into a loping stride behind them. 'Councillor Palpating has addressed the Council,' Wobbli informed her. 'It seems that the Fans-of-Tron are gathering strength. They intend to break away from the Galactic Federal Consolidation, and they repudiate the Jobbi order. Their slogan, somewhat mysteriously, is "Kill or Cure".'

'Sounds nasty.'

'There's little chance they will be able to do the Consolidation any real damage,' said Wobbli. 'We hold all the central positions. Indeed, Councillor Palpating is hoping to get himself elected Military Commander.

He seems confident that it would be an easy matter for somebody in the centre, here, to overwhelm any opposition. Master Yodella agrees with him.'

'I'm sure that's true,' said Pōkme.

'Gosh,' said Jane behind them. He seemed to be about to add something, but his tongue had cloven to the roof of his mouth.

'I must go in to hear whether the vote has gone our way. If it has, we'll soon be leading an army of Jobbi and yellow- and green-armoured troops to the planet of Gstritis to confront the Fans-of-Tron directly.'

It was a heated meeting, and there was much heckling from those delegates to the Council who opposed Councillor Palpating's plans. Luckily for Palpating, an ancient statute declared that councillors had to attend all meetings in person. Although the technology obviously existed whereby all the forty thousand councillors could relate with one another in a virtual mode, this technology was banned within the Council chamber itself. This chamber was, therefore, an absolutely titanic space: nearly eighteen kilometres from roof to its deep-sunken floor. The array of transparent cubicles holding the hordes of councillors stretched like a massively extended piece of optical art, like a vast sheet of chain mail curved around the inside of an empty barrel.

Heckling could only be heard from the Chair's cubicle if it originated from the cubicles immediately to the left, right or the one below. None of these councillors (who were all Palpating's friends) heckled.

'Since there is no opposition to my proposal,' Palpating spoke into the voice amplifier, 'there seems little point in delaying matters with a vote.' Far below him the faces of councillors distorted in rage and hatred were only visible to those who carried telescopes. Palpating inserted his own ear plugs, pressed a button in his cubicle, and his voice was projected through the enormous ceiling speakers at a volume loud enough to carry through the entire hall.

The Councillor's cubicle was protected by a speaker mounted on its top, that broadcast an inverted waveform of his words. This cancelled out the wave front of the shock-boom caused by the amplification. Few other cubicles had any protection. As their reinforced glass shattered, the councillors' many ears (on many parts of their alien bodies) started bleeding like that final slap on the glass bottom of the ketchup bottle that finally dislodges gouts of the red stuff.

'Excellent,' said Palpating, rubbing his hands together as he left the scene of carnage.

Later, Pōkme presented her end-of-session accounts

to Yodella himself, in the Jobbi central building. 'I
think you'll find that I have been able to maximise
your tax-deduction threshold,' she said.

'Excellent, this is,' said Yodella. 'Well, you have
done, Amidships. Come with us you must, to the
planet Gstritis, to be able to confirm for Tax Office
purposes the rebate liability per-head allowance protocols for our soldiery.'

'You intend to declare your entire army against
your tax liability?' said Amidships, in a matter-of-fact
voice.

'Deed, in,' said Yodella.

'Very well. This will be my final assignment to the
Jobbi order. After this my indenture will be at an
end.'

'True this is,' said Yodella. 'Ay-*iiiiii*! Ay-*iiiiii*!
Ay-*iiiiii*!'

Pōkme was given a cabin aboard the lead destroyer
of the Galactic Federal Consolidation battle fleet. She
was on the same corridor as Wobbli K'nobbli, Jane
Seespotrun and Master Yodella, and only a little way
from Councillor Palpating himself.

During the flight Pōkme could not help realising
two things. One was that the Councillor – one of the
most influential politicians in the Galaxy – was very

interested in young Janey. The old politician had spent a great deal of time with the young Jobbi, talking with him, listening to him gush. The other thing she could not help noticing was that Jane Seespotrun had developed a crush on her of an embarrassingly intense sort.

Shortly before landing on Gstritis, she passed him in a corridor, on her way back to her quarters to retrieve her tax manuals.

'Pōkme!'

'Janey! How are you! We haven't really had a chance to talk on this flight, have we?'

'I've been pretty busy,' said Seespotrun. 'Chancellor Palpating has been helping me perfect my skills with the Farce.'

'He's a very dedicated man.'

'He's ace,' said Jane with great passion. Then, as if conscious of having said too much, he blushed strawberry-red and looked away. Pōkme tried an 'I'll see you later, Janey, only now I've got to . . .' But, as if he had arrived with brutal suddenness at the moment of long-delayed action, Jane lurched forward and grabbed her elbow.

'I really fancy you, Pōkme,' he blurted. As soon as he had spoken he blushed purple, and looked to one side. 'I wrote you this poem . . .' He held out a rather tattered piece of flimsy; it looked as though it had been crumpled and smoothed out several times. Upon it was written:

> I am a worm, you are the sun
> I love you Pōkme, you are my everyone
> I love you like the stars and the moon
> If you could love me back that would really be a boon.
> Oh! Pōkme! Tell me your answer true!
> Do you love me as I love you!
> Do you?
> Say you do!
> Ooo!
> Do-be-do-be-doo!
> Me and You too!
> Our love could be a glue
> (to bind us together, I mean).

'Oh, Janey,' said Pōkme, reading the words. 'That's sweet. I'm really flattered – really I am. But . . .'

'Oh don't say "but"—' squealed Jane, putting his hands to his face and stomping through a three-hundred-sixty degree turn right there.

'Janey, I'm very fond of you, I really am, but . . .'

'No, *don't say "but"*—' shrieked Jane. 'Don't finish that part of the sentence! Don't crush my hope, don't crush my heart! Leave me with hope.'

'Jane,' said Pōkme, softly but firmly. 'I'm thirteen years older than you. That's just too big a gap . . . really. You're very nice, you really are, and maybe in ten years . . . I don't know.'

'Then there is hope!' cried Jane, crossing his arms over his chest, and adopting a facial expression somewhere between agony and happiness.

'It would be much better if you stopped putting me on a pedestal and went out with a girl your own age . . . don't you think? I'm sure the right girl is out there for you somewhere.'

Jane looked abashed, and then his face started to crumple in lines and clenches. Rather than cry before her, he turned on his heel and loped away along the corridor.

Later that same day, Pōkme was sipping a solitary coffee in the ship's canteen when Wobbli K'nobbli joined her.

'Are you ready for the coming battle, Madame Tax Assessor?' he asked, punching the code for a thimble of coffee into a passing Float-o-mat Drinks Dispenser.

'It won't be my first,' she said. 'But hopefully it will be my last.'

'A death wish, Ms Amidships?' said Wobbli, horrified.

'No – what I meant was that this assignment will mark the end of my indenture as a tax official. After it is complete I can return to my world and the utter obscurity of ordinary existence.'

'Ah,' said Wobbli. 'I see. Are you keen to disappear from public view?'

'Not at all,' sighed Pōkme. 'I would *love* to stay on Metropolanet, to become involved in real politics, perhaps to become a senior official – even (although I know this is impossible) ruler of the Galaxy. But there's no chance of it. The only pathway would be to become the Councillor of Ya!Boo!; and that would take twenty years of campaigning and political glad-handing on my home world; and even if I became Councillor I would be right at the bottom of the pecking order of the Galactic Federal Consolidation. I'm doomed to live out my days as a nothing, a nobody.'

'I sympathise,' said Wobbli. 'I too am doomed to obscurity.'

'But you are a Jobbi!'

'A very junior one. I have many enemies on the Jobbi Council, who will ensure that I never achieve a very high level in the order. In a year or so I will be sent on a semi-permanent secondment to a dead-end world at the back of beyond, and so the council will be rid of me. I've even visited the world in question: Tatuonweiner. You were there, of course. You know that it's an utterly miserable place. There I shall live my lonely, monk-like life, probably in some sort of desert hermitage.' Wobbli sighed. 'Still,' he added, trying to lift his own spirits. 'A Jobbi knight is not supposed to crave glory, so I'm sure I'll be happy.'

They both looked out through the viewing port. 'Sir Jobbi,' Pōkme asked. 'Will this battle be dangerous, do you think?'

'It will. The evil Lord Tyrannical is masterminding opposition to the Jobbis, and he has created a vast army.'

'Lord Tyrannical?'

'Yes. He used to be a Jobbi, you know. But I think he found it hard going at the Jobbi Academy, what with a surname like that. There was a certain amount of ribbing, and eventually he decided to go with the flow and convert to the Dark Side.'

'Is he very powerful?'

'Oo, yes. But we have Yodella with us; he is a great master of the Jobbi arts. And there's Jane Seespotrun – he may be young, but he's phenomenally gifted. A prodigy when it comes to pratfalls and creative slapstick, and well beyond his years in truncheon work.'

'He—' said Pōkme, uncertain whether she should

reveal this fact, 'he – declared his love for me, you know.'

'He never!' said Wobbli, grinning with surprise. 'Blimey. When?'

'Earlier today. Wrote me a poem.'

'A Jobbi is not supposed to be indulging in those sorts of . . . passions you know,' said Wobbli. 'What did *you* say?'

'I said I was flattered, but that I didn't think of him that way. He's still only a kid.'

'He is,' agreed Wobbli. 'Although one day he will grow up, and then he'll become one of the most powerful Jobbis in the Galaxy.'

'One day,' said Amidships, nodding.

Chapter Two

In which this portion of the adventure is, rather rapidly, brought to a conclusion. I'm only allowed so many pages, you see. Keep the costs down, they said. Philistines

Gstritis was a barren, red-rock world, striated across its surface with caverns, crevasses, crevices, in which vices were created, asses were craved and 'cav', the local currency, was earned. The Fans-of-Tron had constructed a vast robot army in a giant crater, with the help of the local winged aliens. These beings, shaped like man-sized Daddy-long-legses, or Daddies-long-legs, or whatever the plural is, were savage and violent.

There was a great deal of fighting. Sadly, I don't really have time to go into this fighting (see above), although there was an awful lot of it. Great big space-ships swooping close to the ground, scattering laser fire like sparks from a sparkler; smaller, vespine spaceships following arabesque flight paths, locked in dogfights with other vespine spaceships. Thousands of foot soldiers, some cloned, some robotic, fought fiercely. Battle sowed new black clouds in the sky from horizon to horizon.

In a side action the Daddii-longus-legii aliens captured Wobbli, Jane and Amidships and carried them away from the battle to a huge gladiatorial arena. Here they planned to kill these three, acting on the orders of the sinister Lord Tyrannical. They chose a markedly inefficient method of execution. Instead of simply cutting off their heads, or shooting them with guns, they tied them to posts and released giant reptiles into the arena to devour them. Jane's command of the Farce was more than enough for these beasts. He accidentally got free of his shackles, and tried to hurry to lend assistance to Pōkme. Instead of reaching her he clumsily ran into the pole to which he had been tied – with such force that he knocked it over. The pole, lying on the ground, had a spar projecting at right angles from its top. The closest giant reptile, lumbering across the ground towards Jane's supine body, trod on this up-sticking spar with a forepaw, causing the pole to pivot and lurch upwards, rather as a garden rake might do, thereby braining the monster and knocking it into unconsciousness. The second and third lumbering monsters did exactly the same thing.

At this point the Jobbi army arrived and rescued them all. It was almost too Farcical to be believed.

After his forces lost the fight in the stadium, Tyrannical leapt upon his hoverbike and zipped away over the desert. Wobbli, Pōkme, Jane and Palpating boarded a hoverchopper and zoomed after him. They swerved and ripped through the sky. Tyrannical flew into a cave, and his pursuers followed.

Inside they came across the patrician Lord of Evil struggling to get off his hoverbike. 'I seem,' he told them, 'to have got my boot snagged in this stirrup.'

'You are our prisoner now, evil Tyrannical,' said Wobbli, stepping forward with his lightsword at the ready.

'Are are prisoner?' queried the Dark one.

'*Are*,' repeated Wobbli, enunciating more clearly, '*our* – prisoner.'

'Very well,' Tyrannical replied, sighing. 'The game is up. It's a fair cop. You have me bang to rights. I surrender.'

Jane unsnagged Tyrannical's boot from the stirrup and Wobbli fitted him with forcefield handcuffs.

'You shall pay, Tyrannical, for your evil,' Wobbli announced.

'I'm sure I will,' Tyrannical replied, calmly. 'Although what you call "evil" seems to me the necessary path.'

'Pah!' scoffed Wobbli.

'Pah!' scoffed Jane.

'You both live according to the morality of the Jobbi Order,' observed Tyrannical. 'But when one has seen through to the true nature of the cosmos – as I have – then such a code seems . . . somehow irrelevant. You know what I mean, Palpating, don't you . . .'

The Councillor, who had been standing in the shadows, stepped forward. 'Hello there.'

A rather awkward silence settled on the group.

'So,' said Tyrannical, after a while. 'It'll be prison for me, will it?'

'I'm afraid so,' said Palpating. 'You have plotted against the Galactic Federal Consolidation. You and your mysterious "Fans-of-Tron" organisation.'

There was another silence.

'I mean,' Palpating added. 'You have.'

'I have,' agreed Tyrannical.

There was another pause. It stretched, sagged, and became very awkward indeed.

'The *weather* on this planet is . . .' Wobbli began.

'*I've* got a question,' said Pōkme, at the same time.

341

They broke off together.

'After you,' said Pōkme.

'No, no, you first, please,' insisted Wobbli with a forced smile.

'Well,' said Pōkme. 'I was just wondering . . .'

Everybody was looking at her. A little intimidated, she trailed off.

'What?' prompted Tyrannical.

'It's just a stupid question,' said Pōkme, blushing a little. 'I was wondering *why* your mysterious organisation is called Fans-of-Tron.'

Everybody looked at Tyrannical.

'It's not a stupid question at all,' he replied, affably. 'It's a very good question. I'm just not sure you want to know the answer to it.'

'Well now that I've asked it . . .' said Pōkme.

Tyrannical looked, slowly, from face to face. 'I will happily answer this question,' he said. 'But I warn you – it will change everything for you.'

'Let me get this straight,' said Wobbli, stepping forward. 'You're saying that if you tell us, in straight-forward terms, why your gang is called what it's called, then our *whole perspective of the cosmos* will change?'

'Yes,' said Tyrannical, quietly.

'Well go ahead,' said Wobbli, grinning disbelievingly. 'I'm eager to hear what you have to say.'

For several minutes Tyrannical was silent. Finally he said, 'You remember *Tron*, of course? The visual artwork?'

'From the twentieth century?' clarified Pōkme. 'Of course. We were taught it at school. It's a great literary classic.'

'You remember what it is *about*, though?'

'Yes.'

'Well,' said Tyrannical. 'Well.' He was silent for a further minute. When he started speaking again there was something different in his voice; something almost throbbing with significance, an almost hypnotic tone.

'Look at the galaxy in which we live,' said Tyrannical, addressing his small audience. 'Just *look* at it. Does it seem real to you? Of course not.'

'What do you mean?' said Jane.

'What do I mean? Come. It's too obvious. You know the classics of Old Earth culture? Of course you do; we *all* do. They are the masterworks that shape our schooling, the word-art and the visual-art from the Golden Era, the twentieth century.'

Nobody could see what this had to do with anything. After a long pause Pōkme said: 'of course.'

'You know the Bond movies and the advertisements for fruit in tins, and most of all you know the *Star Treks* and the *Dunes*, the *science fiction*?'

'Naturally,' said Wobbli. 'We are all of us cultured people, educated in the classics.'

'Well then, you must know the *Matrix* films.'

'Of course.'

'They provide the key – to the true nature of this so-called reality.'

'I don't see what you're trying to insinuate . . .'

'You don't? When it is so obvious? When it is *so* obvious that this so-called world which we inhabit, in which we run around and bump into one another, is nothing but a tissue of quotations from the works of science fiction? Pick a world, from the many worlds in our Galaxy. Metropolanet is from Asimov's *Foundation*. Tatuonweiner is from Herbert's *Dune*. This person quotes – without even realising it – from *The Hitch-Hiker's Guide to the Galaxy*. These spaceships have exactly the contours of ships from *Babylon 5*. Those aliens are exactly like the ones in *Predator*. Is there anything in our world that doesn't have an antecedent in science fiction? Yes, there are some things. Are those things original to our cosmos? No, they are not original to our cosmos: they are drawn from another set of artworks from the Golden Age: from Monty Python, from slapstick comedy, from Bennihil. Is there anything else? No – *nothing else. Everything* in our world is derived from one of those two sources. Our world is a science-fiction template, modified by a twentieth-century comic sensibility. Don't you see it?'

Nobody said anything.

'I suppose,' Tyrannical went on, 'that familiarity has drawn its usual veil over our eyes, and our minds. Our noses are pressed so close up against the canvas of quotation and allusion that we no longer see it for what it is any more. Yet what it *is*, is inescapable. We cannot avoid the truth.'

'What truth?' asked Wobbli.

'That we are living in a virtual reality, an artificial world constructed out of the orts and scraps of twentieth-century science fiction, flavoured by bits and pieces of comedy.'

'That's preposterous,' blustered Wobbli.

'Is it, my young Jobbi? I don't think it is. Palpating knows that I speak truly. He has known for a long time.'

Everybody looked at Palpating.

'I'm afraid it's true,' said the Councillor, in his soft voice. 'Tyrannical is quite correct. Our world is a complex illusion, a detailed programmed reality.'

'It seems that our consciousnesses are trapped in this second-hand reality,' said Tyrannical. 'As in Philip K Dick, or as in the *Matrix*, our bodies are elsewhere whilst our minds roam about this virtual

Galaxy. And this imaginary world – which so many of us take for real – this programmed world seems to have been designed, cobbled together I would say, by somebody who really, *really* likes the twentieth-century science fiction and comedy. This programmer has drawn on what he, or she, knows and likes, and looked no further.'

'But – *why?*' asked Pōkme, in an anguished voice.

'Ah,' said Tyrannical. 'That is indeed the most pertinent question. It is also the question hardest to answer adequately. Our – *programmer*, let us call him – our jailer, perhaps – we know he has read H Beam Piper's *Little Fuzzy* and seen *2001* and *Metropolis*; we know he loves *Dune* and Asimov and E E "Doc" Smith's interplanetary superweapons. We can deduce all this from the cosmos in which we find ourselves, this Galaxy in which every SF cliché is rolled up together to make a textured reality. But the one thing we cannot deduce is – why. What did we do to find ourselves imprisoned in this reality?' Tyrannical shrugged. 'Perhaps you know, Councillor Palpating? For I confess I do not.'

'I know one thing,' said Palpating, softly. 'I know an ordinary person has no chance of deciphering this puzzle, this rebus. But I find myself wondering – could a person at the very top of things . . .'

'A powerful person,' agreed Tyrannical.

'The most powerful person in this virtual cosmos – a president, say, or emperor – I wonder whether such a person might not be better placed to uncover this great truth?'

'I see,' said Wobbli, turning to face Tyrannical. 'Is that why you went over to the Dark Side of the Farce? Is that why you have plotted to accumulate power at any cost?'

'Is it?' said Tyrannical, offhand. 'Perhaps it is. It's hard to be precise. I believe my initial conversion to the Dark Side of the Farce was predicated upon my realisation that I was trapped inside this virtual world. It seemed to me then, and it seems to me now, that the least I could do was *oppose* this sham. To fight it, to attempt to wreck it, to destroy. What else was I to do? To collaborate with it? To go along with it, meekly, whilst the mysterious programmer pushed us around like clockwork toys? No! I resist.'

'Except,' Pōkme pointed out, 'that your attempts to wreck the virtual reality in fact rebound upon the people trapped within that virtual reality. You don't injure the fabric of this imaginary cosmos; you only injure people.'

'That,' said Tyrannical, 'is indeed a problem. Well, I have surrendered. My particular rebellion is at an end. Perhaps all rebellions are doomed from the beginning; every rebellion must end.'

'If what you say is true,' said Wobbli, who was still struggling with the concept, 'then we must alert the Galactic population.'

'Must we? I suppose so. I think you'll find that they won't care. As long as they can get on with what is important – living, loving, party-going – they are happy. Why would it matter to them whether the backdrop to their lives is a real reality or a simulated reality?'

At this point there came a cry from the cave-mouth: ' Tyrannical!'

It was Master Yodella.

'Found you I have! Your rebellion *end* I will.'

'Wait,' called Wobbli. 'Master Yodella, it's alright, he has surrendered to . . .'

But Yodella, crying yodella-*i-heeeee*, was oblivious, as if he could not hear Wobbli's words. Terrier-like, the tiny green figure leapt through the air. His light-sword flared with light, briefly; with one stroke Yodella broke it against the rock floor of the cave; and, following through with a fluid movement, the Jobbi Master jumped up and severed Tyrannical's head from his neck with the jagged end.

The head bumped onto the floor rather like a

football, albeit an irregularly-shaped football with a bony core and filled with fluid.

'Master!' cried Wobbli. 'He had already surrendered!'

'He had?' said Yodella. 'Had he? Dear, oh. Mind, never.' He strolled out of the cave, whistling *Yankee doodle dandy* with the notes backwards.

Chapter Three

On Ya!Boo!

Councillor Palpating and Pōkme Amidships were strolling by the turquoise lakeside on Ya!Boo! In the distance, Jane Seespotrun was trying to skim pebbles over the calm waters. 'It's so hard to accept,' Amidships was saying, 'that all this, which seems so *real* – that it's nothing but an elaborate computer simulation of reality?'

'I'm afraid it's true, my dear,' said Palpating.

'But I feel devalued . . . as if my life doesn't really count.'

'You shouldn't feel that way, my dear girl. Tyrannical, before his unfortunate demise, did make one very important point. It's our *consciousnesses* that matter, not the environment in which we find ourselves. There's validity in our thoughts, in our hopes, dreams, loves and passions. Our minds are the same.'

'I suppose so,' she replied. 'I suppose we must go on living, as before. Only the question nags at my mind. *Why?*'

'Why, yes,' agreed Palpating. 'Why is a very good

question.' They had come to a marble bench. 'Shall we
sit?'

'Yes.'

For a while the two of them simply sat, breathing
in the air which, although it wasn't real, still tasted
cool and fragrant in their mouths; admiring the view
which, though artificially constructed, was still beautiful. The plop-plop-plop of Jane's pebble skimming
over the water was just audible.

'You're unattached, I think?' asked Palpating
shortly, in his quiet voice. 'No partners? Boyfriends,
girlfriends, significant others?'

'Not *really* any of your business, I'd say,' replied
Amidships, smiling pleasantly.

'No, quite, quite,' conceded the Councillor. He
looked, theatrically, away into the middle distance.
'It's just that I happen to know young Seespotrun has
– what shall we say? Developed a tender passion for
you.'

Despite herself, Amidships blushed a little. 'I
know,' she said. 'He told me he'd got a bit of a crush
on me. It's kind of awkward.'

'You do not reciprocate the sentiments?'

'Jane's good-looking, and kind of fun to be
around,' said Amidships. 'And his Farcical powers
are impressive. And entertaining. But – love him?

He's just too young. Who knows, maybe in five years. Or ten.'

'Well,' said Palpating smoothly. 'I may have a proposition to put to you. In the way of a business proposition. I want you to think carefully about it before you reply. And before I say anything else, I want to make it plain: I intend to become the most powerful individual in the Galaxy before very long. And I intend to make young Seespotrun my deputy.'

Amidships held her breath. A chill seemed to have settled over the scene. 'That,' she said, eventually, 'is quite an announcement to make.'

Palpating waved his hand dismissively, and adjusted his bowler hat. 'You know I'm not merely boasting; I'm speaking the plain truth. It's an inevitability. The Council is in the palm of my hand already.'

'You'd need a big hand for that!' Amidships joked, trying to lighten the mood.

'Not a big hand,' said Palpating, darkly. 'Just a big palm.'

Amidships tried briefly to work out what this meant, but couldn't fathom it.

'Allow me, my dear,' said Palpating, 'merely to tell you a few home truths. As it stands, I shall soon be the most powerful person in the cosmos, and Jane

Seespotrun the second most powerful. Were a young woman to *marry* my second-in-command, she would be in a position of enormous influence. She would be close to the centre of power. She might,' and here Palpating's soft voice became even softer, 'be in a position to find out more about this SF-based universe in which we are trapped . . . maybe even find a way out . . .'

For a long moment, and despite her better instincts, Amidships's eyes grew wide with the possibilities.

'I can see you are interested, my dear,' said Palpating, getting to his feet. 'I can see it in your eyes. Just think it over, that's all I ask. And remember this: although you do not, perhaps, find young Jane very attractive right now, they do say that *power* can be a very effective aphrodisiac. And he will become very powerful in due course.'

'I don't understand,' said Amidships. 'What do *you* get out of this?'

'What do I get? I get to keep my powerful young deputy happy. I get to say to him "you want Amidships? I'll get you Amidships", and thereby impress him with my power to command and bind him to me with bonds of gratitude. That's what I get. Goodbye my dear. Oh – and one more thing.'

Amidships's head was reeling. 'What?'

'That list of SF classics, from which this enormous, complex simulation had been derived – you remember it? *Dune, Foundation, Tron, Hitchhiker's Guide to the Galaxy . . .*'

'I remember,' said Amidships.

'There was one SF text that Tyrannical didn't mention, but which is in fact the most important of all. Most important because it underlies everything else.'

'And what's that?'

'*Carcinoma Angels*,' said Palpating, smiling as if at some secret joke.

'I'm afraid I haven't read it,' said Amidships.

'You haven't? That's a pity. Because it's really most illuminating, for circumstances such as ours. Goodbye my dear.'

Episode Three:

REVENGE OF THE RETURN OF THE SON OF PSMYTH RIDES AGAIN: THE NEXT GENERATION – THE EARLY YEARS

LORD TYRANNICAL WAS DEAD AND THE FANS-OF-TRON HAD BEEN CONTAINED. AND YET THE DARK SIDE OF THE FARCE – THAT HIDEOUS PERVERSION OF JOBBI PRINCIPLES KNOWN ONLY AS 'THE PSMYTH', STILL SPREAD, TENTACLE-LIKE, THROUGH THE GALAXY. ON A THOUSAND WORLDS, DARK DEEDS WERE DOING AND INDEED DONE. NOBODY KNEW WHERE THE CENTRE OF THIS DARK POWER MIGHT BE. IT WAS A MYSTERY. I MEAN, OBVIOUSLY, *YOU* KNOW WHO THE SECRET LORD OF THE PSMYTH IS, IT'S PALPATING OBVIOUSLY; BUT YOU'VE GOT THE BENEFIT OF HINDSIGHT, HAVEN'T YOU. YES, YES, JANE SEESPOTRUN TURNS INTO DARK FATHER; AND YES COUNCILLOR PAL-PATING TURNS INTO THE IMPERIAL EMPEROR AND THE OPEN EMBODIMENT OF EVIL, AND SO ON. WHAT I'M SAYING IS THAT PEOPLE *AT THE TIME* COULDN'T SEE IT. THEN AGAIN, THERE WAS THE STARTLING REVELATION, IN THE LAST EPISODE, THAT THE WHOLE GALAXY WAS NOT SO MUCH REAL, MORE A *MATRIX*-STYLE VIRTUAL REALITY, CONCOCTED BY WHO-KNOWS-WHOM OUT OF QUOTATIONS FROM TWENTIETH-CENTURY SCIENCE FICTION, FOR WHO-KNOWS-WHAT PURPOSE. THAT WAS UNEXPECTED, THOUGH, WASN'T IT? GOOD GRIEF. DO YOU THINK THAT PARTICULAR REVELATION'LL HAVE SOME CONSEQUENCES FOR THE NEXT EPISODE? WHAT DO YOU RECKON?

'You've got kind of fat,' said Jane Seespotrun, as he walked arm-in-arm with his wife, the beautiful, full-figured mature woman Pōkme Amidships. They strolled along a marble palisade beside a turquoise lake, past the red and yellow fruiting blooms of the rhinodendron bushes, on the garden planet of Ya!Boo!

'I *beg* your pardon?' returned Pōkme.

'Kind of,' said Janey, looking over the water, 'fat.'

'Janey,' she replied. 'I think it's time to be open with you.'

'What do you mean?'

'I'm pregnant, Janey.'

'Gosh!'

'Well yes. In fact, I've been pregnant for eight and a half months now.'

'Is that good?'

'Um . . . *I* think so.'

'Right. Will you get better?'

'Better? Janey, I don't think you understand . . .

pregnancy is a state in which a child develops in a female's uterus.'

'Crikey! Can I go play with the paravideo game console now? Please?'

'Janey, in a minute. This is important. You do know what happens when pregnancy comes to an end?'

'Only I've got this new game, *Brian Lara Croft IV* – it's a combination cricket-simulator and zombie-shoot set inside an ancient Mayan pyramid. It's just wizard.'

'Look, for just one minute I want you to be grown-up about this. When this child is born, you and I are going to have to look after it: to raise it. It's a big responsibility . . .'

'Alright, *alright*,' said Jane Seespotrun, twisting away from his wife's arm, 'you don't need to keep going on about it. I'll help you raise the stupid child. Can I go and play the paravideo *now*?'

'Alright. Give me a kiss first . . .'

But Jane had run lopingly away. Princess Amidships stood looking after him, a mixture of affection and infuriation on her face. From behind one of the rhinodendron bushes a familiar figure stepped: Wobbli Bony K'nobbli. He stepped beside the Princess. 'Has he gone?'

'Off to kill zombies in a computer-constructed

virtual reality,' said Pōkme, sighing. 'I sometimes wish that he'd grow up just a little.'

'Well,' said Wobbli, slipping his arm around Pōkme's waist. 'If he's going to be submerged in his Vid-R, that at least gives us a little time together . . .'

Later, in a white marble chamber with a broad casement looking over a broad sunlit fields of feathergrass, Pōkme and Wobbli were lying on a large bed together. Curtains of white samite billowed like jellyfish at the open window. From a hidden speaker there came the soothing sound of lute music.

'I hate,' said Wobbli, 'that you're married to him. I hate that you can't marry me.'

'I know,' said Pōkme. 'You don't need to be jealous, you know. He's sweet, in his way; but he *is* only a kid. He's not a mature man, like you. But let's look at the two sides. On the one hand, there's Jane – he's Palpating's favourite disciple, and when Palpating seizes control of the Senate (apparently that's set for next Thursday) he will become second-in-command. If I am his wife, and you his friend, then we will have tremendous opportunities for influence. And influence, at that level, means power. On the other hand, there's you – and much as I love you, Wobbli, you're a junior Jobbi, concerned largely with arcane

359

and piffling matters. You're mistrusted by many on the Council because your accent keeps wobbling from Cheltenham to Edinburgh-Morningside. And I'm just another civil servant from a rural backwater world. Without this leg-up we'd never be in the position we are now in. If you and I were married we'd be condemned to a life of poverty and exclusion from the corridors of power. It's better this way.'

'He has got a temper on him,' said Wobbli. 'Your husband. Only a kid he *may* be, but he's taller than me, more muscled and considerably less arthritic . . . if he finds out about us two . . .'

'He won't.'

'But if he does?'

'He won't,' repeated Pōkme, firmly. 'We will just have to make sure he never does. Do you understand?'

'Well I'm certainly not going to tell him.'

'Or anybody.'

'No – or anybody.'

'Promise?'

Wobbli sighed. 'Pōkme, a Jobbi's promise is a powerful thing; an utterly binding thing. If I promise, then I can never break that promise.' Amidships looked sternly at him. 'And,' he added, 'I promise.'

'Good,' she said, moving her pregnant but still highly desirable body closer to his.

*

Later, when they were lying in one another's arms restfully for the second time that afternoon, Pōkme said, 'it's strange.'

'What is?'

'All this,' she gestured with her eyes at the window.

'What – the curtains?'

'I mean, everything in the cosmos. To think it's all nothing but a metaphor – an elaborate virtual reality. It seems *so real*.'

'It *is* real. It's real to us, and we're what matters. Besides, you're forgetting: the consciousnesses within this Virt-Re are *actual* consciousnesses. *We're* real – our thoughts, our dreams, our loves and desires. That's all real. As a great philosopher once said: *cogito ergo sum*. I think, therefore I can add up. And *I* think that you and I add up to something special, regardless of whatever environment we find ourselves in. You need to hold on to what's important.'

'I suppose so,' replied Pōkme, taking hold of something important. 'But that's why we must get to the top – or at least *close* to the top – of the structures of power. We need to be in a position to find out everything we can about this science-fiction virtual reality. We need to find if we can get *out* . . .'

'From where I am right now,' cooed Wobbli, 'staying in looks pretty good.'

Days passed. One day a Council shuttle dropped through the perfect blue sky, bearing the Councillor. He made his way into the palace, and up the marble stairs.

'Good afternoon, young Jobbi,' said Councillor Palpating, stepping through the doorway into Jane Seespotrun's rumpus room.

'Golly! Hello!' said Jane, leaping up from the floor (on which he had been lying stomach-down, playing *The Sims: Recursive*). 'How wonderful to see you!'

'You know, young Jane, I regard myself as your patron.'

'I'll always be phenomenally grateful to you for everything you've done for me, sir,' gushed Jane. 'If it weren't for you, I don't suppose I would ever have been able to woo my beloved, or to have accumulated so much power and respect.'

'We help each other, my friend. We help each other. I draw on your strength in the Farce. You make an excellent deputy. Together we're a team.'

'It's awfully nice of you to say so,' said Jane, beaming.

'I do say so. I just saw Amidships, walking along the marble promenade.'

'Isn't she wonderful!' said Jane. 'I'm so lucky to have her – I know I owe it all to you sir.'

'And I hear you're soon to be a father?'

'That's right. The scans say the child is a boy. I've already decided on a name – Luke. What do you think?'

'I think it's a wonderful name. Actually I wanted to have a chat about something else. You know that this Thursday . . .'

Jane's grin grew even wider. He waggled his eyebrows suggestively, and tapped the side of his nose with one long finger. 'Nuff said, sir,' he said. '*I* know. I'll be there, sir. At your side.'

'Yes,' said the Councillor. 'Well, without the amateur dramatics, we both know that on that day I shall use Council protocols to have myself declared Emperor for Life, and have my opponents imprisoned. And you shall be my deputy. Yes? Second in command of the whole Galaxy?'

'Yes sir!' beamed Jane. 'I'm looking forward to it most awfully.'

'Well – there's one final piece of the political puzzle I have yet to explain to you. Take a seat, dear boy, and I'll tell you all about it.'

Jane sat down. Palpating similarly lowered himself into a chair.

'Now,' the Councillor said. 'You've heard, I'm sure, of the Dark Side of the Farce? The Lords of the Psmyth?'

'Yes sir,' said Jane, his brow creasing in disapproval. 'Awful coves.'

'That is the common prejudice,' agreed Palpating. 'So how would you feel if I told you that I, in fact, were one of their number? That, in fact, I was the chief architect of Psmyth power?'

'I'd be pretty jolly ghastly-flabbered, to be honest, sir,' said Jane, looking simultaneously puzzled and astonished – a combination of emotions that few faces can pull off, but which Jane Seespotrun managed with ingenuous ease.

'Let me tell you something about the Dark Side, my boy,' said Palpating. 'After I've explained the true nature of things, you may decide that, of the two sides it's the better side to be on. For one thing you need to know my true name. It's Dark Charlie . . .'

He talked on. And as he talked, Jane Seespotrun's eyes grew wider and wider.

Things changed after that. Amidships was only too aware that her young husband had become gloomier;

as if moving from a sunny to a gloomy portion of his extended adolescence. He took to wearing black, and lurking in his room for long stretches of time. When the chief maid (a Keflapod woman called Psoriasis) tried to get inside to change the sheets and clean up a bit, Jane shooed her away.

The big Thursday came. Jane boarded a shuttle with Palpating and flew away to Metropolanet, to help his mentor seize power in the Council.

Whilst he was away Psoriasis finally got a chance to tidy up his room. And it was while she was doing that she came across Jane's diary. Naturally, she flicked through it; and twenty minutes later she was standing before her mistress with a concerned look on her face.

'Your husband,' she said. 'He has gone over to the Dark Side. It's in his diary.'

'No!' exclaimed Amidships. 'Show me.'

Friday 13th. Got up. Had pop tarts. Finally mastered the chord change from G* to A$-minus on the Altarian electro-lute. Have decided what my name will be as an evil Lord of the Psmyth. Since I'm to be a father now, I figured Dark Father. It's got a good ring to it, I think. All evil Lords of the Psmyth have to have the first name Dark. Which I think is pretty excellent actually, and certainly a better name than Jane, which I've always felt is something of a girlie name, actually. Anyway, Councillor Palpating tells me that Wobbli Bent and Amidships will never join the Dark Side, and therefore they must be sent to a prison world, or perhaps executed, we'll work that out later. Last week that would have bothered me, especially Amidships who's really nice. But she's got so fat (pregnant I know, but what's the difference?) I've kind of gone off her a bit actually – and besides: once you're on the Dark Side, you can't be influenced by mere personal or emotional connections, that's what my pal Palpating tells me.

'Great Thog!' cried Amidships. 'We must tell Wobbli Bent K'nobbli, straight away!'

Far away, on Metropolanet, the coup went entirely according to plan. All of Councillor Palpating's – *Emperor* Palpating as he now was – enemies had been despatched to the prison world. An attempt to arrest the new Emperor, a desperate last throw by the out-going Council, was thwarted by a dazzling display of Farcical slapstick from Palpating's young sidekick. The Council guards were all knocked unconscious with a plate of ham sandwiches, a chair and a pencil.

By Friday the new Emperor had established his cronies in all positions of power on Metropolanet, and was flying back with Seespotrun to Ya!Boo!.

'Now we must deal with your wife, my friend,' Palpating announced. 'She cannot be trusted.'

'It is a pity,' said Seespotrun. 'But I suppose it's the way the cookie crumbles.'

'Cookies, yes. I propose we imprison her on Prison World XII. Wobbli K'nobbli we can send to Prison World III – it's less pleasant there, but he's a Jobbi knight, so he should have the wherewithal to cope with the hardship.'

'Would I be able to visit Amidships from time to time?' Seespotrun asked, tentatively.

'My dear young apprentice,' said Palpating, sternly. 'Remember what we talked about. I hope you're not allowing sentiment to affect you? The Dark Side cannot afford sentimentality.'

'You're right of course,' said Seespotrun, in a low voice.

'No, I think it's best if you don't visit. Unless – of course – unless she changes her ways, and is prepared to join the Dark Side. But I don't think we should hold our breath on *that* count. We both know how unlikely that is.'

'But,' said Jane. 'There's the child. My son . . .'

'I shall take care of the child,' whispered Palpating. 'Leave his upbringing to me.'

'But,' said Jane. 'He's my child, after all.'

'Very well,' said Palpating, looking a little crosser. 'If you *really* want to be saddled with the night-time feeding, the nappy-changing, the colic, the vomiting, all the actual business of raising a child?'

Jane thought about this. 'I suppose not,' he said, reluctantly.

'Wouldn't you rather perfect your High Scores on *Zapping Zombies at Zombie Zoo*? Practise the Dark Side? There's a trick I can teach you that will enable you to crush peoples' windpipes without even touching them! – you'll like that.'

That sounded like a much more productive use of time. 'Golly,' said Jane. 'That *does* sound more exciting than changing nappies,' he said.

'You shall be reunited to young Luke when he is an adult,' Palpating promised. 'This I guarantee. And when he is fully grown, I foresee that he will join us in the Dark Side of the Farce. Then you, he and I will rule the Galaxy as a triumvirate.'

'A what?'

'A three-way power-sharing structure.'

'Wizard! Can I go play my electric Altarian lute now? I got the Death Metal songbook and singalong cassette in the post this morning.'

'Off you go.'

Jane Seespotrun ran off to his cabin.

Palpating sat, looking through the viewing window at the scratchy pattern of stars stretched by the topological impossibilities of hyperspace travel. His eye seemed to take everything in, as if, truly, he could own it all as his personal property: as if he could put it in his pocket. Whether that was because his pocket was large, or because the whole simulated *Tron*-like universe was small, was unclear.

Shortly the craft slipped out of hyperspace and into orbit around Ya!Boo!

'We must leave, *now*,' insisted Wobbli for the seventieth time. 'Your husband – and the new Emperor – could return at any time.'

'I can't leave now,' panted Amidships. 'It so happens that *now* I'm right in the middle of labour. Uggggnnn!'

'*Push*, my lady,' said Psoriasis. 'Push!'

'I am pushin-nnnn-nnnngggg-ggggg,' Amidships replied.

Wobbli paced the birthing chamber. 'We can't afford to wait,' he muttered.

The Keflapod nursemaid tutted crossly. 'My lady won't be ready for a spaceflight for several weeks,' she insisted. 'The shock of hyperspace would kill her.'

'Weeks?' moaned Wobbli. 'That's terrible! Palpating and your husband will be here in *hours*. What can we do?'

Amidships had reached a calm point between contractions. She puffed noisily as Psoriasis mopped her sweating brow. 'The timing is unfortunate,' she agreed. 'If the contractions had held off for only a couple of days, we could have got clean away. But, as it is, I don't see what we can do.'

'Never mind *us*,' said Wobbli. 'What about our child? We cannot allow him to fall into the clutches of the Dark Side.'

'You could take him,' said Amidships, in a low voice. 'When he's born. Take him and a milk synthesiser and a nappy fabricator far away – you can go, even if I cannot.'

'Leave you? Never!' cried Wobbli.

'Think *straight*,' said Amidships. 'That way you and the baby will both be safe. You can go somewhere far away – you can organise resistance to this sinister New World Order.'

'But what about you? And, besides – when your husband sees his child has gone, he'll search the whole cosmos to recover him.'

'Perhaps you're right,' said Amidships crossly. 'It's only an – ararrrrgh! Ggnnnngh!'

Psoriasis bent over her mistress and tried to ease the pain of her parturition.

'Excuse me, Psoriasis,' said Wobbli. 'If you don't

mind me asking. What's that large unsightly lump on the back of your head, between your two tentacles?'

'Is this the time?' Amidships gasped, wide eyed, 'for a question like that? Gggggggggg.'

'That?' replied Psoriasis, feeling round the back of her head with her left hand even as she mopped her mistress's face with her right. 'I'm not sure to be honest. A daughter, I think.'

'A *daughter*? You mean, that's your child *growing* there?'

'Sure. That's how Keflapods give birth. Makes more sense than your crazy human way if you ask me – all this pain and blood and pushing? No thanks. With us, a new baby just grows on the back of the head. When it's ready it buds off.'

'And then?'

The Keflapod shrugged. 'Don't know. Don't care. We leave them to fend for themselves.'

'As soon as they're *born*?'

'That's the Keflapod way, yes.'

'Darling,' said Wobbli, taking Amidships's hand. 'I think I've got an idea . . .' The last syllable of this last word transformed into a cry of 'aaargh!' as Amidships, her body wracked by a new contraction, squeezed his hand hard enough to pop his knuckles.

❀

After his ship touched down on the Municipal Ya!Boo! landing strip, the new Emperor left Seespotrun on board in his cabin, and made his way alone to the palace. He walk bow-legged, his cane bowing out in his right hand. As he neared the main gate he indulged himself in one quick move – a sideways jump into the air, as if pivoting on his right hand on top of his cane, and a quick kicking together of his heels, before landing again on two feet and walking on.

He strode through the gates of the palace, up the broad stairs, and into Pōkme's chambers. Amidships was sitting in her bed, cradling a small child in her arms.

'Palpating!' she exclaimed in a not-pleased-to-see-you sort of voice. He had grown a small moustache. 'What are you doing here?'

'Just popping in for a visit, my dear,' said Palpating, greasily. 'Do you mind if I sit down?'

'I'd rather you didn't,' replied Amidships. 'I know your true motives, Palpating. I know you have aligned yourself with the forces of Darkness. I know that you are one of the Psmyth, and that now you have seized control of the Council you will probably become an evil tyrant, and attempt to purge the Jobbi utterly from the cosmos.'

'You seem to know a great deal,' said Palpating pleasantly. 'And I think I will help myself to a seat, despite your inhospitality.'

'You won't get away with it,' said Amidships, hotly.

'The seat? Or the plot to seize power? I've already got away with the latter, my dear; and that means that, as the Galaxy's most powerful individual, I can do what I like with any chair I come across.'

'I know you've seduced my husband to the Dark Side of the Farce!' exclaimed Amidships. 'He's too young and hot-headed to think clearly. He's a straw blown in the breeze. You seduced him!'

'In a purely political sense, yes. But I'm being rude – I haven't complimented you on your child!' He was on his feet and at the bedside in no time at all. 'A beautiful baby – oh! A *girl*, is it?'

'That's right,' said Amidships, defiantly.

'But the scans indicated a boy . . .'

'They were wrong.'

Palpating looked hard at Amidships. 'I see. Jane was expecting a son, you know. He's got a name for him already. Not that I care a pin one way or the other. It's not as if he's ever going to actually see the child . . .'

'You monster!'

'Yes. You see, young Jane is very powerful with the Farce, and will be a crucial ally in my campaign for Galactic domination. But, as you said, he is hotheaded, changeable, easily swayed. I will need some leverage to persuade him to remain loyal to me. You and your child will do very nicely. My personal troops are, as we speak, landing in the courtyard. Shortly they will take you and your daughter to a certain prison planet. Don't worry; you'll be very well looked after. Spacious, though secure, quarters. All the food and entertainment you need. You can even take your droid with you for company. And comfort breaks.'

'Lock me away all you like!' cried Amidships defiantly. 'I'll never succumb! I'll wilt and die in captivity . . .'

'Perhaps you will, my dear, in a few years,' said Palpating offhandedly. 'It hardly matters. The robots on the prison world will be able to raise the child, and it's the child that matters. As long as Jane knows that I control his child, he will never dare betray me. And so, my dear, neither you nor your lovely offspring will ever be allowed to escape – not until young sweetums there, in your arms, is fully grown up.'

'I see you have grown a moustache, Palpating,' said

Amidships, fiercely. 'It appears you have modelled it on Adolf Hitler – how appropriate!'

'My dear,' said Palpating, pleasantly. 'You are barking up the wrong tree entirely.'

Wobbli K'nobbli cradled his son in his arms as his spacecraft whipped through the complexities of super-subspace. He was heading for Tatuonweiner, where he had located a couple of adoptive parents. He had considered raising the child himself; but, he realised, that might draw too much attention to the lad. No, better to give him to the Svennsons, in a wilderness on the outskirts of a dead-end town in an economically impoverished world. Wobbli resolved to stay nearby, perhaps building himself some sort of hermitage, just to keep an eye on things – at least for the time being. When the threat from the Power of the Psmyth had been defeated by the remaining Jobbi Order (and Wobbli was confident that victory would come soon) then he would re-emerge into the Galaxy at large. But until that time, he would lie low.

He hoped he would only have to wait until Amidships could escape, and join him on Tatuonweiner. And he was sure that Amidships would find a way to escape from Palpating's clutches. He wasn't sure how, but she would surely find a way . . .

'You are the embodiment of evil!' Amidships exclaimed.

'On the contrary, my dear,' Palpating was whispering. 'I'm not evil. And I will tell you why I am not evil. I will tell you exactly what I told young Jane – the thing that persuaded him to join me, and my side of the battle. You know, Jane Seespotrun may be young, but his heart is in the right place.'

'I used to think so,' retorted Amidships. 'Until I learnt he had joined with *you*.'

'But he has joined me because he thinks he is doing the right thing. He now knows what I know – the secret of the Cosmos.'

'Secret!' scoffed Amidships. 'What secret?'

'You know, of course, that our life is not an actual life; not an *authentic* life. That we are living in a metaphor, a metaphor drawn from the works of twentieth-century science fiction. Yes?'

'You forget: I was there,' said Amidships. 'When Tyrannical came up with all that.'

'Once we realise that we are living a virtual world, the natural thing is to wonder – what's outside? Tyrannical assumed that there must be a programmer, that our consciousnesses must have been deliberately inserted into this place. But the truth is – somewhat different.'

'You told me once,' said Amidships, 'that *Carcinoma Angels* . . .' She trailed off.

'You still haven't read that one, have you, my dear? No, I thought not. Even though it might open your eyes. We are all resistant to the truth; it is in our nature. Our consciousnesses yearn to believe in the world in which we find ourselves. Even when we know – as you know, my dear; as I have known for a long time – even when we know that our world is in fact merely *a metaphor for something else*, we continue to ignore the obvious.'

'The obvious?'

'Come, my dear. Look at the facts – look at the clues. There is *order* in the Galaxy, and there is *disorder*. The two things are in conflict. There is authority, and those who fight against authority, who devote themselves to rock and roll, to excess, to indulgence.'

'What do you mean, *clues*?'

'How does *order* manifest itself? Phagocyte police cruisers. The elimination of the free radicals. White blood cells. And how does *disorder* manifest itself?'

He seemed to be waiting for an answer from Amidships. 'I don't know,' she said, eventually.

'In *disease*. Each enemy of order manifests a different disease. This rebel embodies *leprosy*. That one, bent and wobbly, is *arthritis*. This young tearaway is *acne*, with his running spots. These enemies of the state embody, variously, astigmatism, influenza, cancer, dwarfism, nominal aphasia. Here is a person whose whole existence is determined by whole-body hirsutism. Is there any person associated with this movement who is not embodied by illness, sickness, disease? It is epitomised by the Jobbi: the group whose leader is in fact nothing more than a three-foot-high quantity of animated phlegm.'

'Yodella . . .' breathed Pōkme.

'Did you wonder why he so *conveniently* appeared just as Tyrannical was telling us the true nature of the cosmos? Why he came in at precisely *that* moment to silence him forever? Because he does not want us to understand the true nature of things, that's why.'

'But the Jobbi . . .' said Pōkme, unable to comprehend the notion.

'The whole movement is faecal waste. Health inside a body is order, balance, harmony. Disease on the other hand is slapstick, disaster, cells colliding with other cells, organs collapsing. The Farce.'

'But the Jobbi Order has brought peace to the cosmos . . .'

'The peace of a coma victim. The Jobbi Order is the problem, not the cure. But cure, however little you like the fact, is *the other side.*' Palpating shook his head. 'People are so short-sighted! You *know* the cosmos you inhabit is a metaphor, rather than a reality. But you do not ask yourself what is it a metaphor *for*? The answer is obvious, once you think it. This cosmos, this universe, is a body. This body is a battleground between disease and health. Indeed, this body is almost dead – for so long the Jobbi have dominated things that the cosmic corpus is at death's door. And the terrible truth is: once it dies, we all die with it, for it is the horizon of our entire being. Infection has spread from cell to cell, from world to world, until the disease is almost total. Almost – but not quite. Because another agent has been introduced; a cocktail of drugs, we might say; a power that shadows the ubiquitous infection. You call it the Dark Side, but it is here to save, to cure.'

'The whole universe?' said Amidships. 'A single person? And we are the inner workings? It's . . . incredible.'

'This battle between the forces of Order and the forces of the Farce – it's not an *ethical* battleground, my dear; it is something more straightforward than that. It is the battleground between health and disease. The one side is smoking, drinking, partying, having promiscuous, unprotected sex – fun, yes, but it leads to death. Health is less fun; it is order, discipline, routine, eating your greens, taking the stairs rather than the elevator. Less fun. But it is *life*.'

'I,' said Amidships, 'I don't know what to say.'

'I don't expect you to say anything, my dear. I don't even expect you to change, my dear. I don't expect you to betray your friends. You didn't choose to be a germ, any more than I chose to be an antibody. That's just the way it is. But now that I have seized control, I shall manufacture white blood cells and fight the infections on all fronts. I shall reclaim this body for health. And although you cannot help but oppose me, you must pray that I succeed. For if I fail, then the entire cosmos will die, and with it every consciousness inside it.'

'But the science fiction . . . the twentieth-century comedy . . .'

'The things that our cosmic body cares about. The shaping forces in his, or her, mind. Merely the meta-phorical grammar of our cosmic body's thoughts, the grammar that determines our existence.'

Amidships stared into space. She tried to disbelieve Palpating, but somehow she could not. She felt the truth of his words; they chimed with something she had always known.

'That was a long speech, for me,' he croaked. 'My voice is almost gone – soon it will be gone altogether. That is the price I pay for my new position. I wrestle with infectious agents, and it's given me a *shocking* sore throat. But you understand now why your husband felt he had no choice but to join the Dark Side. Unlike you he is not trapped by sentimental attachment to agents of disease.'

'It's a lot to take in,' said Amidships, in a cowed voice, 'It's not every day that a person learns the secret of the cosmos.'

'Indeed, not.'

'But why *fight*? Killing and oppressing people,' Amidships said. 'Why not just *tell* the citizens of the cosmos the true nature of reality?'

'They would not accept it, in the mass. They live within the logic of the metaphor, so they must be fought within the logic of the metaphor. How else could it be? If I were to inform your handsome Jobbi friend Wobbli K'nobbli that he is actually a manifestation of arthritis affecting the joints of the cosmic being – do you *really* think he would simply say "how terrible, I must lie down and die"? Of course not. It is not in the nature of the disease elements to simply give up. They must, I'm afraid, be actively defeated. And you, my dear: you must choose whether you intend to tell your young child the truth, or to keep her in ignorance. She will grow up to embody a disease, you know; so if you force her to accept the truth it may erode her identity and destroy her. But knowing what you know, can you hide the truth from her?' He got to his feet. 'Goodbye my dear. I'm sorry to say that we won't meet again.'

Coda

'Oh Master,' said Dark Jane, as he fitted the black skull-helmet onto his head. 'Do you believe we can defeat the incursion – the infections? Can we save the cosmic body?'

'Of course we can, my young friend,' whispered Palpating. His voice was almost entirely gone now – his throat painfully rasped and sore. His words sounded like paper slipping over paper. 'Of course we can. With you at my side, organising the forces of counter-infection, we will purge the cosmic body of disease.'

'Sorry—' said Seespotrun. 'I didn't quite catch that . . . your voice is very low.'

'I know,' breathed Palpating. 'I will soon have no voice at all; and then I will need to develop some different way of communicating with you. But for now, my young apprentice, let us go to work.'

'I am confident,' mumbled Seespotrun, fitting the mask into place. 'Wait,' he added, 'this plastic is muffling my words.' He fumbled round the back of the helmet for an amplifier switch. 'AH,' he said, finally. 'THAT'S BETTER. NOW – AH YES,

MASTER. I AM CONFIDENT WE WILL DEFEAT THE FORCES OF INFECTION.'

'We must,' said Palpating. 'Or the cosmic body will literally sicken and die. We need a co-ordinated and centralised attack. But do not be anxious, my young friend. I intend to provide strong leadership.'

'PARDON?' said Seespotrun.

'Oh look. I'll write it down.' He pulled a piece of black rewritable plastic from a nearby drawer, and scribbled upon it:

I MAY SEEM FRESH-FACED NOW
BUT I PROMISE YOU THIS, MY FRIEND:
I DON'T INTEND TO BECOME ONLY A
MEDIOCRE DICTATOR . . .

He grinned, and flipped the rectangle over:

I INTEND TO BECOME
THE GREAT DICTATOR